MW01039995

Motorbooks International
Authentic Restoration

JAGUAR E-TYPE
6 & 12 Cylinder
RESTORATION GUIDE

Dr. Thomas F. Haddock

MBI Publishing Company

First published in 1997 by Motorbooks International Publishers & Wholesalers, 729 Prospect Avenue, PO Box 1, Osceola, WI 54020-0001 USA

© Thomas F. Haddock, 1997

All rights reserved. With the exception of quoting brief passages for the purposes of review no part of this publication may be reproduced without prior written permission from the Publisher

Motorbooks International is a certified trademark, registered with the United States Patent Office

The information in this book is true and complete to the best of our knowledge. All recommendations are made without any guarantee on the part of the author or Publisher, who also disclaim any liability incurred in connection with the use of this data or specific details

We recognize that some words, model names and designations, for example, mentioned herein are the property of the trademark holder. We use them for identification purposes only. This is not an official publication

Motorbooks International books are also available at discounts in bulk quantity for industrial or sales-promotional use. For details write to Special Sales Manager at the Publisher's address

On the front cover: A late 1967 U.S. spec Series I Jaguar E-Type coupe in primrose yellow. *Matt Stone*

On the back cover (clockwise from top left): The black vinyl dash of a late 3.8-liter car; the sparkplug wire organizing system of a Series II 4.2-liter car; the mirror of an early 5.3-liter Series III car; serrated locknuts were used instead of spring lock washers in some applications.

Library of Congress Cataloging-in-Publication Data
Haddock, Thomas F.
    Jaguar E-Type 6 & 12 cylinder restoration guide/Thomas F. Haddock. --2nd ed.
        p. cm. --(Authentic restoration guides)
    Rev. ed. of: Jaguar E-type six-cylinder restoration & originality. 1991.
    Includes index.
    ISBN 0-7603-0396-7 (pbk.: alk. paper)
    1. Jaguar E-type automobile--Conservation and restoration. I. Haddock, Thomas F. Jaguar E-type six-cylinder restoration & originality. II. Title. III. Title: Jaguar E-type six and twelve cylinder restoration guide IV. Series: Motorbooks International authentic restoration guides.
TL215.J3H33   1997
629.28'722--dc21   97-44430

Printed in the United States of America

CONTENTS

INTRODUCTION

This book has grown out of my long-standing interest in E-Type Jaguars, going back to the 1960s when what we now call the "Series I" E-Type was a current car. Since 1969 I have owned many E-Types, and have seen, studied, and worked on numerous others. In addition, since 1975 I have kept a register of currently existing examples of early E-Types that later expanded to include all E-Types. In recent years my interest has expanded to include the V-12 cars.

Since the release of the first edition of this book, which dealt only with the six-cylinder E-Type variants, I have continued to collect information on these cars, and this material is contained in this second edition. In addition, I now include the final version of the E-Type, the Series III V-12, in this analysis. The book now treats the full E-Type production of approximately 72,511 cars.

I have divided the E-Types into five basic categories. Most fundamental is the distinction between the six-cylinder 3.8-liter cars, the six-cylinder 4.2-liter cars, and the V-12 5.3-liter cars. Within the 4.2-liter group, I make a distinction between Series I, Series I 1/2, and Series II cars. I assume the reader has an understanding of the basic specifications of the cars in each of these divisions. However, chapter 1 gives a brief description of the basic models, and discusses questions of production quantities and serial numbers. In addition, any of the standard works on E-Types (e.g., Skilleter, Harvey, Porter, or Jenkinson) describe the basic specifications of the different varieties of E-Types. Russ' work focuses exclusively on the Series III cars.

The subject of this book is the variation of the production specifications within each of these five model runs. It is not my goal to discuss in detail the myriad changes that took place between these divisions. For this reason, it is important that the divisions be well chosen.

A problem occurs, however, in the case of the so-called Series I 1/2 cars. The overlap that occurs between various Series I and Series II features within Series I 1/2 production makes it an ill-defined category. I have thus made what seemed a logical definition of the Series I 1/2, and while it may not be universally accepted, it is at least a working basis against which to discuss production variations.

Sources of information on the E-Types include official publications, such as the manuals and spare parts catalogs (both in binder and microfiche forms), as well as the many other standard publications on the subject. In addition to these sources, I have extensively used books and magazine articles, both modern and contemporary with the manufacture of the car, correspondence with the Jaguar factory, and personal experience with numerous E-Types.

Chapters 2 through 4 present information from those sources that cite the serial numbers at which various design changes commenced. I have listed these entries in order of increasing chassis, engine, and transmission numbers.

The history of the Jaguar E-Type has been told many times (e.g., the two Skilleter books, Harvey, Porter, Jenkinson), and even the technical history (listings of detail production changes) has been outlined several times since it was first briefly done in the April 25, 1968, issue of *Autocar*, and in the March 21, 1970, issue of *Motor*. Unlike previous work, however, this book deals exclusively with the technical specifications of the E-Type, and has as its goal a very exhaustive and detailed examination of the evolution of these cars. The information I have gathered from all sources, whether associated with serial numbers or not, is presented in chapters 5 through 10, sorted by the area of the car in which the change occurred. This constitutes the main body of the book.

I should note at this point that it is not my intention to give reasons for changes, nor in fact any general history of the cars. Discussion of the motivation for each change is beyond the scope of this book, which is intended mainly as a descriptive work. I will try to indicate *how* the cars were, and not *why* they were that way, which is a much larger topic. However, in some instances I may include small bits of information on the motivation for a particular change.

Chapter 11 presents new material on the various fastening devices used in the E-Type, while chapter 12 contains updated information on the cars, based on the register of E-Types I began in 1975. This register lists E-Types I have located or about which I obtained information. Due to my particular interest in the early cars, it is weighted in that direction.

The main change in the second edition of this book is the treatment of the V-12 Series III cars. Due to the significant technological differences between the V-12 cars and their six-cylinder predecessors, I considered them outside the scope of my subject in the first edition. Also, at that time they were not so old, and thus did not seem of as much historical interest. They are, however, clearly part of the E-Type story, and I have included them in this edition.

Due to the detailed nature of this subject, it is impossible to write a book that is absolutely accurate and complete. What I have done here is to extend the state of knowledge of this broad subject by recording my latest information on these cars. As I stated in the first edition of this book, this is an ongoing work, and I welcome input from readers about any errors or omissions there may be. I am always interested in corresponding with owners of unrestored, original E-Types.

I would again like to thank the numerous owners and enthusiasts who have assisted me in the compilation of both the first and second editions of this book through the sharing of their information and allowing me access to their cars. This book is principally the result of the examination of hundreds of cars, and without their kind assistance it could never have been written.

Chapter 1

OVERVIEW OF MODELS
AND SERIAL NUMBERS

During the 14-year production run of the Jaguar E-Type, five distinct models were produced. Each of these was available in roadster, coupe, and, in some cases, 2+2 body styles. Good discussions of the basic models can be found in numerous books, so I do not wish to dwell long on the subject here. However, a brief overview is needed to serve as a baseline against which to reference the detail production changes that are the subject of this book.

The following is a quick history of the basic models in which the E-Types appeared. For information on the motivations for the model changes and the effect they had on the overall character of the car, I refer the reader to the numerous books found in the references.

Since so many of the production changes discussed in this book are referenced to the particular serial numbers at which they occurred, it is important to have a good grasp of the serial-number system used for the chassis and large components. This will be included in the following discussion of each model.

The Series I 3.8-Liter Cars

The 3.8-liter cars represent the E-Type in its earliest and roughest form, nearer to a sports car than the GT it evolved into. Introduced in early 1961, the 3.8-liter cars were the first E-Types to go into production. Thus, there were more specification changes during their production than in any other E-Type model (given that the so-called Series I 1/2 is taken to be a separate model). There are several distinct sub-varieties, which I will discuss at the end of this section. Offered in only the roadster and two-seater coupe versions, these early cars suffered from many teething problems, including poor seating and an antiquated gearbox. They had the overall flavor of the traditional British sports car, with a generator (instead of an alternator), positive-ground electrical system, and a rather stark interior.

Four independently running chassis serial number-series were used for the 3.8-liter cars, separate ones for right- and left-hand drive (RHD, LHD) and for coupes

The outside bonnet latches typical of the early 3.8-liter Series I cars are seen in this side view of serial number 875026. The tires, exhaust resonators, and convertible top are not original.

The aluminum trim on the console and dash center is typical of the early Series I 3.8-liter cars, shown here on 875026. The early, flat dash top is evident. The seats of the 3.8-liter cars do not have any adjustment for rake.

Left side of the engine compartment of Series I 3.8-liter 875026. The early corrugated-aluminum breather pipe can be seen coming from the left front of the cylinder head. The early multipiece throttle linkage and the wide sealing flange on the fiberglass air-intake box are evident as well. The spark-plug wires are absent here.

and roadsters. The starting serial numbers for each of these series was:

RHD Roadsters:	850001
RHD Coupes:	860001
LHD Roadsters:	875001
LHD Coupes:	885001

It is important to note that the rate of production in each of these categories was not the same, and the numbers advanced much faster in the high production-rate groups. Thus, for example, the one-hundredth LHD roadster may have been produced before the fourth RHD coupe.

The total production of 3.8-liter E-Types was:

RHD Roadsters:	942
RHD Coupes:	1,798
LHD Roadsters:	6,885
LHD Coupes:	5,871

This amounted to a total of 15,496 3.8-liter E-Types. As with all the production numbers, there is some uncertainty here.

The engine numbers for the 3.8-liter cars ran from R1001-X, where X was a 7, 8, or 9, which denoted the compression ratio of the engine (7:1, 8:1, or 9:1). Later on during engine production, the "R" prefix was changed to "RA." This denoted a shift in the four-digit engine numbering system, with the new number system shifted down by 9000.

The transmission numbers ran from EB101JS, and the body numbers ran from R1001 for the roadsters and V1001 for the coupes.

As mentioned, the 3.8-liter production run had several identifiable subgroups. The first, and most interesting, of these is the so-called First 500. These cars were produced up to and including serial numbers:

RHD Roadsters:	850091
RHD Coupes:	860004
LHD Roadsters:	875385
LHD Coupes:	885020

This indicated a production of 91 RHD roadsters, 4 RHD coupes, 385 LHD roadsters, and 20 LHD coupes, for a total of 500 cars.

These 500 cars are different in many ways from the cars that followed them in production. It is believed that a production lull occurred after 500 bodies had been delivered to the factory, and the factory used this opportunity to make some improvements. While I do not have any hard evidence for this, several suggestive quotes are found in the current literature. In *The Jaguar E-Type: A Collector's Guide*, Paul Skilleter stated: "In fact, an almost fortunate hold-up caused by a delay at the bodyworks enabled Jaguar to rectify a number of obvious faults noticeable in the prototype production cars (which the motoring press sampled and whose comments perhaps helped Jaguar in this respect) before many cars had left the factory." *Road & Track* magazine of September 1961 noted that, "While it is unfortunate that a strike at the body plant has delayed production, this lull may prove to be beneficial, in that Jaguar can make the few obvious corrections that are needed before real production commences." The strike is also referred to in Porter's *Jaguar E-Type: The Definitive History*.

The most pronounced feature of the First 500 cars is the hood-latch mechanism, which is operated from outside the hood with a T-key. This key is similar to those used on numerous postwar British cars, and it goes in keyholes on each of the lower rear corners of the front fenders. The keyholes are covered with teardrop-shaped escutcheons, as used on Jaguar Mk V fender skirts and the trunk lids of early Triumph TR roadsters, and they are very prominent. For this reason, the First 500 cars are often referred to as "outside hood-latch" cars or "outside bonnet-latch" cars.

While these exterior hood latches are the most pronounced of the differences between the First 500 cars and their successors, there are numerous others. Even within the First 500 cars there are many changes in specifications. This is discussed in more detail in chapter 2.

Another well-known early subgroup is the so-called "flat-floor" cars, distinguished by the basically flat cockpit flooring in front of the seats. The floors were not truly flat, having support grooves pressed into them, but they were flat compared to the floors of the subsequent cars, which were comprised of separate, dished-down troughs. These cars were produced up to and including serial numbers:

RHD Roadsters:	850357
RHD Coupes:	860175
LHD Roadsters:	876581
LHD Coupes:	885503

This indicated a production of 357 RHD roadsters, 175 RHD coupes, 1,581 LHD roadsters, and 503 LHD coupes, for a total of 2,616 cars.

The 876581 serial-number car is cited in most references as the final flat-floor LHD roadster, but in the factory parts catalog, J.30 of June, 1963, 876381 is cited. Normally I would accept the parts catalog as correct, and assume the error lies with the other sources. However, since all sources agree with the 876581 number, I am citing it here.

The end of the flat-floor cars came in early 1962.

In 1963, after production was well under way, a series of 12 lightweight, aluminum-bodied roadsters was produced for competition purposes. These are extremely interesting cars, possessing such features as aluminum blocks and vented aluminum hardtops. On a detail level, however, these racers have little relation to the production E-Types and fall outside the scope of this book.

In the last year's production of 3.8-liter, the cars incorporated several of the features of the soon-to-be-released 4.2-liter cars. These included an upholstered center dash and console with storage compartment armrest, armrests on the doors, sculpted windshield L-post trim, and even an all-synchromesh transmission for the very late cars.

The external appearance of Series I 4.2-liter coupe serial number 1E.30488 is basically identical to that of the 3.8-liter cars that preceded it. With the introduction of the 2+2 in 1966, two closed bodystyles were available. The glass-covered headlights were a feature of all but the last Series I cars.

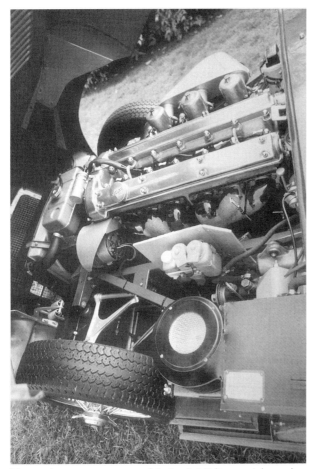

A general view of the interior of Series I 4.2-liter 1E.13003. The improved seats were a welcome feature on the 4.2-liter cars. All 4.2-liter cars had black trim on the center of the dash. All two-seater Series I 4.2-liter cars were fitted with armrests. The shift boot on this particular car should be the rubber type, not leather.

This side view of Series I 1/2 4.2-liter 1E.34580 differs from the early Series I cars only in the absence of headlight covers.

The engine compartment of Series I 4.2-liter serial number 1E.13003. A negative-ground electrical system came in with the introduction of the 4.2-liter, as is noted on the yellow label on top of the heater box. The intake manifold of the 4.2-liter engine was a single unit, as opposed to the complex arrangement used on the 3.8-liter cars. The battery and tires are not original.

A more detailed discussion of 3.8-liter subgroups is given in my *Early E-Type Production and Registration Handbook*.

While the tremendous appeal of the 3.8-liter cars tended to overshadow their failings, the improved 4.2-liter version was very welcome when it was introduced in 1964.

The Series I 4.2-Liter Cars

The new 4.2-liter cars were very different from their predecessors. In addition to the change in the engine, the generator was replaced with a more modern alternator, the electrical system was changed to positive ground, the seats and gearbox were replaced with more up-to-date versions, the brake system was reworked, and the interior trimming was redone to give the car a more sophisticated look. The exterior appearance was essentially unchanged.

The change in the engine was more than just a boring-out of the cylinders. Numerous changes took place, including relocating the cylinders in the block, and changing the intake manifold from a multipiece construction to a single-piece construction.

The new fully synchromesh gearbox is often cited as the main improvement of the 4.2-liter cars over their 3.8-liter predecessors. It is interesting to note that in *Autocar* magazine of May 14, 1965, the 4.2-liter E-Type with synchromesh gearbox was originally announced as an alternate model to the still-produced 3.8-liter E-Type with the old gearbox. The new 4.2-liter model was listed as going for about £66 more for the roadster and £78 more for the coupe.

In 1966 a third variety of body style was made available with the introduction of the 2+2. This elongated-wheelbase version of the coupe had a raised roof line and dropped floor to increase interior room. The two small back seats had a squab that could be moved forward to cover the seat-bottoms if more rear luggage area was needed. While this car was welcomed by some larger owners, or those with small children, it clearly had less of the sporting character possessed by the two-seater versions. The domesticated nature of the 2+2 was enhanced by the availability of an optional automatic transmission that could not be ordered on the two-seater cars.

The cast-aluminum rear crossover pipe of the first generation of emission-controlled engines is seen here on Series I 1/2 4.2-liter 1E.17271.

The large-type Series I 1/2 dash of 1E.17271 was very similar to the early Series II dash. Early Series I 1/2 cars had a dash similar to the late Series I. Like the early Series II cars, the late Series I 1/2 cars did not have door armrests. The shift knob is not original here.

Like their predecessor, the 4.2-liter cars initially had four independently running chassis serial-number series. With the introduction of the 2+2 body style in 1966, two more series were introduced to bring the total to six series. The starting serial numbers for each of these series was:

RHD Roadsters:	1E.1001
LHD Roadsters:	1E.10001
RHD Coupes:	1E.20001
LHD Coupes:	1E.30001
RHD 2+2s:	1E.50001
LHD 2+2s:	1E.75001

As in the case of the 3.8-liter cars, the rate of production in each of these categories was not the same. The total production of 4.2-liter Series I E-Types was:

RHD Roadsters:	1,182
LHD Roadsters:	8,366
RHD Coupes:	1,957
LHD Coupes:	5,813
RHD 2+2s:	1,378
LHD 2+2s:	4,220

This amounted to a total of 22,916 4.2-liter Series I E-Types.

The engine numbers for the 4.2-liter Series I cars had a 7E prefix, and an X suffix, where X denoted the compression ratio, as in the case of the 3.8-liter engines.

The transmission numbers had an EJ prefix, and the body numbers had a 4E prefix.

The Series I 1/2 Cars

These cars represent a transition between the classic Series I cars, which all had basically the same exterior appearance, and the Series II cars, which were the final result of the 1968 U.S. automotive safety and pollution-control regulations. While the Series I 1/2 cars might be considered a subgroup of the Series I cars, I feel they are better described as an independent model in their own right. These cars are often identified by low-set uncovered headlights. However, some late Series I cars had the open headlights and apparently no other Series I 1/2 features.

The serial-number systems of the Series I 1/2 cars are a continuation of those for the Series I cars. According to Skilleter, the Series I 1/2 cars began with the chassis numbers:

RHD Roadsters: 1E.1864
LHD Roadsters: 1E.15889
RHD Coupes: 1E.21584
LHD Coupes: 1E.34250
RHD 2+2s: 1E.50975
LHD 2+2s: 1E.77645

Skilleter also states that the U.S. federal-specification cars were introduced in January 1968 at chassis numbers 1E.15180 for the LHD roadsters and 1E.34583 for the LHD coupes. These numbers do not jive with the above numbers given for the introduction of the Series I 1/2, with the roadster number being earlier and the coupe number being later. In addition, it is believed that the introduction of the open-headlight cars occurred at the same chassis numbers cited above as the beginning of Series I 1/2. Thus, I presume Skilleter took the introduction of the open headlights to be the beginning of the Series I 1/2 cars. There are, however, open-headlight cars with numbers earlier than those cited as the introduction of the open headlights. For example, 1E.15267 was supplied with an open-headlight hood, but would not, according to the serial numbers above, be a Series I 1/2 car.

The general Series I 1/2 confusion is further illustrated by Skilleter's statement that the Series I 1/2 specification changed continuously throughout its production run from late 1967 to early 1968, and thus it is impossible to truly define a particular Series I 1/2 configuration. In keeping with this generally confused situation, in *Original Jaguar E-Type*, Philip Porter lists a slightly different set of Series I 1/2 beginning serial numbers.

Taking the first U.S. specification cars as the beginning of Series I 1/2 is another approach. This is supported by a discussion in the January 13, 1968, *Motor*, where a Series I 1/2, with rocker switches, is discussed as

The plastic leaping Jaguar medallion, seen here on Series II Roadster 2R.14615, is a feature of the later Series II cars. Interestingly, it gives these last six-cylinder cars the appearance of the first cars with the outside bonnet latches. The luggage rack mounted on 2R.14615 is not an original feature.

being the completed new car, modified to comply with U.S. federal demands. From this reference, it would seem the earlier changes (e.g., open headlights) were only a step toward the full Series I 1/2 specification. Since the main driving force behind the introduction of the Series I 1/2 cars was the introduction of the U.S. regulations, it seems reasonable to consider the first cars to meet these specifications as the beginning of the Series I 1/2 category. However, I will adopt Skilleter's serial numbers as the beginning of Series I 1/2.

The Series II Cars

While the Series I 1/2 kept Jaguar in the U.S. market for the 1968 model year, a more integrated response to the new U.S. regulations was being developed for model year 1969. This new model was for a time referred to as the Mk II in *Car* and in *Road & Track*, but came to be officially known as the Series II, probably to avoid confusion with the Mk II sports sedan. With this new name came the designation of Series I and Series I 1/2 for the earlier cars that had previously been known simply as E-Types.

The changes in the Series II cars were not focused exclusively on the U.S. regulations and included numerous unrelated improvements. For example, the air-intake aperture was increased for better cooling, and there were changes in the braking system.

With the introduction of the Series II, the E-Type's exterior appearance noticeably changed for the first time. Not only was the enlarged and reshaped air-intake readily apparent, but the rear-end bodywork and trim were changed to increase bumper protection and accommodate the larger lights required by the new regulations. While these changes typically improved functionality, it is generally regarded that they degrade the original purity and beauty of the car. The cars were offered in the same three body styles as the late Series I and Series I 1/2 cars.

With the introduction of the Series II came a new serial numbering system. It followed the same pattern as the preceding systems, with the models broken down as follows:

RHD Roadsters:	1R.1001
LHD Roadsters:	1R.7001
RHD Coupes:	1R.20001
LHD Coupes:	1R.25001
RHD 2+2s:	1R.35001
LHD 2+2s:	1R.40001

Other than the battery, the restored 4.2-liter engine compartment of Series II serial number 1R.7944 is very original. Here is the standard ribbed camshaft covers of the Series II cars. The Jaguar symbol is cast into the cam cover of 1R.7944. When the ribbed cam covers first appeared, this nameplate was a separate casting. This car is typical of the mid-production U.S.-specification cars, with two Stromberg carburetors but no crossover pipe.

To further specify details of an individual car, pre-fixes and suffixes were used in the numbering system. A prefix P was used to denote that the car was fitted with power steering. A suffix BW for Borg Warner was used to denote that an automatic transmission was fitted. This was only available on 2+2 cars.

The total production of Series II E-Types was:

RHD Roadsters:	775
LHD Roadsters:	7,852
RHD Coupes:	1,070
LHD Coupes:	3,785
RHD 2+2s:	1,040
LHD 2+2s:	4,286

This amounted to a total of 18,808 4.2-liter Series II E-Types.

Engine numbers for the Series II cars ran for the first time in E-Type production in two series:

Two seat chassis:	7R.1001-X
2+2 chassis:	7R.35001-X

The X denoted the compression ratio, as before. The later cars used letters to denote the compression ratio.

Transmission numbers had a KE prefix, and the body numbers had a 4R prefix.

The Series III Cars

As the Series II E-Type continued in production, the progression of emission control regulations reduced the power of the six-cylinder XK engine, while at the same time the other ever-tightening crashworthiness regulations increased the weight of car. To address the resultant decrease in performance, as well as to get the newly developed V-12 engine into production, the final version of the E-Type, the Series III, was introduced. While the Series III was originally announced as available with both the new V-12 as well as the old 6-cylinder XK engine, in practice only a few XK-engined Series III cars were produced at the outset, and from there on only the V-12 was fitted to Series III cars. Because these six-cylinder cars were not truly production cars, they will not be treated in this book.

This last version of the E-Type was yet again heavier and longer. The previous short wheelbase of the roadsters and coupes was discontinued and only the long wheelbase of 2+2 was still offered, in the new Series III roadster as well as the coupe. Since the roadster now had the longer wheelbase chassis, it, too, was available with the optional Borg Warner automatic transmission, as available in the coupe. As before, a suffix BW for Borg Warner was used to denote that an automatic transmission was fitted.

The new engine was an all-alloy, single overhead cam V-12, with in-line valves and a displacement of 5,343 cc. It had four Stromberg carburetors and an electronic ignition system. The front subframe was widened and reenforced to accommodate the larger V-12. Due to the extensive use of alloys, the V-12 weighed fewer than 100 pounds more than its six-cylinder predecessor.

A general view of the interior of Series II 1R.7944. The headrest seen here is typical of U.S.-market cars. Typical features of all Series II cars include a lockable glovebox door, rocker switches, and sun visors. The steering wheel of 1R.7944 shows the brushed finish on the aluminum spokes, and black horn trim ring, used on the Series II cars. Earlier Series II cars had nonilluminated labels, or no labels at all. The shift knob is not original.

This longer and heavier car rode on a 3.25-inch wider wheelbase (accomplished at the rear by employing 420G components) and was standard with power steering to assist with the additional weight, and a smaller dished, 15-inch-diameter leather steering wheel replaced the 17-inch-diameter wood-rimmed wheel of the prior cars.

On the exterior, there were numerous visible changes. Perhaps the greatest of these was the new egg-crate grille and additional air intake situated below the main aperture. Other noticeable changes included wheel-arch flares to accommodate the larger wheelbase, and, initially, a four-outlet exhaust. A chrome V-12 escutcheon was attached to the trunk lid. As production proceeded, the bumper overriders were also dramatically changed to meet the ever-tightening U.S. regulations. Changes to the chassis included larger diameter and thicker front brake discs, cooling ducts on the rear discs, and anti-dive geometry for the front suspension. Due to the greater fuel consumption of the V-12, the fuel tank capacity was increased from 14 to 18 gallons.

As in the case of the Series II, most people feel the changes degraded the appearance of the car, and moved it further from the sports-car category toward the grand-touring category.

Following the system used on the earlier E-Types, the 5.3-liter cars had independently running chassis serial-number series. Since all the cars had the long wheelbase of the 2+2, there was no longer two separate coupe body styles. Thus the cars were numbered in

The new egg-crate grille and the additional air intake situated below it immediately identifies UD1S.21221 as a Series III car. The fender flares were added to accommodate the wider wheelbase, and the longer doors and convertible top are the result of the increased wheelbase used on all models of Series III.

The interior of UD1S.21221 is very similar to that of the 6-cylinder Series II cars that preceded it. One striking change is the dished, leather-rimmed steering wheel, which is a marked departure from the large-diameter wood-rimmed used in the Series I and II cars. While this roadster is fitted with the four-speed manual transmission, the lengthened wheelbase used on all Series III cars made the option of an automatic transmission available on roadsters for the first time.

The all-aluminum V-12 was a tight fit in the E-type engine compartment. Two rain shields were fitted to direct water that came in the hood louvers. On this late model car, UD1S.21221, the footwell fresh-air duct intakes can be seen mounted above the tops of the front shock absorbers. Also, this later engine has the JAGUAR name applied on a sticker to the cam covers, instead of being cast in as on earlier engines.

four separate series. The starting serial numbers for each of these was:

RHD Roadsters:	1S.1001
LHD Roadsters:	1S.20001
RHD Coupes:	1S.50001
LHD Coupes:	1S.70001

A suffix BW for Borg Warner was used to denote that an automatic transmission was fitted, although now, due to all body styles having the long wheelbase, this option was available on roadsters as well as coupes. As before, the rate of production in each of these categories was not the same. The approximate total production of 5.3-liter Series III E-Types was:

RHD Roadsters:	1,872
LHD Roadsters:	6,120
RHD Coupes:	2,116
LHD Coupes:	5,183

for a total of 15,291 5.3-liter Series III E-Types.

The engine numbers for the 5.3-liter Series III cars had a "7S" prefix.

The transmission numbers had an "KL" prefix, and the body numbers had a "4S" prefix.

A significant subgroup of the Series III cars was the "last 50." These were the last E-Types produced, and they each carried a commemorative dashboard plaque mounted on the glove compartment lid with this inscription, "This is one of a special series of fifty right-hand-drive cars built to identify the conclusion of manufacture of the Jaguar 'E' Type Sports Car. W. Lyons (signature) Sir William Lyons. President. Jaguar Cars. Coventry. 1974." The very last car, chassis number 1S.2872 with body 4S.8989, had a special plaque inscribed, "This is the last car built after thirteen years manufacture of the Jaguar 'E' Type Sports Cars. W. Lyons (signature) Sir William Lyons. President. Jaguar Cars. Coventry. 1974." and "Chassis No. IS 2872." The factory kept this last car. All of these cars were roadsters, and all were painted black with the single exception of one that was painted green by special order. These last 50 cars closed out the run of E-Types much as the "First 500" 3.8-liter cars started it 14 years earlier in 1961. The placement of plaques on Jaguar sports-car dashboards signed by William Lyons has a precedent in the "Jabbeke Road" speed run plaques fastened to the dashboards of XK-120s and XK-140s.

With this background information on the five basic E-Type models, we are now ready to look at the detailed production changes that took place within these model classifications. The reader will note that this book is not broken up into four sections, but into three, where the first treats the 3.8-liter cars, the second treats all the 4.2-liter cars, and the last treats the 5.3-liter cars. The reason for this can be found in the size of these sections. There are fewer 4.2-liter changes (in Series I, I 1/2, and II cars together) than occurred in the 3.8-liter cars alone.

Chapter 2

3.8-LITER CHANGES BY SERIAL NUMBER

This chapter chronicles the changes listed in the parts book and other published sources. The listing is in order of chassis number, with RHD roadster number (serial number 850001, forward) determining position in the list. For every entry I give the chassis-number (or engine or transmission number, as appropriate) transition point, and a description of the change. In cases where a change is listed only by a single reference other than the factory literature, I cite that reference.

For this listing I used the 3.8-liter E-Type Spare Parts Catalog, Jaguar publication number J.30, reprint of June 1963 (AL1). The original version of the J.30 parts book, issued August 1961, is very early, and does not contain much information for this book in its text. It does, however, contain some information in its illustrations, many of which are different from those in the AL1 reprint of June 1963. This information is given in chapter 4. Since the June 1963 reprint does not go to the end of 3.8-liter E-Type production in 1964, it will not list some of the later changes. At least some of these can be found in the other references used here.

It should be noted that no single source lists all the changes chronicled here. This reflects the somewhat confused state of the "official" production change lists.

The dates cited for the changes not referenced in the parts books are approximate. As Philip Porter noted in *Jaguar E-Type: The Definitive History*, the dates are when dealers were informed, so the changes actually occurred earlier.

Under a given chassis-number heading, several references may list the same change. There is often confusion as to what happened, when it happened, and sometimes even if it happened.

Changes in Order of Chassis Number
850023/4
875026/7
First type of detachable hardtop mounting assembly begins.

850047/8
860001
875132/3

885001
About August 1961, a water deflector was fitted to the front stub axle carrier.

850078/9
About October 1961, a new plastic license-plate holder was introduced. This is listed only in *Jaguar E-Type: The Definitive History*.

850087/8
875299/300
About October 1961, the chrome finisher at the top of the doors was changed. This is listed only in *Jaguar E-Type: The Definitive History*.

850087/8
875309/10
About September 1961, the chrome finisher on the windscreen glass was changed.

850089/90
860003/4
875331/2
885014/5
About October 1961, the handbrake assembly was changed to the auto-adjust type.

850091/2
875373/4
About October 1961, the sealing rubber around the windows was changed.

850091/2
860004/5
875385/6
885020/1
First 500 production ends at these serial numbers. About September 1961, the hood lock, escutcheon, and so on were changed to internal lock. The rubber buffer cushioning the hood sides in the closed position was discontinued; this change was due to the new internal latch.

Numerous other changes were made. The front cover and breather assembly, and the flexible breather pipe to the open vent, were changed to a vent into the air-intake box. The base assembly for the air-intake box was changed to accept the vent. The gas tank was changed with the fitting of a one-piece sump. The fuel pump, bracket, pipe, and filter bracket were changed. The bracket for mounting the fuel filter to the frame was changed. The hood and front fender assemblies were changed with the hood latch moved inside. An extension assembly for the coil bracket was added. The generator was changed (part number 22531/A-C45.PV5/6 changed to 22902/A-C42). The control box and bracket were changed (part number 37304A/RB.310 changed to 37331A/RB.340). Earth cables were added for the cigar lighter. The outer rear hub bearings were enlarged.

It was claimed in *Jaguar International Magazine*, March 1986, that the pressed-in louvers began in October 1961, but this is not the case as this occurred later.

850091/2
875385/6
The hardtop fitting kit was changed.

850103/4
860005/6
875495/6
885025/6
About October 1961, the driveshaft was changed and the driveshaft universal joints were enlarged.

850117/8
875520/1
860006/7
885032/3
About October 1961, the single center drain tube for the trunk lid aperture was changed to two tubes on the right and the left.

850136/7
860007/8
875541/2
885038/9
About October 1961, the rear-suspension coil springs were enlarged, the seats for the springs were changed, and the aluminum packing piece at the top was dropped.

850168/9
860009/10
875589/90
885050/1
About November 1961, the cigar lighter was changed.

850168/9
860009/10
875590/1
885050/1

About November 1961, the support bracket for the rear engine mount was changed.

850178/9
860011/2
875607/8
885058/9
About December 1961, the welded-together exhaust tailpipe assembly was changed to a two-piece assembly.

850209/10
860012/3
875760/1
885085/6
About November 1961, two more rubber corner pads were added to the battery clamp. This is listed only in *Jaguar E-Type: The Definitive History*.

850232/3
860020/1
875858/9
885104/5
About December 1961, the clutch pedal, the bushing in the boss of the clutch pedal, and the housing for the clutch pedal and brake pedal were changed. The brass bush in the brake and clutch pedal housing was changed to impregnated plastic.

875910/1
885124/5
The washers and collars on the connecting lever between the drop arm and the control rod of the throttle linkage were changed.

876014/5
885155/6
The brake master-cylinder assembly was changed.

850238/9
860138/9
876457/8
885384/5
The front subframe assembly and hinge were changed.

860138/9
885384/5
The front subframe assembly was changed on the coupes. In the June 1963 factory parts catalog, a different front subframe assembly is listed as used on all roadsters, and no changes are listed.

The hood hinge was changed on the coupe only. In the June 1963 parts catalog, the later-type coupe hood hinge is listed for use on all roadsters.

850248/9
860020/1
875910/1
885124/5

About January 1962, the spacing collar and washer on the accelerator pedal assembly were changed, and the accelerator-pedal lever assembly was changed.

850253/4
860022/3
875963/4
885142/3

About January 1962, the front suspension assembly was changed. The front and rear brake caliper assemblies were changed from malleable iron to cast iron, and the pistons were changed to have an integral backing plate.

850254/5
860026/7
876014/5
885155/6

About February 1962, the front and rear brake master-cylinder assemblies were changed. The modification gave a more positive location of the rear spring support to the piston.

850254/5
860026/7
876030/1
885160/1

About January 1962, the fuel pipe from the pump and its bracket were changed, with the attachment of the line to the pump by a banjo fitting. This is listed only in *Jaguar E-Type: The Definitive History*.

850273/4
861186/7
878020/1
886748/9

About November 1962, the relay for the fan motor was changed and the forward wiring harness was changed.

850288/9
860028/9
876116/7
885205/6

About February 1962, the tachometer was changed.

850290/1
860032/3
876129/30
885209/10

About February 1962, the front suspension assembly was changed. The brake pad material was also changed.

850300/1
860112/3
876358/9
885317/8

About January 1962, seatbelts were introduced as an option, and seatbelt attachment points were introduced. In *The Jaguar E-Type: A Collector's Guide*, Skilleter

quotes chassis number 875358/9 instead of 876358/9; *Jaguar International Magazine*, March 1986, quotes chassis numbers 850200/1 instead of 850300/1.

850321/2
860121/2
876394/5
885334/5

About February 1962, the front and rear shock absorbers were changed.

850327/8
860138/9
876470/1
885398/9

Calendar year 1961 production ended and 1962 production began.

850356/7
877430/1

About July 1962, the hardtop mounting brackets were changed. This is listed only in *Jaguar E-Type: The Definitive History*.

850357/8
860175/6
876581/2
885503/4

In late winter of 1962, the floor assembly was changed to include heelwells. Note that the June 1963 parts book lists chassis numbers 876381/2 instead of 876581/2, the numbers given in other sources. The Jaguar Service Bulletin lists the body numbers for the change as OTS: 2879/2889, FHC: 1635/1647.

At the same time, Flintkote was added to the front floor. The front carpets were also changed.

860175/6
885503/4

The bracket for the muffler was discontinued.

850376/7
860192/3
876638/9
885571/2

About March 1962, the balance link for operation of the master cylinders was changed.

876664/5
885566/7

About March 1962, a cable for the steering-column lock connector to the instrument panel wiring was introduced along with the combined ignition switch-steering column lock for cars going to Germany.

860194/5
885584/5

About March 1962, the glass and latches for the rear quarter lights were changed. The mounting for the attachment block for the catch arm to the quarter-light frame was changed from brazed to screwed.

850403/4
860231/2
876846/7
885735/6
About March 1962, the spring, covers, plunger, and so forth on the rack and pinion housing and the rack friction damper were changed.

850455/6
876974/5
The hardtop fitting kit was changed.

850474/5
860374/5, including 860365
About May 1962, the accelerator pedal assembly was changed to facilitate heel-and-toe operation.

850474/5
860374/5, including 860365
876998/9
885870/1
About May 1962, the brake pedals were changed. The brake connecting lever was also changed to increase the mechanical advantage; an eccentric barrel nut was installed to adjust the servo arm.

850479/80
860386/7
877044/5
885887/8
About May 1962, the driveshaft was changed, and "sealed for life" universal joints were introduced. A gaiter was fitted to the sliding joint, and the grease nipples on the universal joints and sliding joint were deleted.

850499/500
860435/6
877154/5
885970/1
About May 1962, the horns were changed. The cable to the front lamp connector was changed.

850499/500
860425/6
877275/6
886045/6
About May 1962, the hardware for the rack and pinion assembly was changed; a two-stud mount was introduced for the rack thrust plate, and the studs with self-locking nuts replaced the two hexagon-headed setscrews.

850503/4
860450/1
877182/3
885984/5
About June 1962, the oil seals in the hub carriers,

for the fulcrum shafts, were changed.

860478/9
886013/4
About May 1962, the frame for the door window and the rubber seal and the seal retainer for the cantrail were changed. The headlining on the cantrail and rear trim panels, the headlining, the panel assembly for trimming the windscreen header rail, and the trim panel assembly for the windscreen header rail were all changed. The chrome finishers on the roof gutters were changed.

The casing assembly on the trunk lid and the trunk-lid hinge assembly were changed. The prop supporting the trunk lid in the open position, the pivot bracket on the trunk lid for the prop, and the bracket on the body receiving the prop were all changed. The striker and safety catch for the trunk-lid lock and the screw for the interior light were changed. The glass, the hinge, and the catch for the quarter light were changed.

The door shells and hinges were changed. In *The Jaguar E-Type: A Collector's Guide*, Skilleter cites this change with chassis numbers 860475/6 instead of 860478/9. The fuel filler box and its lid were changed. Skilleter cites chassis numbers 860475/6 instead of 860478/9.

The rear fender assembly, the tail panel below the trunk lid, the trunk gutters, the casing assembly at the rear side of the luggage compartment floor, the roof panel assembly, the windscreen header panel assembly, scuttle top panel and windscreen pillars, the cantrail panel assembly, the drip bead on the cantrail panel assembly, the windscreen pillar assembly, the underframe, the closing panels under the screen pillars, the outer skills, the roof panel, the rear fenders, and the trunk lid were changed. The support panel for the trunk lid aperture was also changed.

About June 1962, the glass in the trunk lid (clear or Sundym), and the chrome finisher at the top of the rubber seal for the trunk window were changed. In *The Jaguar E-Type: A Collector's Guide*, Skilleter cites this change with chassis numbers 860475/6 given instead of 860478/9. This was part of the extensive rework of the coupes that took place at these chassis numbers.

Several other changes occurred about June 1962 as well: The front subframe assembly and hood hinge were changed. The sealing rubber around the trunk-lid aperture was changed from one piece to two pieces. The stop-tail-flasher lamps were changed to adapt the lights to the altered body panels.

850506/7
877201/2
About May 1962, the door shell assembly was changed, and some cars before these chassis numbers were also modified. The chrome finisher at the top of the doors was changed, and some cars before these chassis numbers may have also been modified.

860580/1
886088/9

About July 1962, the strikers for the luggage-floor hinged extension latches, and the rubber buffers for the extension in its raised position were changed. This is listed only in *Jaguar E-Type: The Definitive History.*

850526/7
860580/1
877355/6
886092/3

About June 1962, the body underframe assembly, floor assembly, and rear-end body shell were changed. This included modifying the rear bulkhead of the body shell to include recesses to allow the seats 1-1/2 inches more rearward travel.

In *The Jaguar E-Type: A Collector's Guide*, Skilleter stated that a temporary modification had been carried out on the driver's side shortly after the introduction of the car.

The seat slides were also changed, as were the mat assembly on the floor behind the seats, the mat assembly on the rear bulkhead panel, and the moquette face piece for the lower bulkhead panel, the casing assembly below the quarter light, the hinged extension for the luggage compartment floor, and the support rail assembly for the hinged extension in its lowered position.

850526/7
860583/4
877354/5
886094/5

In summer or early fall of 1962, the fuel line from the pump to the gas-tank outlet connection was changed from the Vulkollan material to nylon.

850547/8
860646/7
877487/8
886213/4

About June 1962, the lower tubular-shaft steering column was changed to a one-piece forging, and the seal where the shaft passes through the dash was changed.

850547/8
860646/7
877488/9
886218/9

About June 1962, the clutch master cylinder was changed to give more positive location for the main spring support to the piston.

850548/9
860660/1
877518/9
886246/7

About June 1962, the screw jack was changed to the cantilever type with integral handle, and the container for the jack was introduced.

850549/50
850552/3

850554/5
860657/8
877534/5
877544/5
877549/50
886246/7

About July 1962, the rear-end halfshafts were changed from a tubular construction to solid forgings.

850550/1
850552/3
850554/5
860663/4
877534/5
877539/40
877566/7
886262/3

About July 1962, the handbrake assembly on the rear brakes was changed.

850554/5
860663/4
877566/7
886262/3

The handbrake cable assembly was changed.

850555/6
860677/8
877556/7
886282/3

About July 1962, the brake and clutch reservoir assemblies, including their mounting brackets, were changed. There is a slightly different listing for the bracket change in the June 1963 parts book.

877556/7
886282/3

The shield for the reservoirs was changed. The brake reservoir assembly and its bracket were also changed.

850558/9
860691/2
877578/9
886305/6

About July 1962, the three studs on the thrust plate and the mounting rubber for the rack and pinion were changed.

850565/6
860677/8

About July 1962, the mounting bracket for the fluid reservoirs changed. This is listed only in *Jaguar International Magazine*, March 1986.

850572/3
860722/3
877660/1
886381/2

About August 1962, the rubber pads under the

corners and end of the battery clamp were changed to a single pad.

850577/8
860740/1
877735/6
886455/6

About September 1962, the mounting screws for rear calipers to the final drive unit were changed.

850583/4
860832/3
877963/4
886685/6

About September 1962, the rear hubs and hub carriers were changed, and water throwers were added.

850587/8
860862/3
878036/7, including 876665-878036 for cars shipped to Germany
886753/4, including 885567-886753 for cars shipped to Germany

About October 1962, the upper steering column assembly was changed, and felt bearings were replaced with Vulkollan bearings. The lock and ignition switch assembly on the steering column was changed from Neiman to Waso Werken, and a cable was introduced to connect the steering-column lock connector to the instrument panel wiring.

850609/10
860912/3
878301/2
887131/2

About October 1962, the patterns embossed on the aluminum finisher panels on the assembly above the gearbox and on the assembly over the gearbox and driveshaft cover were changed.

861013/4
887316/7

About December 1962, the trunk lid prop and its bracket were changed.

861056/7
888066/7

About February 1963, the interior mirror assembly was changed.

850647/8
861070/1
878936/7
888138/9

A combination screwdriver (Phillips head or conventional) was introduced.

850648/9
861061/2

878888/9
888081/2

About January 1963, the rubber mounts at the rear of the gearbox were changed to a spring mount, except for the following cars: chassis numbers 850653, 850654, 861087, 878895, 878900, 878907, 878908, 878913, 878914, 878915, 878926, 878936, 878937, 878939, 878958, 878986, 879005, 879024, 879049, 888086, 888096, 888101, 888103, 888109, 888113, 888117, 888118, 888120, 888134, 888157, 888178, and 888238. In *The Jaguar E-Type: A Collector's Guide*, and *Jaguar International Magazine*, March 1986, chassis numbers 850646/7 were given instead of 850648/9, and slightly different omission lists are given in some sources.

The heat shield assembly was changed, probably to accommodate the new gearbox mount. Factory parts catalog of June 1963 states that these chassis numbers were fitted with the early shield: 850653, 850654, 861087, 878895, 878900, 878907, 878908, 878913, 878914, 878915, 878926, 878936, 878937, 878938, 878958, 878986, 879005, 879024, 879049, 888086, 888096, 888101, 888103, 888109, 888113, 888117, 888118, 888120, 888134, 888157, 888178, and 888238.

850649/50
861079/80, including 860365
878963/4
888168/9

The brake connecting lever between the pedal shaft and the plate of servo bellows was changed.

850653, 850654
861087
878895, 878900, 878907, 878908, 878913, 878914, 878915, 878926, 878936, 878937, 878939, 878958, 878986, 879005, 879024, 879049
888086, 888096, 888101, 888103, 888109, 888113, 888117, 888118, 888120, 888134, 888157, 888178, 888238

These cars were fitted with the transmission rear-end covers that were fitted to transmissions just prior to EB.8858JS.

850654/5
861085/6
878979/80
888184/5

About March 1963, the brake-fluid reservoir caps were changed, and a level indicator was adopted (the latter must be an error, as the level indicators had been fitted before this time). This is listed only in *Jaguar E-Type: The Definitive History*.

850655/6
879023/4

About March 1963, the seal assemblies at the rear of the wheel arches were changed.

850656/7
861090/1
879043/4
888240/1

About March 1963, the radiator header-tank assembly was changed; the 4-pound pressure cap was changed to a 9-pound one.

The water hose between the engine water outlet and the header tank was also changed. This is listed only in *Jaguar E-Type: The Definitive History.*

861092/3
888256/7

About August 1963, the mat assembly on the luggage compartment floor changed from a two-piece to a one-piece unit.

861098/9
888301/2

About August 1963, the trim panel for the shut pillar, the casing assembly at the side of the luggage compartment floor, and the hinged extension assembly for the luggage compartment floor were changed.

The shut pillar was changed. This is listed only in *Jaguar International Magazine,* March 1986.

The catch operating the quarter lights was changed. The casing assembly below the quarter lights and the quarter-light catches were changed. The casing assembly at the side of the luggage compartment floor and the hinged extension assembly for the luggage compartment floor were changed.

850656/7
861426/7
888759/60
889696/7

About January 1964, a cover was introduced for the brake-fluid reservoir cap. Due to the date, RHD coupe and LHD chassis numbers, and the nature of the change, I think the chassis numbers 850656/7 here should be 850806/7. This is listed only in *The Jaguar E-Type: A Collector's Guide.*

850678/9
861105/6
879131/2
888326/7

About April 1963, various parts in the rear suspension, such as wishbones, mountings at inner fulcrum shafts, and the bracing plate, were changed.

850680/1
861120/1
879159/60
888352/3

About April 1963, a canvas and rubber seal for the left-hand front frame undershield was introduced.

850695/6

861149/50
879291/2
888512/3

About May 1963, the ashtray was changed. This is listed only in *Jaguar E-Type: The Definitive History.*

850701/2
861168/9
879323/4
888542/3

About November 1963, the clock in the tachometer was changed to one fitted with a rectifier. The clock dial is marked CE.1111/01 (except for a few early ones that were marked CE.1111/00 in error). A black sleeve indicates that the clock is fitted with a rectifier. This is listed only in *Jaguar E-Type: The Definitive History.*

850707/8
861171/2
879331/2
888559/60

About May 1963, a keeper plate was added to the antiroll bar bushes. I am not sure if this reference is to the front or rear antiroll bar. This is listed only in *Jaguar E-Type: The Definitive History.*

850708/9
861174/5
879342/3
888566/7

About May 1963, the grab handle and its fixings were changed, and its position was slightly changed. This is listed only in *Jaguar E-Type: The Definitive History.*

850712/3
861177/8
879372/3
888611/2

About June 1963, the engine compartment undershields were increased in size and a cover was placed over the hole in the right-hand-side shield, under the oil filter. This is listed only in *Jaguar E-Type: The Definitive History.*

850713/4
861178/9
879422/3
888657/8

About June 1963, a trim panel was fitted to the hinge face of the door and was retained by the door light-switch striker. This is listed only in *Jaguar E-Type: The Definitive History.*

861178/9
888658/9

About June 1963, "various new items" of trunk-lid trim were added. This is listed only in *Jaguar E-Type: The Definitive History.* I am not sure if this is alluding to the E-Type nameplate, and perhaps a 3.8 plate that may have appeared on some late 3.8-liter cars. I have seen no hard evidence that any 3.8-liter cars left the factory with other than just a Jaguar plate on the trunk lid.

879440/1
888672/3
About June 1963, for cars with 3.54:1 rear ends, the rear end was changed. For cars with 3.54:1 rear ends, the rear brake discs were increased in thickness to 1/2 inch, the brake pad material was changed to Mintex M.59, and the rear calipers were mounted on adapter plates, as opposed to bolted direct.

879460/1
888694/5
About June 1963, for cars with 3.31:1 rear ends, the rear end was changed. For cars with 3.31:1 rear ends, the rear brake discs were increased in thickness to 1/2 inch, the brake pad material was changed to Mintex M.59, and the rear calipers were mounted on adapter plates, as opposed to bolted direct.

850721/2
861184/5
879493/4
888705/6
About June 1963, for cars with 3.07:1 rear ends, the rear end was changed. For cars with 3.07:1 rear ends, the rear brake discs were increased in thickness to 1/2 inch, the brake pad material was changed to Mintex M.59, and the rear calipers were mounted on adapter plates, as opposed to bolted direct.

850722/3
861202/3
879550/1
888759/60
About August 1963, two fork ends replaced the compensator inner-lever link in the handbrake. Some sources cite chassis numbers 850727/8 rather than 850722/3.

850723/4
861186/7
About June 1963, the fan motor relay was discontinued and the front wiring harness was changed. These changes are listed only in *Jaguar E-Type: The Definitive History.*

850723/4
861188/9
879495/6
888697/8
About June 1963, armrests were added to the doors. This is listed only in *Jaguar E-Type: The Definitive History.*

850725/6
861197/8
879550/1
888766/7
About August 1963, the turn signal-headlight flasher switch was changed. The striker plate (I think it is the one in the turn-signal switch) was changed. These changes are listed only in *Jaguar E-Type: The Definitive History.*

850729/30
861203/4
879576/7
888790/1
About June 1963, the filter in the clutch fluid reservoir was changed. This is listed only in *Jaguar E-Type: The Definitive History.*

850734/5
861218/9
879680/1
888885/6
About August 1963, two more windshield-pillar external chrome trim pieces were added. This is listed only in *Jaguar E-Type: The Definitive History.*

879758/9
888966/7
About September 1963, the 3.07:1 rear-end ratio was made standard for Italy, France, Germany, Belgium, and the Netherlands.

850736/7
861215/6
879760/1
888858/9
About August 1963, the console was changed. The new one had an armrest with storage space. This is listed only in *Jaguar E-Type: The Definitive History.*

This change was not made on chassis numbers 850725, 850727, 879531, 879543, 879545, 879546, 879553, 879556, 879562; these cars come before the listed change, so I suppose this means the new consoles were fitted to these earlier cars before it was made standard.

850736/7
861225/6
879820/1
889002/3
About September 1963, the 3.31:1 rear-end ratio was made standard for all countries except Italy, France, Germany, Belgium, the Netherlands, the United States, Canada, and Newfoundland.

850751/2
861253/4
879802/3
889029/30
About September 1963, the front finisher panel was changed from embossed aluminum to leather. This is listed only in *Jaguar E-Type: The Definitive History.* Since the change is from aluminum to leather, I assume this is the front finisher panel to the console, not the dash (which was trimmed in vinyl on the later 3.8-liter cars).

850751/2
861255/6
879892/3
889053/4
(and some prior cars)

About September 1963, the front carpets were changed to a type with a plastic heel pad. This is listed only in *Jaguar E-Type: The Definitive History.*

850754/5
861270/1
879989/90
889095/6

About September 1963, the mufflers and their mounts were changed. This is listed only in *Jaguar E-Type: The Definitive History.*

880025/6
889123/4
(including 879751 to 879808 and 888952 to 888994)

About September 1963, the 3.54:1 rear-end ratio was made standard for the United States, Canada, and Newfoundland.

861274/5
880165/6
889134/5

About November 1963, the wiper arms were changed to carry longer blades. This is listed only in *Jaguar E-Type: The Definitive History.*

850766/7
861294/5
880212/3
889235/6

About November 1963, the A-post rubber seals were changed. On the roadsters, the two-piece seal was replaced by a one-piece seal, and on the coupes, the separate cantrail seal and A-post seals were replaced by a single seal. The seal retainer on the cantrails on the coupes was no longer required after this change. This is listed only in *Jaguar E-Type: The Definitive History.*

850767/8
880290/1

About January 1964, a hole was added to the number-plate panel at the rear to allow access to the trunk-lid latch in case the release cable should break. Access was by using a right-angle 3/16-inch-diameter rod. A rubber seal was inserted in this hole.

850771/2
861324/5
880411/2
889346/7

About November 1963, the carpet fasteners were changed. This is listed only in *Jaguar E-Type: The Definitive History.*

850778/9
861341/2
880458/9
889374/5

About November 1963, the sealing rubber on the door shut pillar was changed. This is listed only in *Jaguar E-Type: The Definitive History.*

850784/5
861363/4
880561/2
889451/2

About December 1963, the differential breather was changed to one with an extension tube on the differential cover.

850785/6
861383/4
880614/5
889503/4

About January 1964, the ashtray was changed. The new one is not interchangeable with the old. This is likely the institution of the large, rectangular ashtray. This is listed only in *Jaguar E-Type: The Definitive History.*

850785/6
861385/6
880618/9
889509/10

About January 1964, the fuel pump was changed. The operating pressure went up. This is listed only in *Jaguar E-Type: The Definitive History.*

850786/7
861388/9
880630/1
889525/6

About March 1964, the radio was changed to use only one speaker. I suspect, however, that at least some earlier cars were delivered with only one speaker. The radio panel part of the console was also changed. These changes are listed only in *Jaguar E-Type: The Definitive History.*

880631/2
889526/7

About April 1964, sealed-beam headlights were adopted for cars going to Brazil, Canada, Chile, Colombia, Cuba, Dominican Republic, Egypt, El Salvador, Greece, Guatemala, Haiti, Hawaii, Jordan, Lebanon, Madeira, Mexico, Newfoundland, Nicaragua, Panama, Persian Gulf, Peru, Philippines, Puerto Rico, Saudi Arabia, Syria, the United States, Uruguay, Venezuela, and South Vietnam. This is listed only in *Jaguar E-Type: The Definitive History.*

850805/6
861423/4
880754/5
889688/9

In late winter or early spring of 1964, the roller-bearing seals in the halfshaft universal joints were changed, and covers for the journal assemblies were added. *The Jaguar E-Type: A Collector's Guide* gives chassis numbers 889697/8 as the LHD coupe chassis for the change, not 889688/9.

850806/7
861426/7
880759/60
889696/7

About March 1964, the protective caps for the brake-fluid level indicators were changed. This is listed only in *Jaguar E-Type: The Definitive History.*

850807/8
861445/6
880834/5
889779/80

About March 1964, the brake pedals were changed to improve attachment to the pedal shaft, and a tab-washer was added to the pinch bolt. This is listed only in *Jaguar E-Type: The Definitive History.*

850808/9
861445/6
880839/40
889786/7

About March 1964, the interior door trim was changed. This is listed only in *Jaguar E-Type: The Definitive History.*

850810/1
861460/1
880870/1
889819/20

About March 1964, the turn-signal-switch clamp bracket was changed from being a part of the switch to being part of the steering column. This is listed only in *Jaguar E-Type: The Definitive History.*

850818/9
861480/1
880982/3
889966/7

About April 1964, the upper steering column bearings were changed from Vulkollan to Elastollan. This is listed only in *Jaguar E-Type: The Definitive History.*

850824/5
861520/1
881152/3
890170/1

About April 1964, the front bush in the rear-suspension radius arms was changed. This is listed only in *Jaguar E-Type: The Definitive History.*

850839/40
861549/50

881202/3
890234/5

About April 1964, the starter solenoid was changed to reduce water leakage. This is listed only in *Jaguar E-Type: The Definitive History.*

850842/3
861556/7
881260/1
890250/1
(and a few earlier cars)

About April 1964, the rubber seals were improved (throughout the car, I assume). This is listed only in *Jaguar E-Type: The Definitive History.*

850856/7
881249/50

About April 1964, the chrome finishers on the top of the doors were changed. This is listed only in *Jaguar E-Type: The Definitive History.*

850858/9
861604/5
881281/2
890317/8

About May 1964, the striker for the turn-signal control was changed. This is listed only in *Jaguar E-Type: The Definitive History.*

861615/6
890339/40

About May 1964, the rear casings at the side of the luggage compartment floor were changed. This is listed only in *Jaguar E-Type: The Definitive History.*

850882/3
861661/2
881437/8
890487/8

About May 1964, the grille bar mounts were changed to incorporate a rubber mount. This is listed only in *Jaguar E-Type: The Definitive History.*

850888/9
881590/1

About August 1964, the chrome finishers at the sides of the windshield were changed. This is listed only in *Jaguar E-Type: The Definitive History.*

850907/8
861719/20
881696/7
890714/5

About October 1964, packing rings were added to the top of the rear springs. This is listed only in *Jaguar E-Type: The Definitive History.*

850907/8
861722/3

881705/6
890721/2

About October 1964, the gas cap was changed. This may be the end of the reeded-edge chrome steel fabricated cap and the beginning of the cast fluted cap. This is listed only in *Jaguar E-Type: The Definitive History*.

850934/5
861780/1
881863/4
890847/8

About October 1964, the feed pipe filter to the fuel pump was changed. This is listed only in *Jaguar E-Type: The Definitive History*.

850934/5
881864/5

About October 1964, the convertible-top cover was changed.

850942
861798
881885
890871

End of 3.8-liter E-Type production.

Changes in Order of Engine Number

R.1008/9

In June 1961, the size of the oil pump was increased for RHD cars. This is listed only in *The Jaguar E-Type: A Collector's Guide*.

R.1075/6

About October 1961, the separate intermediate timing-chain sprockets were replaced by a single-piece unit. This is listed only in *Jaguar E-Type: The Definitive History*.

R.1216/7

About August 1961, the inlet camshaft was changed to have a hole in the base.

R.1458/9

In October 1961, the crankshaft pulley was changed. The new crankshaft pulley was cast iron instead of alloy.

R.1509/10

The dynamo mounting bracket, pulley, and fan for dynamo pulley were changed. The dynamo adjusting link and the bolts securing the timing cover to the cylinder block were changed.

R.1844/5

About October 1961, the dynamo adjusting link was changed and a jockey pulley assembly was added.

R.1845/6

The bolts securing the timing cover to the cylinder block were changed.

R.2563/4

About December 1961, the rear-end crankshaft cover was changed, an asbestos oil seal was added, and the crankshaft was codified accordingly. The cover assembly for the rear of the cylinder block, and the associated hardware, changed.

R.2599/600

About December 1961, the oil thrower at the rear of the exhaust camshaft, the sealing port at the left rear of the cylinder head, and the cover for the left-hand (exhaust) camshaft were changed.

R.2933/4

About January 1962, the air-balance pipe was changed to accommodate the simplified throttle linkage; the air-balance pipe changed from three bosses to two. The slave-shaft assembly for throttle operation was changed to two slave-shafts from the previous arrangement with three slave-shafts using a flexible coupling.

R.3161/2

About February 1962, the big-end connecting-rod bearing clearances were reduced.

R.3690/1

About March 1962, the head stud holes in the cylinder-head gasket were enlarged.

R.3854/5

About March 1962, the spark-plug cables were increased in length and rerouted. The spacers for the spark-plug leads were changed.

R.5000/1

About May 1962, the inlet camshaft was drilled to reduce cold-starting noise.

R.5249/50

About June 1962, the pulley for the water pump and the belt were changed to accept the new duplex belt, and the material of the pulley was changed from aluminum to cast iron. The crankshaft pulley for the fan belt, and the dynamo and jockey pulley assemblies were changed to accept the new duplex belt. The early fan belts were of the single-grooved type, and the later belts were of the wide, double-grooved type.

R.5399/400

About June 1962, the oil-pan filter basket was changed to have four semicircular cutouts.

R.5532/3

About June 1962, the intermediate damper assembly for the upper timing chain was changed.

R.6417/8

About September 1962, the oil-pan drain plug was

changed to steel. This is listed only in *Jaguar E-Type: The Definitive History*.

R.6723/4
About September 1962, the inlet valve guides were lengthened.

R.7103/4
About September 1962, the connecting rods and pistons were changed. The upper pressure ring was chamfered on its inner edge, and a two-part scraper ring introduced. The connecting rods had an oil-spray hole added near the small end, and were marked with yellow paint near the rib.

R.7194/5
About October 1962, the dowels between the bearing caps and the cylinder block were enlarged.

R.7307/8
About October 1962, the crankshaft was changed. This is listed only in *Jaguar E-Type: The Definitive History*.

R.8138/9
About November 1962, the vibration damper for the lower timing chain was changed.

R.8299/300
About November 1962, a quick-lift thermostat with a higher opening temperature was fitted.

R.9520/1
About February 1963, a quick-lift thermostat with a higher opening temperature was fitted.

R.9527/8
About December 1962, the spark plugs were changed to Champion UN.12Y. This is listed only in *Jaguar E-Type: The Definitive History*.

R.9699/700
About February 1963, the dipstick was changed. This is listed only in *Jaguar E-Type: The Definitive History*.

RA.1099/100
About March 1963, the automatic fan belt tensioning system was changed. This is listed only in *Jaguar E-Type: The Definitive History*.

RA.1100/1
The carrier for the jockey pulley was changed.

RA.1381/2
About April 1963, the distributor and vacuum suction pipe were changed.

RA.2077/8
About June 1963, the oil pump was changed, and the oil suction pipe was changed to 3/4 inch instead of 11/16 inch.

RA.2289/90
About August 1963, rubber sleeves were fitted to the spark-plug wires where they enter the distributor cap. This is listed only in *Jaguar E-Type: The Definitive History*.

RA.2463/4
The needle valve and seat in the carburetor float chamber was changed to Delrin, and changes were made in the lid and hinged lever. In *The Jaguar E-Type: A Collector's Guide*, Skilleter cites a date of about June 1963 for this change, and in *Jaguar E-Type: The Definitive History*, Porter cites about April 1964. Based on these dates, I suspect the serial numbers of this change are really 5463/4 instead of 2463/4.

RA.2971/2
About September 1963, the exhaust valves were changed to be made of a different material.

RA.3289/90
About September 1963, the water pump impeller was changed. This is listed only in *Jaguar E-Type: The Definitive History*.

RA.4115/6
About January 1964, the throttle spring bearings in the carburetors were changed to an impregnated plastic material. This is listed only in *Jaguar E-Type: The Definitive History*.

RA.4573/4
About March 1964, the oil-pan drain plug was changed. This is listed only in *Jaguar E-Type: The Definitive History*.

RA.4974/5
About March 1964, the oil filter was changed. This is listed only in *Jaguar E-Type: The Definitive History*.

RA.5633/4
About April 1964, the spark-plug cables were changed. This is listed only in *Jaguar E-Type: The Definitive History*.

RA.5648/9
About March 1964, the pistons were changed to have chamfer and oil drain holes below the control ring (to reduce oil use). This is listed only in *Jaguar E-Type: A Collector's Guide*.

RA.5736/7
About April 1964, the cylinder heads on E-Types and Mk X cars were made the same. This is listed only in *Jaguar E-Type: The Definitive History*. I'm not sure if this means the E-Type head was changed or not.

RA.5800/1
About April 1964, the clutch was changed to the Laycock diaphragm type and the flywheel was

changed to accept either Borg and Beck or the diaphragm clutch.

RA.5885/6
About April 1964, the jockey pulley bracket was changed to have impregnated plastic bushes instead of the brass bushes used earlier. This is listed only in *Jaguar E-Type: The Definitive History*.

RA.6024/5
About May 1964, the lower timing-chain intermediate damper was changed. The new damper was positioned differently and was attached to two tapped bosses on the cylinder block.

RA.6419/20
About August 1964, the front timing cover was changed so that the oil seal could be changed without removing the cover. This is listed only in *Jaguar E-Type: The Definitive History*.

RA.6453/4
About May 1964, the crankshaft damper was changed. This is listed only in *Jaguar E-Type: The Definitive History*.

RA.6603/4
About May 1964, a support was added to the first intermediate bearing cap to support the oil delivery pipe, and this support replaced a lock washer that was on the cap before. This is listed only in *Jaguar E-Type: The Definitive History*.

RA.6745/6
About August 1964, the scraper rings on the pistons were changed for 8.0:1 and 9.0:1 compression-ratio engines. The new rings were Maxiflex 50. This is listed only in *Jaguar E-Type: The Definitive History*.

RA.6833/4
About July 1964, the distributor was changed on the 9.0:1 compression-ratio engines and a plastic ring impregnated with magnetized metal particles replaced the metal magnetic ring in the oil filter assembly. This is listed only in *Jaguar E-Type: The Definitive History*.

RA.7175/6
About October 1964, the intake manifold gasket was changed from cupronickel to a tin-plate material. This is listed only in *Jaguar E-Type: The Definitive History*.

RA.7201/2
About October 1964, the distributor was changed on 8.0:1 compression-ratio engines. This is listed only in *Jaguar E-Type: The Definitive History*.

RA.7323/4
About August 1964, engine-lifting brackets were added to the cylinder head. Some head studs had to be made longer. The spark-plug cables had to be lengthened to accommodate the new engine-lifting brackets. These changes are listed only in *Jaguar E-Type: The Definitive History*.

Changes in Order of Transmission Number
EB.245/6 JS
The rear-end transmission cover and the speedometer driver gear were changed.

EB.1653/4
The dowel screws in the transmission gear-selection mechanism were changed. This is listed only in *Jaguar E-Type: The Definitive History*.

EB.8858/9 JS
About February 1963, the rear-end cover of transmission was changed. This change was related to the change in the rear engine mounting.

Chapter 3

4.2-LITER CHANGES BY SERIAL NUMBER

In this chapter I chronicle the changes listed in various published sources, including the various Jaguar factory parts books. The listing is in order of chassis number, with RHD roadster number (chassis number 1E.1001, forward for Series I and 1R.1001, forward for Series II) determining position in the list. For every entry I give the chassis-number (or engine or transmission number, as appropriate) transition point, and a description of the change. In cases where a change is listed only by a single reference other than the factory literature, I cite that reference.

For this listing I used the spare parts catalog for Jaguar 4.2-liter E-Type Grand Touring models, publication number J.37, November 1965, November 1969 reprint; the spare parts catalog for 4.2 liter E-Type 2+2s, publication number J.38, December 1965; the Jaguar-Daimler Interim Parts List for 1969 Jaguar E-Type open and fixed-head-coupe 2+2 models; the parts catalog for Series II E-Type open and fixed-head coupe, January 1979 (a microfiche reference); and the same published sources as used in chapter 2. The notes appearing at the beginning of that chapter apply here. In particular, note that the dates cited for the changes from *The Jaguar E-Type: A Collector's Guide*, *Jaguar E-Type: The Definitive History*, and *Jaguar International Magazine*, March 1986, are approximate.

Changes in Order of Chassis Number
1E.1011/2
1E.10312/3
1E.20079/80
1E.30251/2
About January 1965, spacers were introduced at the front mounts of the seat slides where they attach to the floor. This is listed only in *Jaguar E-Type: The Definitive History*.

1E.1019/20
1E.10323/4
1E.20081/2
1E.30268/9
The vacuum reservoir was changed.

1E.1038/9
1E.10337/8
1E.20097/8
1E.30291/2
About March 1965, the sealing at the front ball joints was improved.

1E.1039/40
1E.10337/8
1E.20097/8
1E.30292/3
About January 1965, the fittings between the seat slides and the seat were changed. This is listed only in *Jaguar E-Type: The Definitive History*.

1E.1046/7, including 1E.1021
1E.10337/8
1E.20099/100, including 1E.20083
1E.30301/2, including 1E.30271
About February 1965, shields were added to the front brake discs. The left-hand tie-rod lever was changed. The bolt and washer mounting for the front caliper to the stub axle carriers was changed.

1E.1060/1
1E.10359/60
1E.20102/3
1E.30349/50
The cockpit panel assembly at the side of the gearbox was changed. About November 1964, the leather shift boot was changed to a rubber boot.

1E.1062/3
1E.10771/2
1E.20362/3, including 1E.20335
1E.30856/7
The horns were changed.

1E.1069/70
1E.10425/6
1E.20116/7

1E.30401/2

The body shell underframe and rear-end assembly were changed.

1E.20116/7
1E.30401/2

About February 1965, the casing assembly below the quarter lights was changed and the pocket assembly in the casing below the quarter lights was deleted. The cover assembly over the spare wheel and fuel tank and forward luggage floor area were trimmed, and the old luggage floor mat was done away with. The rear-wheel arch covers were changed from moquette trimmed to PVC trimmed. The hinged extension board and its support rail assembly were changed. Some carpets and hardura mats and insulating felts and interior trim were changed.

About March 1965, body shell changes took place. This is listed only in *Jaguar E-Type: The Definitive History*.

1E.1076/7
1E.10429/30, including 1E.10427
1E.20136/7, including 1E.20132
1E.30442/3

About March 1965, the front suspension was changed. The front brake caliper was changed. The front calipers were altered to move the bleed screw to the inner side of the assembly. The hydraulic pipe from the front flexible hose to the front brake calipers was changed.

1E.1103/4
1E.10045/6
1E.20207/8
1E.30033/4

About June 1965, the speedometer cable was changed. This is listed only in *Jaguar E-Type: The Definitive History*.

1E.1151/2
1E.10702/3
1E.20328/9
1E.30771/2

About May 1965, the axle ratio was changed from 3.31:1 to 3.07:1 for all cars except those exported to the United States, Canada, and Newfoundland, which were 3.54:1. Some sources cite chassis numbers 1E.1072/3 instead of 1E.10702/3.

1E.10739/40
1E.30806/7

The 3.54:1 rear-end assembly was changed for cars exported to the United States, Canada, and Newfoundland.

1E.1162/3
1E.10771/2
1E.20362/3, including 1E.20335
1E.30856/7

About June 1965, the forward wiring harness and front lamp harness were changed.

The horns were changed. This is listed only in *Jaguar E-Type: The Definitive History*.

1E.1164/5
1E.20370/1

The forward wiring harness and the instrument-panel wiring harness were changed.

1E.1164/5
1E.10753/4
1E.20370/1
1E.30824/5

About June 1965, the windshield washer bottle was changed to plastic, and pre-timed operation was deleted.

1E.10753/4
1E.30824/5

The instrument-panel wiring harness was changed.

1E.1177/8
1E.10783/4
1E.20396/7
1E.30861/2
For 3.07:1 rear ends
1E.10739/40
1E.30806/7
For 3.54:1 rear ends

About June 1965, the rear-end assembly was changed for cars exported to the United States, Canada, and Newfoundland. About June 1965, the rear end changed to a type with driveshaft flanges as part of the driveshafts. The 3.07:1 rear-end assembly was changed for all countries except the United States, Canada, and Newfoundland.

1E.1201/2
1E.10847/8
1E.20501/2
1E.30889/90

About June 1965, the console was changed. This may be where the vinyl shift boot was introduced.

The driveshaft tunnel changed. This is listed only in *Jaguar E-Type: The Definitive History*.

1E.1225/6
1E.10957/8
1E.20611/2
1E.30911/2
(and some previous chassis)

About June 1965, a speedometer-drive access aperture, with cover, was added to the right-hand-side gearbox side panel. This is listed only in *Jaguar E-Type: The Definitive History*.

1E.1225/6
1E.10957/8
1E.20611/2
1E.30981/2

About June 1965, a rubber sealing plug was added to seal the gearbox apertures. The left-hand water-feed pipe to the heater, behind the dash panel, between the water control valve and the heater radiator, was changed.

1E.1234/5
1E.11165/6
1E.20632/3
1E.31243/4
About November 1965, the rack and pinion assembly was changed. This is listed only in *Jaguar E-Type: The Definitive History*.

1E.1236/7
1E.10978/9
1E.20638/9
1E.31002/3
The rear hub carrier and its oil seal were changed.

1E.1252/3
1E.11048/9
1E.20691/2
1E.31077/8
About September 1965, the front cylinder-head cover and the crankcase breather arrangement were changed from the non-U.S. type to a standard type for all cars. The inlet manifold stud for the water outlet was changed, and a stud and distance piece for the water outlet pipe and breather pipe were added for non-U.S. cars. The base assembly for the air-intake with three trumpets and the adapter for the breather pipe were changed to a standard type for all cars (U.S. cars were no different).

1E.1285/6
1E.11117/8
1E.20752/3
1E.31170/1
About September 1965, the front closing panel assemblies for the cockpit and sills were changed.

1E.1292/3
1E.11120/1
1E.20762/3
1E.31176/7
About November 1965, the rear shock absorbers were changed. This is listed only in *Jaguar E-Type: The Definitive History*.

1E.20851/2
1E.31412/3
About November 1965, the coupe rear-door support went from post-type prop to the hinged type.

1E.1333/4
1E.11157/8
About November 1965, sealing panels were added between the rear bulkhead panel and wheel-arch valances. This is listed only in *Jaguar E-Type: The Definitive History*.

1E.1376/7
1E.11363/4

1E.20899/900
1E.31526/7
About November 1965, the rear coil springs were changed.

1E.1386/7
1E.11546/7
1E.20936/7
1E.31778/9
About March 1966, more mud shielding was fitted to the front frame. This is listed only in *Jaguar E-Type: The Definitive History*.

1E.20938/9
1E.31787/8
About March 1966, a vanity mirror was added to the passenger's sun visor. This is listed only in *Jaguar E-Type: The Definitive History*.

1E.20952/3
1E.31919/20
About February 1966, the coupe window frame seals were changed from felt to a flocked runner.

1E.1408/9
1E.11714/5
1E.20977/8
1E.32008/9
About March 1966, the standard tires were changed to Dunlop SP.41 HR tires, except for cars exported to Australia, Canada, Newfoundland, New Zealand, and the United States. The speedometers were changed to reflect the Dunlop tire change. Special rear-suspension bump stops were used to avoid fowling the new Dunlop tires. These changes are listed only in *Jaguar E-Type: The Definitive History*.

1E.1411/2
1E.11727/8
1E.20995/6
1E.32008/9
The bracket assembly for the rear bumpers was changed. An attachment bracket assembly for the rear bumpers was introduced.

1E.1412/3
1E.11534/5
1E.20992/3
1E.31764/5
About March 1966, the steering assembly was changed (a seven-tooth pinion replaced the eight-tooth pinion) to improve steering when radial-ply tires were fitted.

1E.1412/3
1E.11740/1
1E.20999/1000
1E.32009/10

About March 1966, the brake-light switch was repositioned. The front wiring harness was changed. The rear bumper fittings were changed so that the bumpers could be removed from outside the car. New brake and clutch master cylinders and pedal housings were fitted to standardize the two-seater cars with the 2+2 cars, and the brake-light switch was repositioned. These changes are listed only in *Jaguar E-Type: The Definitive History*.

1E.1418/9
1E.11802/3
1E.21037/8
1E.32039/40

The trimmed base assembly of the seats, and the screws and washers mounting them to the slides, were changed.

1E.1423/4
1E.11885/6
1E.21075/6
1E.32089/90

An O-ring was placed on the hood-lock operating rod to prevent vibration of the rod.

1E.12024/5
1E.32193/4

About December 1965, a hazard warning light (or four-way flasher) was fitted as standard. Porter's *Jaguar E-Type: The Definitive History* cites this change as occurring for U.S. cars in about July 1967.

1E.21133/4
1E.32267/8

About September 1966, the hinged extension board in the luggage area was changed. This is listed only in *Jaguar E-Type: The Definitive History*.

1E.1430/1
1E.12169/70
1E.21139/40
1E.32315/6
1E.50156/7
1E.76000/1

About September 1966, the cooling fan thermostat was changed. This is listed only in *Jaguar E-Type: The Definitive History*.

1E.1457/8
1E.12033/4
1E.21206/7
1E.32200/1

About September 1966, the turn signal-headlight flasher switch was changed. About March 1966, the upper steering column was changed. These changes are listed only in *Jaguar E-Type: The Definitive History*.

1E.1464/5
1E.12521/2
1E.21214/5

1E.32596/7

About September 1966, the air cleaner and its support bracket were changed. This is listed only in *Jaguar E-Type: The Definitive History*.

1E.21222/3
1E.32608/9
1E.50001
1E.75001

The rear defroster switch was changed and a warning light was added. The warning lamp dims when the sidelights are on. Dates of April 1966 and July 1967 were given in various sources for this change.

1E.1478/9
1E.12579/80
1E.21227/8
1E.32631/2

About September 1966, the hood, including front fenders, front bumpers, and heater air-intake plenum, were changed to the type as used on the 2+2s. This is listed only in *Jaguar E-Type: The Definitive History*.

1E.1483/4
1E.12637/8
1E.21234/5
1E.32666/7
1E.50007/8
1E.75074/5

About September 1966, a rubber cover was added to the tops of the brake-fluid warning terminals. This is listed in *Jaguar E-Type: The Definitive History*.

1E.1489/90
1E.12687/8

About September 1966, sun visors were added. This is listed only in *Jaguar E-Type: The Definitive History*.

1E.1489/90
1E.12692/3
1E.21253/4
1E.32684/5

About September 1966, a rubber seat was added to the top of the spring in the rear transmission mount, and the spring retainer was changed. This is listed only in *Jaguar E-Type: The Definitive History*.

1E.1497/8
1E.12716/7
1E.21265/6
1E.32691/2

About September 1966, the illumination color of the instruments and switch label strip was changed from blue to green. This is listed only in *Jaguar E-Type: The Definitive History*.

1E.21311/2
1E.32765/6

About September 1966, the regulator channel for the wind-up windows was changed. This is listed only in *Jaguar E-Type: The Definitive History*.

1E.1544/5
1E.12964/5
1E.21334/5
1E.32887/8

About December 1966, a heat shield was introduced for the headpipes. This is listed only in *Jaguar E-Type: The Definitive History*.

1E.1560/1
1E.13010/1
1E.21341/2
1E.32941/2

About November 1966, the clutch and brake master cylinders were modified to have shorter pushrods, to change pedal angles, and to improve the accelerator pedal angle, and a change was made in the accelerator pedal assembly.

1E.50121/2
1E.75862/3

About December 1966, the screws retaining the chrome beads at the top of the doors were changed to retainers and rivets.

1E.1598/9
1E.13181/2
1E.21379/80
1E.33119/20
1E.50155/6
1E.75991/2

About December 1966, the mufflers changed from being welded to the tailpipes to being clipped to them. This is listed only in *Jaguar E-Type: The Definitive History*. This is an unusual entry, since a similar change occurred earlier during 3.8-liter production at chassis numbers 850178/9, 860011/2, 875607/8, and 885058/9. I am not aware of early 4.2-liter cars having mufflers welded to the tailpipes.

1E.1606/7
1E.13205/6
1E.21387/8
1E.33149/50

About March 1967, the right-hand-side scuttle top casing (underdash panel) was changed from Rexine-trimmed aluminum to fiberboard. This is listed only in *Jaguar E-Type: The Definitive History*.

1E.50422/3
1E.76663/4

The trim panels above the rear door aperture, as well as the headlining, was changed.

1E.50573/4
1E.76888/9

(and certain individual earlier cars) Seatbelts were available for the rear seats.

1E.1657/8
1E.13386/7
1E.21388/9
1E.33139/40

About March 1967, the windshield glass was changed. This is listed only in *Jaguar E-Type: The Definitive History*.

1E.1685/6
1E.13588/9
1E.21441/2
1E.33548/9
1E.50585/6
1E.76910/1

About March 1967, the shift-lever boot was changed to Ambla from the grommet that was used previously. I presume this was the introduction of the third style of shift-lever boot as found on late Series I and early Series II cars.

1E.1685/6
1E.13724/5
1E.21442/3
1E.33643/4

About March 1967, the center scuttle top casing was changed from Rexine-covered aluminum to fiberboard. This is listed only by Porter.

1E.1689/90
1E.13846/7
1E.21450/1
1E.33708/9
1E.50640/1
1E.76933/4

About July 1967, the linkage between the tailpipes was changed from bolted to welded. This is listed only in *Jaguar E-Type: The Definitive History*.

1E.50660/1
1E.76949/50

About July 1967, the upper squab of the back seat was changed. This is listed only in *Jaguar E-Type: The Definitive History*.

1E.50680/1
1E.77376/7

About July 1968, the package trays were changed. This is listed only in *Jaguar E-Type: The Definitive History*.

1E.1692/3
1E.13951/2
1E.21450/1
1E.33774/5

About July 1967, the drain tray on the doors was changed. This is listed only in *Jaguar E-Type: The Definitive History*.

1E.1711/2
1E.14582/3
1E.21472/3
1E.34146/7
1E.50709/10
1E.77046/7

About January 1968, the motif bar and its rubber mountings were changed. This is listed only in *Jaguar E-Type: The Definitive History*.

1E.1723/4
1E.13150/1
1E.21480/1
1E.33090/1
1E.50165/6
1E.75546/7

About July 1967, there were numerous changes in the electrical equipment, an ignition warning light replaced the oil-pressure switch, and the old oil-pressure switch in the cylinder block oil gallery was replaced by a plug. For the 2+2s, at least, the forward wiring harness, the instrument-panel wiring harness, and the alternator harness were changed.

1E.13804/5
1E.33688/9
1E.76921/2

About July 1967, a cover was added to the four-way flasher switch panel (for those cars with four-way flashers). This is listed only in *Jaguar E-Type: The Definitive History*.

1E.1762/3
1E.15109/10
1E.21488/9
1E.34302/3

About July 1967, the rear hub carriers were changed. This is listed only in *Jaguar E-Type: The Definitive History*.

1E.50874/5
1E.77406/7

About July 1968, the diameter of the torsion bars was increased. This is listed only in *Jaguar E-Type: The Definitive History*.

1E.1813/4
1E.11534/5
1E.21517/8
1E.34338/9
1E.50911/2
1E.77474/5

New wheels with the forged center hub and straight spokes were introduced for the chrome wire wheels only. Some sources cite chassis number 1E.15486/7 instead of 1E.11534/5. Dates of May 1967 and July 1968 are cited for this change.

1E.15179/80
1E.34582/3

About January 1968, U.S. federal specification cars were introduced. This is listed only in *The Jaguar E-Type: A Collector's Guide*. It is possible that 1E.15179/80 should be **1E.15979/80.** If this is so, it clears up some of the mystery of Series I cars like 1E.15267 with open lights.

1E.1852/3
1E.15752/3
1E.21578/9
1E.34457/8
1E.50971/2
1E.77601/2

About July 1968, a forged hub was introduced for the painted wire wheels. This is listed only in *Jaguar E-Type: The Definitive History*.

1E.1863/4
1E.15888/9
1E.21583/4
1E.34249/50
1E.50974/5
1E.77644/5

About July 1967, the headlight covers were discontinued. In *Jaguar E-Type: The Definitive History*, Porter stated that about January 1968, the hood was changed to give direct access to the headlights; only chassis numbers 1E.34549/50 are cited instead of 1E.34249/50. This note may be referring to the introduction of the first style of open headlights, commonly thought of as Series I 1/2 headlights. As is noted in chapter 1, Skilleter cites these same chassis numbers as the beginning of the Series I 1/2 cars. Some late Series I cars had open headlights. For example, serial number 1E.15267 is such a car. So perhaps what is being referred to here is the introduction of the Series I 1/2 production, and not just the introduction of the open-headlight cars. This may be the onset of the open headlights for the non-U.S.-market cars.

1E.1886/7
1E.15981/2
1E.21619/20
1E.34602/3

About September 1967, the Powr-Lok differential was discontinued as standard, except for the U.S. 3.54:1 ratio axle. This is listed only in *The Jaguar E-Type: A Collector's Guide*.

1E.1895/6
1E.16009/10
1E.21628/9
1E.34633/4
1E.51016/7
1E.77694/5

About July 1968, the fuel filter was changed to one with more filter area. This is listed only in *Jaguar E-Type: The Definitive History*.

1E.1904/5

1E.16056/7
1E.21661/2
1E.32771/2
1E.51042/3
1E.77700/1

The fuel filter element was changed from gauze to a renewable fiber element. *Jaguar E-Type: The Definitive History* cites a date of about July 1968 for this change, while *The Jaguar E-Type: A Collector's Guide* cites about February 1968. In addition, the latter cites chassis numbers 1E.34771/2 instead of 1E.32771/2, and numbers 1E.50142/3 instead of 1E.51042/3.

1E.1919/20
1E.16098/9
1E.21668/9
1E.34846/7
1E.51058/9
1E.77704/5

About July 1968, the tires were changed to Dunlop SP Sport, and whitewalls were used for cars exported to the United States. This is listed only in *Jaguar E-Type: The Definitive History*.

1E.1925/6
1E.16720/1
1E.21668/9
1E.34850/1
1E.51066/7
1E.77704/5

In early 1968, greased nipples were reintroduced on the halfshaft universal joints. In some references, chassis numbers 1E.16126/7 are cited instead of 1E.16720/1, and numbers 1E.50166/7 are cited instead of 1E.51066/7.

1E.2038/9
1E.21783/4

About April 1968, the dashboard was revised. Heater controls, choke, and switches were changed, a lid was added to the glovebox, and the heater box was changed. I think this is also the introduction of the rocker switches, which I believe was simultaneous with the addition of the glovebox lid (except for the 2+2 cars, which had it earlier).

1E.2050/1
1E.31806/7
1E.51212/3

The radiator was changed to a vertical-flow type, as already fitted to LHD cars. The date for this change is alternately listed as April and July of 1968.

About July 1968, the header tank and cap were changed. This is listed only in *Jaguar E-Type: The Definitive History*.

About April or July 1968, the water pump assembly, the thermostat, and the breather pipe were changed to the type already fitted to LHD cars. The water outlet housing and thermostat housing were changed.

About April 1968, the single cooling fan was replaced by dual cooling fans, as already fitted to LHD cars. This is listed only in *The Jaguar E-Type: A Collector's Guide*.

1E.16537/8
1E.34944/5
1E.77837/8

About July 1968, the water temperature gauge was changed to one with zones only marked, as opposed to the earlier calibrated gauge. This is listed only in *The Jaguar E-Type: A Collector's Guide*.

Series II Chassis

(Note that the prefix is now R)
1R.1012/3
1R.7442/3
1R.20006/7
1R.25283/4
1R.35010/1
1R.40207/8

About January 1969, the alternator was changed to have side-entry cables, for cars not fitted with air conditioning. The alternator harness was changed.

1R.35018/9
1R.40238/9

The handbrake lever assembly was changed.

1R.1053/4
1R.20072/3
1R.35098/9

About February 1969, earless hubcaps were introduced on RHD cars (as on the LHD cars).

1R.7747/8
1R.25430/1

The choke assembly was changed.

1R.1057/8
1R.7795/6
1R.20087/8
1R.25430/1

The screen rail fascia and the defrosting equipment were changed.

1R.1057/8
1R.20094/5
1R.35098/9

About December 1968, a steering column lock was fitted to RHD cars.

1R.1060/1
1R.7829/30
1R.20101/2
1R.25438/9
1R.35098/9
1R.40507/8

About March 1969, the master cylinder spacer

was changed. This is listed only in *Jaguar E-Type: The Definitive History*.

1R.1067/8
1R.7992/3
1R.20118/9
1R.25523/4
1R.35797/8
1R.40667/8
About March 1969, the top part of the gas tank was changed.

1R.1084/5
1R.20094/5
1R.35098/9
About December 1968, a steering column lock was fitted to RHD cars.

1R.1137/8
1R.8868/9
1R.20211/2
1R.26004/5
About May 1969, the perforated leather trim was introduced for the seats, and the headrests were changed. The following cars were also fitted with the early seats: chassis numbers 1R.8870, 1R.8871, 1R.8873, 1R.8874, 1R.8875, 1R.8876, 1R.8877, 1R.8878, 1R.8879, 1R.8880, 1R.8881, 1R.8882, 1R.8883, 1R.9029, 1R.9042, 1R.9069, 1R.9070, 1R.9077, 1R.9147, 1R.9169, 1R.9172, 1R.9174, 1R.9185, 1R.9195, 1R.9255, 1R.9328, 1R.9244 (perhaps this is 9344), 1R.9350, 1R.9396, 1R.9419, 1R.26002, 1R.26007, 1R.26010, 1R.26022, 1R.26023, 1R.26025, 1R.26028, 1R.26033, 1R.26051, 1R.26053, 1R.26057, 1R.26069, and 1R.26078.

1R.9456/7
1R.26319/20
1R.35332/3
1R.42012/3
About August 1969, a composite bracket was introduced to mount the alternator, air-conditioning compressor, and the power steering pump. This is listed only in *Jaguar E-Type: The Definitive History*.

1R.1183/4
1R.9456/7
1R.20260/1
1R.26319/20
The cooling fan cowl was changed. The air conditioning was changed from the early type (which did not permit the fitting of power steering) to the later type. As a special note, the factory parts catalog for open and fixed-head-coupe Series II E-Types states that the later-type installation was also fitted to chassis numbers 1R.1152, 1R.9207, 1R.9451, 1R.9453, 1R.20223, and 1R.20245.

1R.1184/5
1R.20263/4

The upper steering-column assembly was changed.

1R.1187/8
1R.9569/70
1R.20269/70
1R.26386/7
1R.35352/3
1R.42117/8
About June 1969, the hood-lifting springs were replaced by a gas-filled cylinder.

The front subframe assembly changed; chassis numbers 1R.3532/3 and 1R.42117/8 were not included in this change.

1R.1189/90
1R.9594/5
1R.20271/2
1R.26401/2
The radiator was changed.

1R.1195/6
1R.9642.3
1R.20277/8
1R.26428/9
The top water hose from the radiator to the water manifold was changed.

1R.9859/60
1R.26532/3
1R.42381/2
About April 1969, the starter switch was changed to one that isolated some auxiliaries while the starter was cranking.

1R.1243/4
1R.9939/40
1R.20334/5
1R.26575/6
The mounting of the rear brake calipers to the final drive unit changed, and the adapter plate was discontinued.

The final drive unit was changed (chassis numbers 1R.9929/30 were cited in the Series II parts catalog instead of 1R.9939/40, I believe in error).

1R.35421/2
1R.42400/1
About March 1970, the handbrake lever was changed to one with a different material in the pivot pin and lever.

1R.1301/2, and some cars after 1R.1277
1R.10151/2, and some cars after 1R.10114
1R.20365/6, and some cars after 1R.20354
1R.26683/4, and some cars after 1R.26649
1R.35457/8, and some cars after 1R.35440
1R.42559/60, and some cars after 1R.42539
About August 1969, the seat assemblies were adapted to take headrests as an optional extra, but chassis

numbers 1R.35457/8 and 1R.42559/60 were not mentioned in the factory parts catalog.

1R.1325/6
1R.10334/5
1R.20390/1
1R.26755/6
Armrests were added to the doors.

1R.1348/9
1R.10522/3
The sun visor mechanism was changed.

1R.1351/2
1R.10536/7
1R.20424/5
1R.26834/5
1R.35563/4
1R.42676/7
About October 1969, the clock was changed from a mercury-cell type to a battery-operated type. Some references cite chassis numbers 1R.1350/1 instead of 1R.1351/2, and numbers 1R.24424/5 instead of 1R.20425/6.

1R.1392/3
1R.11051/2
1R.20485/6
1R.27050/1
1R.35642/3
1R.42849/50
About January 1970, a ballast resistor was added to the ignition system.
The side-marker lights were changed, but their colors remained the same. The gas tank and cap, as well as the fascia panel assemblies, were changed. Chassis numbers 1R.35642/3 and 1R.42849/50 were not included in these three changes.

1R.1410/1
1R.11302/3
1R.20509/10
1R.27173/4
1R.35647/8
1R.42993/4
About November 1969, the front flexible brake hose was changed.

1R.35649/50
1R.42551/2
About October 1969, a defroster-tube extension was fitted.

1R.35656/7
1R.43164/5
About January 1970, the automatic transmission selector lever was changed. This is listed only in *Jaguar E-Type: The Definitive History*.

1R.11973/4
1R.27480/1
The stop-tail-flasher lights were changed for cars exported to Canada, Greece, Portugal, and the United States only, but the color of the lens remained red.

1R.1586/7
1R.12955/6
1R.20722/3
1R.27869/70
1R.35787/8
1R.43772/3
About April 1970, the fan control thermostat was changed. This is listed only in *Jaguar E-Type: The Definitive History*.

1R.13427/8
1R.28054/5
The side flasher lights changed, for cars exported to Canada and the United States only.

1R.14065/6
1R.28294/5
The headlights were changed for cars exported to Belgium, Czechoslovakia, Holland, Germany, Poland, Rumania, and Switzerland.

1R.1775/6
1R.14120/1
1R.20952/3
1R.28319/20
The headlight dip switch was changed.

1R.1755/6
1R.20954/5
About August 1970, larger-diameter torsion bars were fitted to RHD cars.

1R.35815/6
1R.43923/4
About May 1970, the handbrake lever assembly was changed. The new one was longer and angled upward.

Changes in Order of Engine Number
"7E.1001 to 7E.000" and then "7E.0000 & subs."
The main bearings were changed.

7E.1336/7
About December 1964, the connecting rods were changed. The new rods have a small hole at the small end to spray oil. This is listed only in *Jaguar E-Type: The Definitive History*.

7E.1404/5
About December 1964, the water pump and pulley were changed to make removal easier. The studs and bolts for the water pump were changed to bolts.

7E.1724/5
About January 1965, the inlet manifold was changed. The pressed-in vacuum fitting was replaced with a screwed-in one. This is listed only in *Jaguar E-Type: The Definitive History*.

7E.1881/2
About March 1965, the inlet manifold gasket was changed. This is listed only in *Jaguar E-Type: The Definitive History*.

7E.2458/9
About April 1965, a waterproof cover was added to the distributor. This is listed only in *Jaguar E-Type: The Definitive History*.

7E.2693/4
About April 1965, the oil pan was changed.

7E.2895/6
The exhaust-side cam cover was changed, and the fiber washer on filler cap was changed to an O-ring.

7E.3422/3
About June 1965, the alternator bracket was changed. This is listed only in *Jaguar E-Type: The Definitive History*.

7E.4606/7
The clutch slave cylinder, return spring, and operating rod were changed.

7E.5169/70
About November 1965, the oil filter changed from felt to paper. This is listed only in *Jaguar E-Type: The Definitive History*.

7E.6332/3
The exhaust manifold studs were changed. The bolt holding the timing chain cover to the cylinder block was changed to allow attachment of the alternator shield.
About May 1966, an alternator shield was added.

7E.7297/8
7E.50021/2
About September 1966, a low-lift carburetor can was introduced to reduce engine speed when the choke was put on. This included changes in the jet housing of the carburetors.

7E.7449/50
7E.50021/2
In late 1966 or early 1967, the valve guides were fitted with circlips to ensure their location in the head.

7E.50021/2
The shaft assembly for the intermediate timing-chain sprocket was changed.

7E.50024/5
About September 1966, the intermediate sprocket was changed to cast iron. This is listed only in *Jaguar E-Type: The Definitive History*.

7E.7810/1
7E.50046/7
About September 1966, the clutch disc was made a little convex. The new disc is marked with light blue and purple paint near the center. This is listed only in *Jaguar E-Type: The Definitive History*.

7E.9209/10
7E.50962/3
About December 1966, the cylinder head gasket was changed. This is listed only in *Jaguar E-Type: The Definitive History*.

7E.9291/2
7E.51101/2
About December 1966, the fuel lines from the filter to the carburetors were changed. This is listed only in *Jaguar E-Type: The Definitive History*.

7E.51451/2
About September 1966, the automatic transmission kick-down control rod and cable were changed.

7E.51451/2
The automatic transmission was changed.

7E.10008/9
7E.52154/5
About March 1967, the front seal on the oil pan was changed. This is listed only in *Jaguar E-Type: The Definitive History*.

7E.52275/6
The torque-converter housing was changed.

7E.10956/7
7E.52607/8
About July 1967, the crankshaft damper was changed. This is listed only in *Jaguar E-Type: The Definitive History*.

7E.11667/8
7E.52686/7
About March 1967, oil seals were fitted to the inlet valve guides. This is listed only in *The Jaguar E-Type: A Collector's Guide*.

7E.11818/9
7E.52716/7
About January 1968, the number of bolts holding the bellhousing to the cylinder block was reduced from nine to eight, with the top one being omitted. This is listed only in *Jaguar E-Type: The Definitive History*.

7E.12159/60
7E.53209/10
About January 1968, the adjustor and pivot pin for the clutch-operating rod was changed. This is listed only in *Jaguar E-Type: The Definitive History.*

7E.13500/1
7E.53581/2
About July 1968, the clutch was changed from a Laycock to a Borg and Beck diaphragm type. This is listed only in *Jaguar E-Type: The Definitive History.*

7E.14212/3
7E.53742/3
About July 1968, the connecting-rod bearings were changed. This is listed only in *Jaguar E-Type: The Definitive History.*

7E.16335/6
7E.54361/2
About July 1968, cylinder block heaters were made standard for Canada. This is listed only in *Jaguar E-Type: The Definitive History.*

7E.16754/5
7E.54608/9
About July 1968, the coil was changed to one with a push-in high-tension coil wire, and with "+" and "-" replacing "SW" and "CB." This is listed only in *Jaguar E-Type: The Definitive History.*

7E.17157/8
7E.54836/7
About June 1968, the water pump pulley and belt were changed to increase pump speed. This is listed only in *The Jaguar E-Type: A Collector's Guide.*

7E.17864/5
7E.52452/3
About December 1968, the valve seats were changed. This is listed only in *Jaguar E-Type: The Definitive History.*

Series II Engines
(Note that the prefix is now R)

7R.1345/6
7R.35088/9
About December 1968, the pointer for the timing marks was moved from the bottom of the engine to the left-hand side. This is listed only in *Jaguar E-Type: The Definitive History.*

7R.1837/8
7R.35329/30
The inlet manifold and associated hardware, the carburetors, and accelerator linkage were changed for U.S. and Canada cars only. The heater-hose return pipe at the right-hand side of the cylinder block was changed.

7R.1914/5
7R.35388/9
The cylinder head studs, the cylinder head assembly, and gasket set were changed. The cylinder block assembly was changed (the core plugs and the block heater were changed), and the front timing cover was changed. The water pump assembly was changed.

7R.2082/3
7R.35462/3
The camshaft covers and studs at the front of the head for fixing the camshaft covers were changed for U.S. and Canada cars only. The rear exhaust manifold, the mixture housing on top of the rear exhaust manifold and its associated hardware, and the clip holding the dipstick were changed for U.S. and Canada cars only.

7R.2297/8
7R.35582/3
The oil filter assembly was changed.

7R.2587/8
7R.35730/1
About March 1969, the clutch cover assembly was changed to a new one with stronger springs. In some sources an exception is given for engine numbers 7R.2784 to 7R.2791.

7R.4158/9
7R.36599/600
About May 1969, the camshaft cover mounts at the front were changed to countersunk screws.

7R.4488/9
7R.36957/8
About May 1969, the water pump spindle was changed. This change is listed only in *Jaguar E-Type: The Definitive History.*

7R.5263/4
7R.37488/9
About May 1969, the thermostat was changed from 74 to 82 degrees Celsius. Some sources cite chassis numbers 7R.5262/3 instead of 7R.5263/4, and numbers 7R.37488/9 are not cited.

7R.5263/4
The cooling fan thermostatic switch was changed.

7R.5338/9
7R.37549/50
About May 1969, the pointer for the timing marks on the crankshaft damper was moved from the left-hand side of the engine back to the bottom of the engine (where it had been before), for cars with air conditioning or power steering. This change is listed only in *Jaguar E-Type: The Definitive History.*

7R.5541/2
7R.37654/5
About June 1969, the water drain spigot on the block was changed to a drain plug, and the fiber washer was deleted, but the copper washer was retained.

7R.5546/7
The alternator was changed for cars without air conditioning. The alternator belt for cars without air conditioning was changed to a different type for cars exported to the United States and Canada.

7R.6305/6
7R.38105/6
About August 1969, the engine number stamping was moved from the area above the oil filter to the left-side bellhousing flange, near to the dipstick.

7R.6572/3
7R.38135/6
About August 1969, the oil seal in the speedometer drive gear was changed. This is listed only in *Jaguar E-Type: The Definitive History*.

7R.7503/4
7R.38501/2
About October 1969, the oil pump shaft was changed to one with a pressed-on inner rotor from one with a pinned-on inner rotor. This is listed only in *Jaguar E-Type: The Definitive History*.

7R.7973/4
and 7R.7506
The distributor was changed.

7R.8687/8
7R.38854/5
About November 1969, the camshafts were changed to give quieter valve operation and longer periods between valve adjustments.

7R.8687/8
The cylinder head assembly was changed (this probably just denotes the camshaft change above). The camshaft covers were changed.

7R.8767/8
7R.38894/5
About January 1970, the camshaft covers were changed so that all cars had mounting holes for the emission-control warm-air duct, even if the duct was not fitted.

7R.9709/10
7R.39111/2
About March 1970, the clutch-operating rod was altered to allow greater adjustment tolerances.

7R.10747/8
The release bearing and cup assembly was changed.

7R.13198/9
7R.40325/6
About August 1970, the crankshaft distance piece at the front of the shaft was replaced by a distance piece with an O-ring.

7R.14048/9
About October 1970, the thermostat was changed.

7R.14074/5
About October 1970, the cams were changed so as to have no oil hole in the back. This was to reduce oil consumption.

7R.14268/9
About December 1970, the designation of the compression ratio of the engine was changed from a number to a letter, thus H=high compression, S=standard compression, and L=low compression. This change is listed only in *Jaguar E-Type: The Definitive History*.

Changes in Order of Transmission Number
EJ.245/6
The housing for the rear oil seal and its gasket were changed.
About January 1965, the housing for the rear transmission oil seal was changed. This change is listed only in *Jaguar E-Type: The Definitive History*.

EJ.944/5
About March 1965, the roller bearing on the gearbox constant-pinion shaft was changed.

EJ.3169/70
About September 1965 or February 1966, the constant-pinion shaft was changed to include an oil thrower, and the spacer under the roller bearing was no longer required.

EJ.7919/20
EJS.7919/20
About November 1966, a retaining washer was added to the shift lever.

EJ.11776/7
EJS.11776/7
About July 1967, the spring for the synchromesh thrust members was changed. This is listed only in *Jaguar E-Type: The Definitive History*.

KE.11768/9
KJS.2858/9
About March 1970, the clutch release bearing was changed. The new one can be identified by a ridge in the bore of the thrust pad. This is listed only in *Jaguar E-Type: The Definitive History*.

Chapter 4

5.3-L<small>ITER</small> C<small>HANGES</small> <small>BY</small> S<small>ERIAL</small> N<small>UMBER</small>

Changes in Order of Chassis Number
1S.50064/5
1S.70412/3
The torsion bars and front shock absorbers were changed.

1S.50144/5
1S.71035/6
The rear lights for cars shipped to the United States, Canada, Mozambique, Portugal, Angola, and Greece were changed.

1S.1004/5
1S.50175/6
About July 1971, the brake pedal was changed on cars fitted with automatic transmissions.

1S.1004/5
1S.20024/5
1S.50204/5
1S.71493/4
The center dash clock was changed from a Smiths type to a Kienzle type.

1S.1004/5
1S.20024/5
The wiring harness was changed.

1S.1004/5
1S.20024/5
1S.50227/8
1S.71836/7
The back-up light was changed for cars going to all countries except Algeria, Ivory Coast, Morocco, New Caledonia, Senegal, and South Vietnam.

1S.1004/5
1S.20024/5
1S.50226/7
1S.71729/30
The cooling system plumbing was changed.

1S.1004/5
1S.20024/5
1S.50192/3
1S.71448/9
The cigar lighter was changed.

1S.1004/5
1S.20024/5
1S.50166/7
1S.71233/4
About December 1971, the retaining bolts for both steering-column universal joints were changed to bolts with longer shanks.

1S.50166/7
1S.71177/8
The lower wishbone in the rear suspension was changed.

1S.1004/5
1S.20024/5
1S.50166/7
1S.71247/8
The instrument panel electronics were changed.

1S.1004/5
1S.20024/5
1S.50202/3
1S.71475/6
About November 1971, a removable connector (part number C.33835) was added to the line from the pump to the hood-mounted squirters to make hood removal easier.

1S.50204/5
1S.71493/4
The wiring harness was changed.

1S.50263/4
1S.72169/70
The wiring harness was changed.

1S.1004/5
1S.20024/5
1S.50226/7
1S.71684/5

About December 1971, the battery and its tray and hold-down were all changed, and the colors of the battery cables were changed: positive from red to blue and negative from black to brown. Russ states, however, that his research does not support the battery-cable-color change, and he has observed on Series III cars only the positive cable covered by a white cloth braid and bare braided wire on the negative.

1S.1004/5
1S.20063/4
1S.50263/4
1S.72204/5

The coolant temperature sensor was changed.

1S.1006/7
1S.20075/6
1S.50264/5
1S.72256/7

The clips for the top trim of the main air intake were changed.

1S.1021/2
1S.20090/1
1S.50184/5
1S.71310/1

The front subframe was changed.

1S.1021/2
1S.20090/1
1S.50317/8
1S.72317/8

Changes were made to the ignition system.

1S.20024/5
1S.71485/6

The stop on the accelerator pedal mechanism was changed.

1S.50313/4
1S.72317/8

The front subframe was changed.

1S.1039/40
1S.20090/1
1S.50378/9
1S.72318/9

About March 1972, the choke and heater controls were reconfigured into a symmetrical arrangement.

1S.50590/1
1S.72332/3

The optional electrically heated rear window was changed.

1S.1092/3
1S.20098/9
1S.50591/2
1S.72331/2

About November 1971, the teeth on the ring and pinion gears were modified (the new parts were marked 4HA-016-54 and 4HA-017-54 respectively). At this same point a tag labeled "7.5" was attached to the case.

1S.1112/3
1S.20102/3, for cars not shipped to the United States and Canada
1S.20024/5, for cars shipped to the United States and Canada
1S.50685/6
1S.72333/4, for cars not shipped to the United States and Canada
1S.71369/70, for cars shipped to the United States and Canada

About July 1971, the water temperature gauge was changed. Numerous unofficial sources cite only the chassis numbers 1S.20024/5 and 1S.71369/70 and state that the change was the removal of the red warning marking on the gauge, and that this applied only for cars shipped to the United States. The factory parts books cite the full set of six transition numbers, with U.S. and Canada distinctions, as listed above, but do not describe the change. Possibly there are other changes besides the removal of the red marking.

1S.1151/2
1S.20121/2
1S.50871/2
1S.72356/7

About December 1971, the handbrake was changed.

1S.1162/3
1S.20134/5
1S.50874/5
1S.72449/50

About March 1972, the cable and pinion gear control of the defroster control flap was changed to a cable and connecting rod.

1S.20115/6
1S.72489/90

The interior mirror was changed for cars exported to France.

1S.1178/9
1S.20152/3
1S.50885/6, including 1S.50826
1S.72567/8

The hydraulic brake pipes near the master cylinder were changed.

1S.1178/9

1S.20152/3
The wiring harness was changed.

1S.50885/6
1S.72567/8
The wiring harness was changed.

1S.72624/5
The lights were changed on cars shipped to Italy.

1S.1209/10
1S.20168/9
1S.50967/8
1S.72661/2
About April 1972, the factory began supplying brackets on the center cross beam and the lower mounts of the rear shock absorbers for use during shipping of the car. These were not intended for towing.

1S.20168/9
1S.72660/1
About April 1972, a remote control was added to the external mirror for cars shipped to the United States and Canada.

1S.20168/9
1S.72660/1
About May 1972, seatbelt alarms were added for cars shipped to the United States and Canada.

1S.72660/1
The upper squab of the rear seat was changed for cars shipped to Australia, the United States, and Canada.

1S.72661/2
The headliner used was changed in color from beige to grey.

1S.1211/2
1S.50972/3
The lighting configuration for right-hand-drive cars changed.

1S.51012/3
1S.72660/1
The leading section of the rear quarter windows and the rear body sheet metal were changed.

1S.1231/2
1S.20174/5
1S.51048/9
1S.72686/7
About April 1972, the lock on the steering column was changed from a Britax unit to a Waso unit.

1S.1235/6
1S.20172/3
1S.51015/6
1S.72681/2

About April 1972, fresh-air vents with control levers were introduced.

1S.51015/6, including 1S.51013 and 1S.51014
1S.72681/2, including 1S.72676, 1S.72677, for cars not shipped to the United States or Canada
1S.72660/1, including 1S.72567, 1S.72579, for cars not shipped to the United States or Canada
The body sheet metal was changed.

1S.1235/6
1S.20180/1
1S.51073/4
1S.72690/1
The carpets were changed.

1S.1264/5
1S.20248/9
The wiring harness was changed.

1S.51164/5
1S.72952/3
The wiring harness was changed.

1S.1296/7
1S.20409/10, for cars not shipped to the United States and Canada
1S.20168/9, for cars shipped to the United States and Canada
1S.51225/6
1S.73210/1, for cars not shipped to the United States and Canada
1S.75266/7, for cars shipped to the United States and Canada
The back-up light was changed for cars going to all countries except Algeria, Ivory Coast, Morocco, New Caledonia, Senegal, and South Vietnam, and as noted after the serial numbers above.

1S.1303/4
1S.20557/8
1S.51246/7
1S.73336/7
About June 1972, a support bracket was added between the intake manifold and the front part of the rain shield.

1S.1347/8
1S.20568/9
1S.51262/3
1S.73371/2
About June 1972, the torsion-bar adjuster cam profile was raised.

1S.20711/2
1S.73523/4
The back-up light was changed for cars going to Algeria, Ivory Coast, Morocco, New Caledonia, Senegal, and South Vietnam.

1S.1442/3
1S.20920/1
1S.51317/8
1S.73371/2 or 1S.73720/1

About December 1972, the pinion valve in the rack and pinion was changed. There is disagreement about the changeover numbers for the coupe, so I have listed both sets here.

1S.51415/6, including 1S.51392
1S.73950/1

The body sheet metal was changed.

1S.21028/9, for cars shipped to the United States and Canada
1S.73966/7, for cars not shipped to the United States and Canada
1S.73855/6, for cars shipped to the United States and Canada

The front subframe was changed. It was at this point the front bumper impact tubes were added.

1S.1579/80, including 1S.1550, 1S.1553, and 1S.1555
1S.21169/70

Changes were made to the door sheet metal for cars not shipped to the United States and Canada. Some parts of these changes may not have been restricted to the United States and Canada.

1S.1579/80, including 1S.1550, 1S.1553, and 1S.1555
1S.21169/70
1S.51415/6, including 1S.51392
1S.73950/1, for cars not shipped to the United States and Canada
1S.73855/6, for cars shipped to the United States and Canada

The door latch mechanism was changed.

1S.1659/60
1S.21169/70, for cars not shipped to the United States and Canada
1S.21028/9, for cars shipped to the United States and Canada
1S.51582/3
1S.73966/7, for cars not shipped to the United States and Canada
1S.73855/6, for cars shipped to the United States and Canada

The hood-support subframe (between the hood and the main front subframe) was changed.

1S.21028/9, for cars shipped to the United States and Canada
1S.21727/8, for cars shipped to Germany
1S.73855/6, for cars shipped to the United States and Canada
1S.74400/1, for cars shipped to Germany

The front license-plate mount was changed.

1S.21028/9, for cars shipped to the United States and Canada
The bodyshell was changed.

1S.73855/6
The body sheet metal was changed.

1S.21028/9
1S.73855/6, for cars shipped to the United States and Canada

About January 1974, the rubber bumper overriders were added as a result of the U.S. federal 5 mph impact requirements. While most sources cite 1S.23239/40 and 1S.74585/6 as the introduction of these bumper overriders, the factory parts books seem to cite only chassis numbers 1S.21028/9 (only for cars shipped to the United States and Canada) for the introduction of the rear overriders, and 21028/9 and 1S.73855/6 (only for cars shipped to the United States and Canada) for the introduction of the front overriders. No change in the rear-end sheet metal is cited for coupes. Roadster UD1S.21221, a very original car still in the hands of the first owner, is fitted with rubber overriders and impact tubes on the front, but steel overriders with small rubber pads (and no reenforcing box on the body) on the rear end. Perhaps the rubber overriders came in on the front at 1S.21028/9 and 1S.73855/6 and at the rear at 1S.23239/40 and 1S.74585/6.

1S.21028/9
1S.73855/6

About December 1972, a sealed fuel system was introduced for cars shipped to the United States and Canada. The new system used a carbon canister.

1S.21575/6
1S.74260/1

About March 1973, the 3.31:1 rearend was introduced for cars shipped to the United States and Canada, and the 3.07: was fitted to cars sold in other countries. The 3.54:1 rear end was no longer available on manual transmission cars.

1S.1662/3
1S.21605/6
1S.51609/10
1S.74265/6

About April 1973, the cooling ducts to the rear brakes were changed to increase ground clearance.

1S.1664/5
1S.21661/2
1S.51616/7
1S.74311/2

About March 1973, the fuel filter was changed to one with a metal bowl, and it was located on the right side of the trunk bulkhead.

1S.1697/8
1S.21790/1
1S.51618/9
1S.74457/8
The choke control was changed.

1S.1700/1
1S.21850/1
1S.51618/9
1S.74515/6
The windshield squirter nozzles were changed.

1S.1740/1
1S.21984/5
1S.51654/5
1S.74626/7
The air-distribution knobs were changed from the old serrated types (as used on Series II E-Types and S-Type sedans) to a type with raised knurling, and the vertical anodized metal labels were riveted next to the choke and heater controls. There is uncertainty about the 1S.51654/5 and 1S.74626/7 numbers, with some sources citing 1S.51655/6 and 1S.74627/8.

1S.1740/1
1S.22045/6
1S.51317/8 or 1S.51616/7,
1S.74311/2 or 1S.74661/2,
About March 1973, the four-outlet tailpipes were replaced by tailpipes with two outlets. There is disagreement about the changeover numbers for the coupe, so I have listed the two sets of cited changeover numbers here.

1S.1775/6
1S.51705/6
The lighting configuration for right-hand-drive cars changed.

1S.22271/2
1S.74768/9
From about March 1973, cars sold in West Germany had engines meeting the ECE 15 European emission specification.

1S.51761/2
1S.74822/3
The rear lights were changed.

1S.22333/4
The lighting configuration changed for cars shipped to the United States and Canada.

1S.2125/6
1S.23237/8
1S.52008/9
1S.75183/4
The horns were changed.

1S.2125/6
1S.23237/8
1S.52008/9
1S.75183/4
The front roll-bar mounts were changed.

1S.23239/40, for cars shipped to the United States and Canada
The wiring harness was changed, and changes were made to the dashboard switchgear and the seatbelt warning system. The bodyshell was changed.

1S.2449/50
1S.23418/9
From about October 1974, cars sold in all countries except the United States, Canada, and Japan had engines meeting the ECE 15 European emission specification.

1S.2449/50, for cars not shipped to the United States and Canada
1S.23418/9, for cars not shipped to the United States and Canada
1S.23239/40, for cars shipped to the United States and Canada
The manual and automatic transmission housings changed.

1S.2484/5
1S.23758/9
The bodyshell was changed for cars not shipped to the United States and Canada.

1S.2808/9
1S.25320/1
The antiroll bar couplings were changed.

1S.25467/8
The lighting system was changed for cars shipped to countries other than the United States, Canada, Italy, and France.

Changes in Order of Engine Number
7S.2251/2
The wiring harness was changed.

7S.2823/4
About December 1971, the carburetor gaskets were changed to a new style having insulating properties. The new gaskets were pink, and after they were fitted the separate insulators were no longer required.

7S.3708/9
The starter motor was changed.

7S.3904/5
The cast "JAGUAR" name in the front of the cam covers was discontinued. In its place was a flat region in the casting with a gold-and-black sticker with the name

"JAGUAR" printed on it. This change occurred at about the transition from 1973 to 1974 model years.

7S.4020/1
The thrust bearings were changed.

7S.4064/5
The bolts for the crankshaft pulley were changed.

7S.4097/8
The starter motor was changed.

7S.4336/7
The automatic transmission was changed.

7S.4509/10
About December 1971, the thrust bearings on the crankshaft were altered to have beveled corners on their inner side. The new bearings were gold colored.

7S.4663/4, including 7S.4560 to 7S.4621, emission-control engines
The balance-pipe and gulp valve plumbing between the left and right intake manifolds was changed for cars shipped to the United States, Canada, and Japan, with automatic transmissions. The thermostat housing and the distributor were changed.

7S.4663/4
The engine lifting-rings were changed. The early rings were cast and the later rings were fabricated from sheet steel.

7S.4663/4, including 7S.4560 and 7S.4621, excluding 7S.4879
Changes were made to the dipstick and its mounting hardware.

7S.4663/4 for cars shipped to the United States and Canada
7S.4879/80 for cars not shipped to the United States and Canada
The carburetors and the air-filter retaining bolts were changed.

7S.4879/80, non-emission-control engines
The thermostat housing and the air balance pipes were changed. The thermostatic vacuum system, the intake manifold and its hardware, and the distributor were changed.

7S.5501/2
The pistons were changed.

7S.6309/10
About May 1972, the pistons were changed to a lighter version.

7S.7000/1
About May 1972, the starter motor and flywheel (for manual transmission cars) or driven plate (for automatic transmission cars) were changed.

7S.7154/5
About June 1972, the oil-feed holes were deleted from the con-rod big-end bearings.

7S.7376/7
C35165 was changed to C37963.

7S.7377/8
The oil line plumbing to the heads, the oil pressure sender unit mounting, and the wiring harness were changed.

7S.7559/60
About August 1972, a printed-circuit ballast resistor was introduced (Lucas number 47229).

7S.7685/6
Vacuum tubing was changed.

7S.7784/5
About October 1972, the water pump and its hoses were changed, as was the mount for the power-steering pump.

7S.7855/6
About October 1972, the oil holes in the small ends of the con rods were discontinued.

7S.8178/9 for cars shipped to the United States and Canada
7S.8670/1 for cars not shipped to the United States and Canada
The air filter retaining bolts were changed again, and changes were made to the fuel-delivery system and carburetors.

7S.8178/9, for cars shipped to the United States and Canada
Exhaust gas carburetor preheat was added and the carburetor float-chamber vents were changed. The engine breather configuration and the air-cleaner adapters were changed.

7S.8188/9
About December 1972, the main bearings were changed to a new version with better lining material.

7S.8443/4
About February 1973, the thermostatic vacuum switch (and related plumbing) on the right rear coolant pipe was discontinued on non-emission-control engines.

7S.8670/1

The balance-pipe and gulp valve plumbing between the left and right intake manifolds was changed for emission-controlled cars shipped to Sweden, Japan, and EEC countries. The thermostatic vacuum system and the air cleaner adapters were changed for cars other than those going to the United States and Canada.

7S.8833/4

The engine mounts were changed.

7S.8929/30

The automatic transmission changed, and the vacuum tubing was changed.

7S.8981/2

Changes were made to the gearbox.

7S.9033/4, emission-control engines

About February 1973, the air-injection pump was altered on emission-controlled engines. The new pump incorporated an air filter. Changes were also made to the air distribution pipes at this point.

7S.9678/9

About February 1973, the ballast resistor and coil were moved to the right rear of the engine. This made the drive belts easier to get at.

7S.9696/7

The wiring harness was changed.

7S.9714/5

About February 1973, the modified Model 12 Borg-Warner automatic transmission was introduced. This was the same transmission used on the XJ12.

7S.9733/4

The exhaust gas carburetor preheat was changed.

7S.9336/7

The thermostat housing was changed.

7S.10798/9

About May 1973, the crankshaft was changed to the one used on the XJ12.

7S.12064/5

About July 1973, the oil pump was changed to one with a different housing.

7S.12546/7

The thermostat housing was changed.

7S.13501/2

The throttle linkage was changed.

7S.13999/14000

(associated with gearbox number KL.6771/2)
About October 1973, synchromesh sleeves were changed.

7S.14000/1

The rear transmission mount was changed, and the firing-order sticker applied to the air cleaner was standardized. Prior to this, U.S. and Canadian market cars had different stickers. Also, the wiring harness and thermostat housing were changed. The thermostatic vacuum system was changed for emission-control cars shipped to the United States, Canada, and Japan.

7S.14340/1

(associated with gearbox number KL.7097/8)
About October 1973, the gearbox countershaft was changed. The new one was made of a different material.

7S.14662/3

The throttle linkage was changed.

7S.16209/10

About February 1974, a high-load coil and an amplifier were specified.

7S.17073/4

About November 1974, the tappets were changed.

Changes in Order of Transmission Number

KL.4240/1

About January 1973, there was a change in the needle bearings.

KL.6771/2

(associated with engine number 7S.13999/14000)
About October 1973, synchromesh sleeves were changed.

KL.7097/8

(associated with engine number 7S.14340/1)
About October 1973, the gearbox countershaft was changed. The new one was made of a different material.

Chapter 5

3.8-LITER BODYWORK AND INTERIOR COMPONENT CHANGES

This chapter lists the production changes organized by component classification rather than by order of serial number. In addition, I have included production-change information that is not referenced to serial number. This additional information comes from many sources, including early magazine articles and road tests, advertising literature, driver's handbooks and factory service manuals, recent books and articles written about E-Types, personal observations of many unrestored, original cars, and word-of-mouth. It is used to support and append the information of chapter 2.

While the articles I have used for research are mainly those written at the time the cars were new (and thus show only cars in their factory-original condition), in some instances I have gathered information from modern magazine articles or pictures. This was done with care. Similarly, some information was gathered from restored cars. This was done sparingly, and only in cases

where I trusted the accuracy of the restoration. On the whole, though, research on currently existing cars was confined to carefully preserved originals.

Using unofficial sources, such as books and magazine articles, may seem an odd way to gather information on a subject such as this. One would expect the factory to simply have production records that could be transcribed. There are two reasons this is not the case. First, during a portion of the time this book was being written, the factory was without a historian, and was not able to offer much historical information (their historian, A. J. A. Weyth, had always been helpful to me, and supplied material for this book, but he had recently died. Karen Miller of Jaguar North America was helpful, but the company archives still need organization before much information can be retrieved).

Several writers had preceded me in obtaining official lists of production changes from the factory, and I

A Lucas PL headlight. These lights employed a separate bulb, and were fitted to non-U.S.-market cars. The three support arms hold a chrome reflector in front of the bulb. The enameled crest in the center is marked "LUCAS" and "PL."

Lucas sealed-beam headlights were fitted to U.S.-specification cars. These units are marked "LUCAS" in the center of the lens, but otherwise have the standard appearance of typical U.S. sealed-beam bulbs.

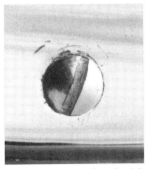

Some cars were fitted with slot-type headlight cover retaining ring screws, while others used the Phillips type.

The Phillips-type headlight cover retaining ring screw.

used their works to supplement the factory parts-book information of chapters 2 and 3. Their listings are similar, but do not exactly agree with each other, nor with the factory spare-parts catalogs. In those cases where a change is listed only by a single reference, other than the factory literature, I cite that reference.

The second reason for basing my work on as many sources as possible is that, even when it is available, the factory-supplied information is not always complete and accurate. Throughout production of the E-Type (and especially the early 3.8-liter cars), numerous production changes occurred. After studying the subject for a number of years, it has become apparent that many of these changes were not official and were not recorded well, if at all. There are production variations in the cars, such as the change in the shape of the necks of the convertible-top hold-down clasps, or the change in the shade of gold paint used to paint the cylinder head, that do not appear in any official lists (in fact, the factory has stated that the early pumpkin-colored gold cylinder heads never existed, and that only one shade of gold paint was used). Thus, I decided that the only way to properly treat this subject would be to use as many sources as possible.

In some instances, information given here on the serial-number-related changes is sketchy. For example, it may be stated that a change occurred in a given component at a specific serial number, without any mention of what the change is. This is a result of the nature of the available research materials, which sometimes cite that a change occurred, but don't say what it was. Even though 5 factory-published parts catalogs, more than 80 previously published works, and hundreds of cars were examined to complete this work, some such entries were unavoidable.

The illustrations used here and through chapter 10 are different from those used in chapter 1. Each of these black-and-white figures is meant to illustrate the one specific feature discussed in the caption. Other features that show are incidental and may or may not be original. They should be disregarded. Unlike the illustrations in chapter 1, I will not always cite unoriginal features when they show up.

This marking was used on the glass headlight covers.

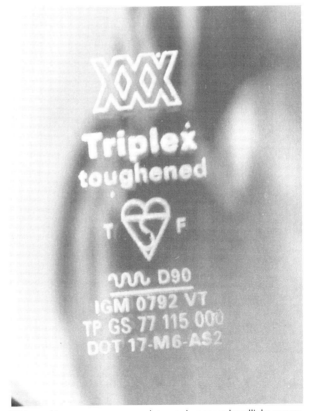

This marking appears on some later replacement headlight covers.

The outer chrome trim of an early license-plate light clearly showing the "BUTLERS ENGLAND" marking.

"LUCAS L. 705" showing on a later license-plate chrome trim.

In addition, even though the differences between the basic models (3.8-liter, 4.2-liter Series I, Series I 1/2, and Series II) are depicted in the color photographs, chapter 1 is not meant to be an exhaustive and detailed comparison of these four models. The goal of this book is to discuss the production changes *within* these four basic model groups, not *between* them. However, in some instances where I feel it would be especially helpful, I have illustrated differences between these basic model groups in the black-and-white figures of chapters 5 through 10.

The reader should be aware that when references are made to model years, these are unofficial and loosely defined. The cars were not shipped from the factory as 1963s or 1964s, but merely as E-Types. However, some changes coincide well with the production of a given model year, and occasional references will be made in this manner.

Exterior: Headlights and Trim

The headlight trim rings were black on at least one prototype car, which was likely serial number 850002, a prototype assembled by the experimental department. After the first few prototypes, I am not aware of any design changes in the chrome trim rings.

The headlight units themselves were Lucas, either PL.700 or other types, depending on country of destination. However, some early cars apparently were equipped with non-PL lights. One example of this, 77 RW, was an early 1961 test car. Another example is a coupe with black trim rings, reputed to be the first coupe, pictured in The *Jaguar E-Type: A Collector's Guide.*

In *Autocar*, April 26, 1963, it is stated that the "full beam of the lamps is good and penetrating, apparently unhindered by the toughened glass covers to the lamp wells. On early cars these were of transparent plastic material." I have never seen plastic covers on an early car, nor have I found any other references to this. I think this is likely an erroneous statement, and that all lenses were glass.

Changes at chassis numbers 880631/2 and 889526/7: About April 1964, sealed-beam headlights were adopted for cars going to Brazil, Canada, Chile, Colombia, Cuba, Dominican Republic, Egypt, El Salvador, Greece, Guatemala, Haiti, Hawaii, Jordan, Lebanon, Madeira, Mexico, Newfoundland, Nicaragua, Panama, Persian Gulf, Peru, Philippines, Puerto Rico, Saudi Arabia, South Vietnam, Syria, the United States, Uruguay, and Venezuela. This change is listed only in *Jaguar E-Type: The Definitive History.*

Parking and Brake Lights and Trim

Changes at chassis numbers 860478/9 and 886013/4: The stop-tail-flasher lamps were changed. This occurred about June 1962, and the change was to adapt the lights to the altered body panels. This was part of the extensive rework of the coupes that took place at these chassis numbers.

The taillight lens colors varied as a function of the country the car was to be delivered to. For cars shipped to the United States, both lenses were red. For all other cars, the stop-taillight lens was red and the flasher lens was amber.

License-Plate Lights and Trim

The license-plate lights on the early cars were marked "BUTLERS" instead of "LUCAS" as on later cars. Otherwise, they are similar to the later lights.

The Butler lights were supplied at least as late as serial number 875109, engine numbers R.1138-9, which had two Butlers, and serial number 860084, engine numbers R.3137-9, which had a Lucas on the left and a Butler on the right.

From research of surviving cars, serial numbers 875026, 875109, 875166, 875407, 876052, and 876270 all had two Butler lights, 860084 had one Butler and one Lucas (perhaps the Lucas was a later replacement), and 860005 had two Lucas lights.

Jaguar International Magazine, March 1986, stated that early license plate light covers were black and

Some 3.8-liter cars were fitted with taillight reflectors with distinctly different patterns.

This close-up view shows the unusual pattern of these alternate reflectors. Note the central dividing line and central symmetry are lacking here. Contrast this pattern to the standard pattern illustrated in Figures old 5-240 and 250.

This standard taillight lens reflector shows a pattern that is symmetrical, but different on either side of the vertical center line.

This close-up view of the standard taillight reflector lens shows a dividing line down the center where the left and right patterns come together.

marked Butler—Made in England, not Lucas. This is the only reference I have found to license plate lights being black, and I have never seen any black ones. I am not sure if some left the factory black, like the headlight trim rings on the first few prototype cars, or not.

Back-up Light and Trim

There were at least three back-up light configurations: no back-up light at all, mounted beneath the left bumper, and mounted under the license plate in the center. The central mounting is the common, with the left mount and no light configurations appearing on only a few of the earliest cars. The change to the conventional centrally mounted back-up light took place early on.

A back-up light mounted on the left side of the license-plate aperture is seen on the Geneva shows car, serial number 885005, in *The Jaguar E-Type: A Collector's Guide,* and in *Motor* magazine, March 22, 1961. This car appears to have no back-up light in some illustrations,

An early wiper arm showing rivets.

but I think this may be due merely to the angle of the pictures.

In *Jaguar E-Type 3.8 & 4.2 6-cylinder, 5.3 V-12,* by Denis Jenkinson, the back-up light is seen mounted in the center on a roadster (with body number 2892 crayoned on the license plate area). LHD roadster serial number 875026 has a center-mounted back-up light. In the same source, early RHD E-Type, called chassis number 45, (I suppose 850045) is shown in a current photograph with a central mounted back-up light, and an early roadster, claimed to be chassis number 12, is seen with a centrally mounted light.

Wiper Arms, Blades, and Windshield Squirter Nozzles

The wiper arms on early cars came in two types: with two rivets showing on the outside of the lower part of the arm, and without rivets.

Changes at chassis numbers 861274/5, 880165/6, and 889134/5: About November 1963, the wiper arms were changed to carry longer blades. This change is listed only in *Jaguar E-Type: The Definitive History*.

The original wiper blades were Aermic. A common replacement for these blades are the Rainbow blades.

I am not aware of any changes to the squirter nozzles.

Bumpers

Some of the early cars appear in pictures without bumper overriders. For example, this is seen on car license plate number 9600HP (claimed to be serial number 885002) in *Classic and Sportscar*, April 1986. In *Jaguar E-Type: The Definitive History*, 9600HP is shown without overriders, and Porter states that the overriders were removed to enhance top speed. Bumpers without overriders were likely never a production configuration, and aside from a few early examples, all production 3.8-liter E-Types seem to have had the same bumper overriders.

However, the configuration without overriders may have been considered for the early cars. A rear bumper is illustrated this way in a line drawing in Jaguar handbook numbers E.122/1 and E.122/6.

An unusual front overrider is shown on a coupe, stated to be the "first one" in *The Jaguar E-Type: A Collector's Guide*. A similar unusual large overrider is also shown on the right rear of an early coupe. These strange and asymmetric overriders are likely bumper protection experiments, and bear no resemblance to those found on any production cars.

T-Key Hole Covers

A few early cars are pictured without T-key hole covers. Other than these few illustrations (probably of one or a few prototype cars), I am not aware of any T-key

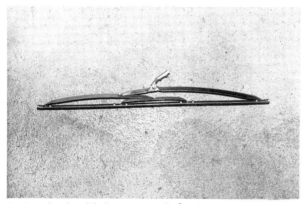

An Aermic wiper blade, as originally fitted to 3.8-liter cars.

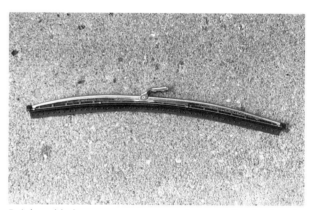

Rainbow blades were a common replacement for the Aermic, and many cars are seen fitted with these. Some Aermic blades were made in this style.

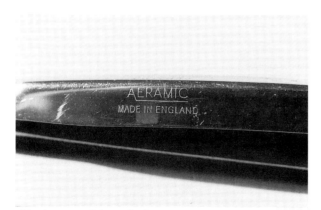

This close-up of the end of an Aermic wiper blade shows the stamped-in markings.

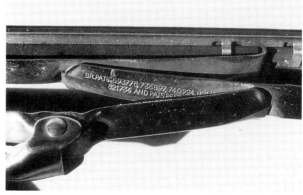

The patent markings found on the Aermic wiper blades.

hole cover changes. All evidence indicates the covers were of the pear shape as found on Mk V Jaguar sedan fender skirts, and early Triumph TR trunk lids.

The pear-shaped covers are marked on the back with "WB Birmingham" in a box, sometimes a heart symbol, and a number M1121/X, where X represents a variable single digit. I presume the M1121 is the part number, and the suffix is a mold or revision number. I have seen this last digit range from 2 to 6. M1121/2 appears on an original-looking cover from a 1950 Mk V; a cover, which I believe to be an original from serial number 875026, is marked M1121/4. Two NOS (new-old-stock) covers I acquired in 1975 are marked M1121/6.

One cover I acquired from a Mk V Jaguar sedan is marked M1121/4, with a heart in a circle with some small letters, a small 1, and the WB symbol. Another is marked M1121/2, without the heart symbol, with a small 2, and with the WB symbol.

Various reproductions have been made of these covers. In 1975 I bought some that were cast in a brasslike material, instead of the original pot metal. They were chrome plated and looked like the originals, but the greater density of the brass caused the

hinges to break. There were no markings inside these covers.

More recently, in 1988, I purchased reproduction covers made of a material with a density similar to that of the original cover. These are marked on the inside with M1121/6, the WB symbol, a small 2, and two recessed holes about half the diameter of the four push-pin ejector holes. There is no heart symbol.

The round-type T-key covers, such as found on XK120 fender skirts, are frequently used as replacements for the original pear-shaped covers. I have seen no evidence suggesting they were ever fitted to the early E-Types at the factory.

Changes at chassis numbers 850091/2 860004/5, 875385/6, and 885020/1: About September 1961, the bonnet lock, escutcheon, and so on were changed to internal lock.

Vent Trim

I am not aware of any changes in this trim piece at the rear of the hood. On the cover of *Car and Driver*, May 1961, the chrome trim was absent on an early or prototype car, but I doubt this reflects how any production cars were made.

Outside of a T-key hole cover. This one shows some of the pitting typical of these chromed castings.

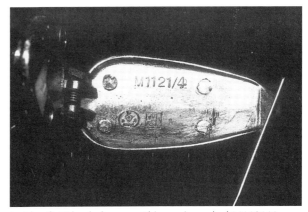

Inside of a T-key hole cover. This one is marked M1121/4.

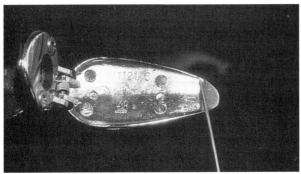

Inside view of a reproduction cover, marked M1121/6. Note that the four ejector-pin marks stick out further than on the original, and that two additional small ejector-pin marks are on either side of the center. Also, the heart-in-a-circle symbol is not present.

The depression running along the bottom edge of this early door-top trim strip was a feature of some of the early cars, although not all had it.

A door-top trim strip without the depression running along the bottom.

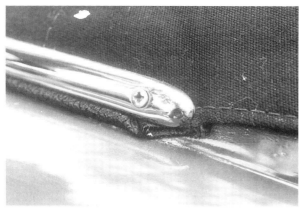

A later convertible-top chrome strip without a lip. The four convertible-top cover retaining hooks are typically found fitted under these strips.

Door Handles

Holes are seen instead of door handles on illustrations of a few prototype cars, but this configuration likely does not reflect the state of any production cars. Other than these examples, I am not aware of any door handle variations.

Top Door Trim

Changes at chassis numbers 850087/8 and 875299/300: About October 1961, the chrome finisher at the top of the doors was changed. This change is listed only in *Jaguar E-Type: The Definitive History*.

Changes at chassis number 850506/7 and 877201/2: The chrome finisher at the top of the doors was changed. This occurred about May 1962, and some cars before these chassis numbers may have also been modified.

Convertible-Top Trim

The chrome trim strip that runs around the rear of the convertible top (where it tacks to the rear of the cockpit) has a lip running along it on some early cars. The early-type strip was used on serial number 875109, but by 875954 it was replaced with the later type.

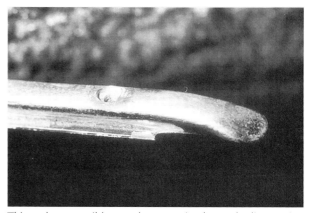

This early convertible-top chrome strip shows the lip running along the bottom. This lip presumable played a role in the retention of the convertible-top cover, as the four hooks found on later cars to retain the cover were absent on the earlier cars.

I suspect this lip was used to help retain the convertible-top cover, and the four hooks seen on some later cars were introduced as an alternate to the lip when it was removed. These hooks are mentioned in the factory spare parts catalog, June 1963 version, but with no cutoff serial numbers, as if they were on all 3.8-liter E-Types.

However, while these hooks were present on serial number 876577, they are apparently absent in all early 3.8-liter roadster photos.

External Markings and Decorative Trim

All 3.8-liter cars had only the usual horizontal grille bar in the front aperture, and the chrome "JAGUAR" nameplate on the trunk lid as external markings to identify the car.

Changes at chassis numbers 860478/9 and 886013/4: The chrome finishers on the roof gutters were changed. This was part of the extensive rework of the coupes that took place at these chassis numbers.

From research of surviving cars: Serial number 876577 had only a JAGUAR nameplate on the trunk lid, 879325 and 887129 had JAGUAR and E-TYPE nameplates on their trunk lids, and 879093 had JAGUAR, E-TYPE, and 3.8 nameplates on its trunk lid.

Changes at chassis numbers 861178/9 and 888658/9: About June 1963, "various new items" of trunk-lid trim were added. This change is listed only in *Jaguar E-Type: The Definitive History*. I am not sure if this is alluding to the E-TYPE nameplate, and perhaps a 3.8 plate, that may have appeared on some later 3.8-liter cars. I have seen no hard evidence that any 3.8-liter cars left the factory with other than just a JAGUAR plate on the trunk lid.

Changes at chassis numbers 850734/5, 861218/9, 879680/1, and 888885/6: About August 1963, more windshield-pillar external chrome trim was added (two more pieces). This change is listed only in *Jaguar E-Type: The Definitive History*.

Changes at chassis numbers 850856/7 and 881249/50: About April 1964, the chrome finishers on

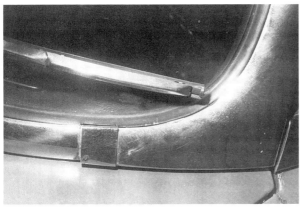

The small, rectangular chrome strip characterizes the early three-piece L-post trim. The chrome strip running along the lower front of the windshield is thicker than on later cars with the two-piece trim.

This is the first style of the two-piece L-post trim. The L-post chrome trim comes to a pointed termination, while on the earlier cars the strap was used to cover a blunt end. The lower windshield trim strip is now narrower.

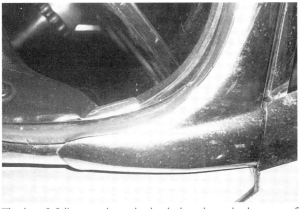

The late 3.8-liter roadsters had a bulge along the bottom of the L-post trim. This served to integrate it with the chrome trim along the top of the roadster doors.

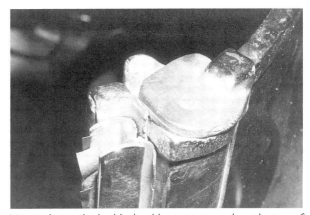

Very early cars had a black rubber cap screwed on the top of the windshield post.

the top of the doors were changed. This change is listed only in *Jaguar E-Type: The Definitive History*.

Changes at chassis numbers 850882/3, 861661/2, 881437/8 and 890487/8: About May 1964, the grille bar mounts were changed to incorporate a rubber mount. This change is listed only in *Jaguar E-Type: The Definitive History*.

Changes at chassis numbers 850888/9 and 881590/1: About August 1964, the chrome finishers at the sides of the windshield were changed. This change is listed only in *Jaguar E-Type: The Definitive History*.

Windshield and Pillars

On early cars, a hard rubber pad was screwed to the top of the L-post. This is found on cars at least as late as serial number 875235, but seems to be gone at least by 876577.

On early cars, a chrome strap went over the interface between the chrome trim of the L-post and the early-style wide chrome strip running along the bottom of the windshield. Later, this strap was omitted, the chrome strip was made narrower, and the wind-

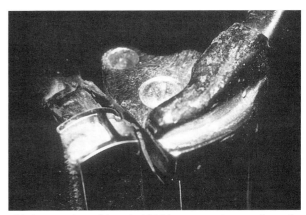

This later version of the windshield post cap does not have the rubber cap.

shield pillar trim was given a pointed tip.

From research of surviving cars: Serial numbers 875026 and 875109 had the wide trim and strap, 876577 had the narrow trim and no strap.

Pictured in Jenkinson's book is a car with the early multipiece throttle linkage, with a pointed L-post chrome trim, and no strap. This throttle linkage was discontinued at engine numbers R.2933/4, so the pointed L-post trim likely came in before this.

The trim strip along the bottom of the windshield is missing altogether in illustrations of numerous early cars, at least one of which was serial number 850002. I think these illustrations reflect one or a few prototype cars, and not the configuration of any production cars.

Changes at chassis numbers 850087/8 and 875309/10: About September 1961, the chrome finisher on the windscreen glass was changed. I believe this is referring to the removal of the strap.

The L-post trim was changed again late in 3.8-liter production to a type with a bulge along the bottom, in the 4.2-liter fashion.

Changes at chassis numbers 850888/9 and 881590/1: About August 1964, the chrome finishers at the sides of the windshield were changed. This change is listed only in *Jaguar E-Type: The Definitive History*. I believe this is referring to the introduction of the bulge.

Changes at chassis numbers 850734/5, 861218/9, 879680/1, and 888885/6: About August 1963, more windshield-pillar external chrome trim was added (two more pieces). This change is listed only in *Jaguar E-Type: The Definitive History*.

Side Windows, Trim, Frames, Winding Mechanisms, and Sealing Rubber

Some early roadsters did not have the chrome channel guide at the front of the window aperture to guide the window up. 77 RW (likely 850001) is seen in early photos with this guide, while 850004 is illustrated with a guide.

Changes at chassis numbers 850091/2 and 875373/4: About October 1961, the sealing rubber around the windows was changed.

Changes at chassis numbers 860478/9 and 886013/4: The frame for the door window was changed. This was part of the extensive rework of the coupes that took place at these chassis numbers.

Changes at chassis numbers 860478/9 and 886013/4: The rubber seal and the seal retainer for the cantrail was changed. This was part of the extensive rework of the coupes that took place at these chassis numbers.

Changes at chassis numbers 861098/9 and 888301/2: The shut pillar was changed. This change is listed only in *Jaguar International Magazine*, March 1986.

Changes at chassis numbers 861098/9 and 888301/2: The casing assembly below the quarter lights was changed. About August 1963, the quarter-light catches were changed.

Changes at chassis numbers 850766/7, 861294/5, 880212/3, and 889235/6: About November 1963, the A-post rubber seals were changed. On the roadsters, the two-piece seal was replaced by a one-piece seal, and on the coupes the separate cantrail seal and A-post seals were replaced by a single seal. The seal retainer on the cantrails on the coupes was no longer required after this change. This change is listed only in Philip Porter's *Jaguar E-Type: The Definitive History*.

Changes at chassis numbers 850778/9, 861341/2, 880458/9, and 889374/5: About November 1963, the sealing rubber on the door shut pillar was changed. This change is listed only by Porter.

Changes at chassis numbers 850842/3, 861556/7, 881260/1, 890250/1, and a few earlier cars: About April 1964, the rubber seals were improved (throughout the car, I assume). This change is listed only by Porter.

Wing Vents

The wing vent clasps came in at least two types. The early type was similar to the sort found on the rear windows of Mk II sedans. The later one was the usual type found on subsequent 3.8-liter E-Types. The early latch was likely a feature of the prototype cars.

Changes at chassis numbers 860194/5 and 885584/5: About March 1962, the glass and latches for the rear quarter lights were changed. The mounting for the attachment block for the catch arm to the quarter-light frame was changed from brazed to screwed.

Changes at chassis numbers 860478/9 and 886013/4: About May 1962, the glass, the hinge, and the catch for the quarter light were changed. These changes were part of the extensive rework of the coupes that took place at these chassis numbers.

Changes at chassis numbers 861098/9 and 888301/2: The catch operating the quarter lights was changed again.

Rear Window

The rear defogger was available as of April 1962.

Changes at chassis numbers 860478/9 and 886013/4: About June 1962, the glass in the trunk lid (clear or Sundym), and the chrome finisher at the top of the rubber seal for the trunk window were changed. In *The Jaguar E-Type: A Collector's Guide*, Skilleter cites this change with chassis numbers 860475/6 given instead of 860478/9. This was part of the extensive rework of the coupes that took place at these chassis numbers.

Front License-Plate Mount

On home-market (British) cars, the front number plate was applied directly to the front of the hood, while at least two arrangements were used for mounting the front license plate on U.S. market cars. On the early cars, two small chromed-steel straps were screwed to the bottom of the air-intake aperture. The tops of these straps were bent over and folded around the lower lip of the aperture.

Later these straps were replaced by a mount incorporating a pivoting arrangement with a connecting rod, connected to the front subframe. When the hood was raised, this pivoted the license plate upward and kept it from hitting the ground. It is interesting to note that sometime after the introduction of this pivoting

Front license-plate mounts appear to have been an afterthought on the early U.S.-market cars. The tops of these two straps are bent around the lower edge of the air-intake aperture, and the bottoms are retained by sheet-metal screws.

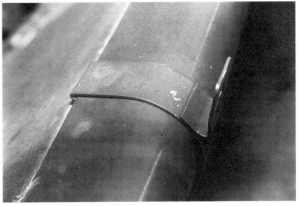

This close-up of an early strap-type license-plate mount shows its spot-weld fabrication.

On later U.S.-market cars, a pivoting front license-plate mount was used to prevent fowling of the plate on the ground when the bonnet was opened. In this illustration, the bonnet has been removed from the car. The end of the connecting rod, where it attaches to the bonnet frame, is seen on the left.

The attachment point of the connecting rod on the front frame. The threaded rod is broken off in this illustration, but the machined bracket is seen pinned to the lobe on the frame member.

Once the pivoting front license-plate mechanism was introduced for the U.S.-market cars, the connecting-rod hole in the lower part of the bonnet was apparently standardized for all production. This hole is on an early RHD coupe without any front license-plate mounts.

This speedometer calibrated in miles per hour was standard for cars going to countries using the English system.

Speedometers calibrated in kilometers per hour were standard for cars going to continental Europe and other countries using the metric system.

The very early brake warning lights had red plastic lenses. Note that the lens here has been melted and distorted by the head of the warning lamp bulb. This is typical of these early lenses, and is likely why they were later replaced with glass lenses.

A later brake warning light with the red glass lens. This lens could stand up to the heat of the bulb.

mechanism, cars not fitted with a front license plate mount had the same oval connecting-rod hole in the sheet metal beneath the air-intake aperture.

From research of surviving cars: Serial numbers 875026 and 875109 had the strap mounts, 860084 had no straps but an oval connecting-rod hole, and 876577, 879325, and 889076 had the tilting mount.

License-Plate Holder

Changes at chassis numbers 850078/9: About October 1961, a new plastic license-plate holder was introduced. This change is listed only in *Jaguar E-Type: The Definitive History.*

Interior: Instruments and Controls

Different speedometers were supplied with different rear-end ratios, and whether the car was calibrated in miles per hour or kilometers per hour.

Changes at chassis numbers 850288/9, 860028/9, 876116/7, and 885205/6: About February 1962, the tachometer was changed.

Changes at chassis numbers 850701/2, 861168/9, 879323/4; and 888542/3: About November 1963, the clock in the tachometer was changed to one fitted with a rectifier. The clock dial is marked CE.1111/01 (except for a few early ones that were marked CE.1111/00 in error). A black sleeve indicates that the clock is fitted with a rectifier. This change is listed only in *Jaguar E-Type: The Definitive History.*

Switches and Controls

The May 1961 issue of *Road & Track* stated that "The fan, of course, has its own switch on the instrument panel." I have never seen such a manual control switch, and this is the only reference to it I have found. It does not appear on the dashboards of cars in any early illustrations I have seen, nor have I seen it on any car.

Changes at chassis numbers 850725/6, 861197/8, 879550/1, and 888766/7: About August 1963, the turn-signal-headlight flasher switch was changed. This change is listed only in Porter's *Jaguar E-Type: The Definitive History.*

Changes at chassis numbers 850725/6, 861197/8, 879550/1, and 888766/7: About August 1963, the turn-signal-switch striker plate was changed. This is listed only by Porter.

Changes at chassis numbers 850810/1, 861460/1, 880870/1, and 889819/20: About March 1964, the turn-signal-switch clamp bracket was changed from being a part of the switch to being part of the steering column. This change is listed only in *Jaguar E-Type: The Definitive History*.

Changes at chassis numbers 850858/9, 861604/5, 881281/2, and 890317/8: About May 1964, the striker for the turn-signal control was changed. This change is listed only by Porter.

Indicator Lights

It is likely that a few of the early cars were fitted with a reverse-engagement light on the dash above the heater controls.

A light above the heater controls is seen in various illustrations of early prototype coupe interiors. In the late 1960s or early 1970s, I saw an early roadster that had a clear-lens light in this location that lit up when reverse was engaged. I did not record the chassis number, and have never seen another like it. I presume a reverse-engagement warning light is what is illustrated in the early pictures.

Some early brake-warning light lenses were red plastic, and would melt when the bulb was left on for a long time. These lenses were later replaced with glass lenses.

From research of surviving cars: Serial numbers 875026 and 875109 had the plastic lenses, and 875954, 875958, and 876052 had the glass lenses.

Cigar Lighter

The cigar lighter came in basically two types. The early type is of the sort seen in older Jaguars, with an all-plastic body. The later type is a multipiece unit, and is of a smaller diameter than the early unit. The early and late lighters are not interchangeable in the sockets.

Changes at chassis numbers 850168/9, 860009/10, 875589/90, and 885050/1: The cigar lighter was changed. This occurred in late fall or early winter of 1961.

Changes at chassis numbers 850091/2, 860004/5, 875385/6, and 885020/1: Earth cables were added for the cigar lighter.

The early, large-diameter cigar lighter. This is the style used in Jaguar cars prior to the E-Type.

The later, small-diameter cigar lighter. The early and late lighters are not interchangeable in their sockets.

The round-headed Wilmot-Breeden FS-type key was used on the early cars.

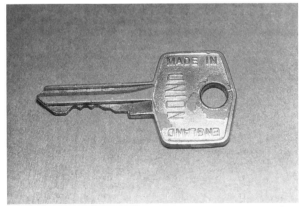

The square-headed Wilmot-Breeden FP-type key was used on later cars.

Ignition Switch and Key

A single key was used for the ignition and the door locks, and it was changed late in 3.8-liter production. Both early and late keys are Wilmot-Breeden, but the early type is the round-headed FS, while the late type is the square-headed FP.

Changes at chassis numbers 876664/5 and 885566/7: About March 1962, a cable for the steering-column lock connector to the instrument panel wiring was introduced along with the combined ignition switch-steering column lock for cars going to Germany.

Changes at chassis numbers 850587/8, 860862/3, 878036/7, and 886753/4 (and 876665-878036 and 885567-886753 for Germany only): The lock and ignition switch assembly on the steering column was changed from Neiman to Waso Werken, and a cable was introduced to connect the steering-column lock connector to the instrument panel wiring.

Grab Handle

Changes at chassis numbers 850708/9, 861174/5, 879342/3, and 888566/7: About May 1963, the grab handle and its fixings were changed, and its position was slightly changed. This change is listed only in *Jaguar E-Type: The Definitive History*.

Steering Wheel and Column

On the early cars, the steering wheels were round in cross section, lacking the scooped-out thumb trough, and with exposed aluminum on the inner circumference. I am not aware of any deviations from this design in the early cars.

Later cars had a steering wheel with a scooped-out thumb trough running around the inner front of the wood ring, and with no aluminum showing on the wood section. The cross section of the early wheel is much fatter than that on the later wheels.

From research of surviving cars: Serial numbers 875954, 875958, 876289, 876577, and 885733 had the fat cross-section wheel, and 879325 and 887576 have the scooped-out wheel.

Changes at chassis numbers 876664/5 and 885566/7: About March 1962, a cable for the steering-column lock connector to the instrument panel wiring was introduced (for Germany only). This was the introduction of the combined ignition switch-steering column lock for cars going to Germany.

The early steering wheels were round in cross section, and had the aluminum support ring showing on their inner circumference.

Later steering wheels had a thumb groove cut in the wood, and the aluminum support ring was completely embedded in the wood.

Front view of the locking steering column, as fitted to German-market cars.

Front view of the top mount for the rearview mirror mount on a very early roadster. Note the chromed spacer screwed in between the mount and the windshield.

This top view of the two-piece top mirror mount shows the spacer's position between the mount and the top windshield frame.

Changes at chassis numbers 850547/8, 860646/7, 877487/8, and 886213/4: About June 1962, the lower tubular-shaft steering column was changed to a one-piece forging, and the seal where the shaft passes through the dash was changed.

Changes at chassis numbers 850587/8, 860862/3, 878036/7, and 886753/4 (876665-878036 and 885567-886753 for Germany only): About October 1962, the upper-steering-column assembly was changed, and felt bearings were replaced with Vulkollan bearings.

Changes at chassis numbers 850587/8, 860862/3, 878036/7, and 886753/4 (876665-878036 and 885567-886753 for Germany only): The lock and ignition switch assembly on the steering column were changed from Neiman to Waso Werken.

Changes at chassis numbers 850810/1, 861460/1, 880870/1 and 889819/20: About March 1964, the turn-signal-switch clamp bracket was changed from being a part of the switch to being part of the steering column. This change is listed only in *Jaguar E-Type: The Definitive History*.

Changes at chassis numbers 850818/9, 861480/1, 880982/3, and 889966/7: About April 1964, the upper-steering-column bearings were changed from Vulkollan to Elastollan. This change is listed only in *Jaguar E-Type: The Definitive History*.

Pedals

The clutch pedal was changed at chassis numbers 850232/3, 860020/1, 875858/9, and 885104/5.

Changes at chassis numbers 850474/5 and 860374/5 (except 860365): About May 1962, the accelerator pedal assembly was changed to facilitate heel-and-toe operation.

Changes at chassis numbers 850474/5, 860374/5, 876998/9, and 885870/1 (except 860365): About May 1962, the brake power lever and pedals were changed to increase the mechanical advantage.

Changes at chassis numbers 850807/8, 861445/6, 880834/5, and 889779/80: About March 1964, the brake pedals were changed to improve attachment to the pedal shaft, and a tab washer was added to the pinch bolt. This change is listed only in *Jaguar E-Type: The Definitive History*.

Mirror and Mounts

The upper retainer for the roadster rearview-mirror mounting rod on some early cars had an extra plate screwed to it. Later cars had a single-piece unit.

I have seen this early plate on serial number 875026, but not on 875109. It is a small detail and does not show up well in photographs, so I have found no evidence of it in any references.

Changes at chassis numbers 861056/7 and 888066/7: About February 1963, interior mirror assembly was changed.

Interior Lights

Changes at chassis numbers 860478/9 and 886013/4: The screw for the interior light was changed.

Handbrake Lever

I am not aware of any design changes to the handbrake lever.

This one-piece roadster mirror rod mount was introduced early in production, and is typical of most roadsters. Note that the thick section is wider than on the early mount.

The white plastic defroster vent of the early cars.

Dash Top

The early cars had dash tops that were much thinner than those on later cars. I am not sure how long this was continued.

From research of surviving cars: Serial numbers 875958 and 876052 had the flat dash top, while 879325 had the fat dash top.

Defroster Ducts

The plastic plenums for the defroster ducts are found in both white and black plastic.

Dash Materials and Trim

There are several variations in the dash trim materials used both for the center dash and the two outer sections.

The earliest standard for the center of the dash was a circular-pattern aluminum. Around the 1963 model year, this was changed to incuse-crossed-pattern aluminum. The final version of this trim was black vinyl, as used on the rest of the dash.

In *Original Jaguar E-Type*, Porter mentions a third variety of the patterned aluminum trim with "lozenge-shaped" dots.

Front view of the later one-piece roadster mirror rod mount.

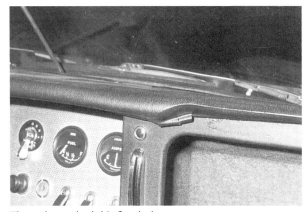

The early cars had this flat dash top.

The fat dash top of the later cars. This is the common type; all the reproductions I have seen have been in this style.

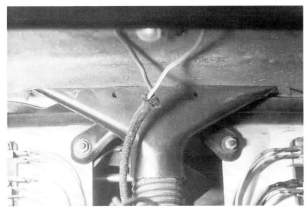

A later black plastic defroster vent.

A view of the porous textured dash covering material on a very early car. This may not have been standard on all early cars.

The typical wrinkled textured dash covering material as found on later cars.

Changes at chassis numbers 850609/10, 860912/3, 878301/2, and 887131/2: About October 1962, the pattern embossed on the aluminum finisher on the instrument panel was changed.

There may have been some early exceptions to this progression. In *Car and Driver*, May 1961, an early roadster is shown with black center trim, as opposed to the usual circular-pattern aluminum. This car is pictured many places in the magazine, and, judging from the pictures and identification in Porter's *Jaguar E-Type: The Definitive History*, it appears to be serial number 850002, a car built by the experimental department.

The leather trim came in on the lower part of the console before the aluminum was replaced on the front part of the console and the center section of the dash.

Changes at chassis numbers 850751/2, 861253/4, 879802/3, and 889029/30: About September 1963, the front finisher panel was changed from embossed aluminum to leather. This change is listed only in *Jaguar E-Type: The Definitive History*.

There were variations to the vinyl trim used on the outer two sections of the dash. One early and original car has a porous pattern to the dash trim material, quite different from the usual wrinkled pattern seen on most cars. The pattern is hard to determine from the pictures in the literature, so I don't know if this was a fluke, or the way some early cars were.

In *Jaguar Sports Cars*, Skilleter claimed that the fascia has a black "crackle" finish. I am not sure exactly what this means, but I suspect it is referring to the later-style wrinkled vinyl covering.

There were additional dash trim changes. On the later cars, a curved, chrome trim piece was at each end of the dash, where it joined the L-post trim.

Another change was the addition of chrome mounts on the grab handle.

Glovebox

The early cars came with plastic glovebox inserts. They appear to be fiberglass, coated with the same fuzzy material used on the later cardboard gloveboxes.

With the possible exception of a few prototypes, all the early cars had this circular-pattern aluminum trim on the dash center and console.

Later on in production, this cross-pattern aluminum trim was used.

The last style of center dash trim used on the 3.8-liter cars was black vinyl, as used on the Series I 4.2-liters.

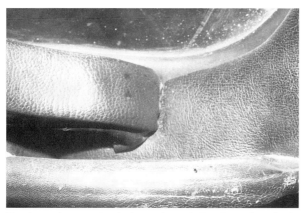

On the early cars, the dash top butted directly against the L-post trim, and there was no chrome trim at the ends of the grab bar.

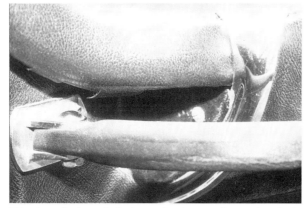

This view of a later dash shows the chrome trim used at the L-posts, and the later-style chrome grab-bar mounts.

The early cars had glovebox inserts molded from plastic. As with the later cardboard inserts, the inside was covered with a fuzzy black material.

The fabrication seams and pop-rivets are evident on this cardboard glovebox from a later car.

This rear view of a cardboard glovebox shows its folded construction.

The earliest ashtrays had an oblong shape.

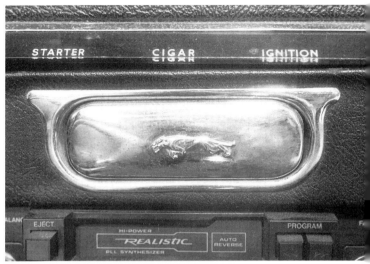

Later, two small "wings" were added to the upper part of the ashtray. I suspect this was to help determine which side was up during assembly, as some of the early ashtrays were inserted upside down.

The last style of 3.8-liter ashtray was the sliding-tray type, as used in the early 4.2-liter cars.

From research of surviving cars: Serial numbers 875026 and 875109 had the plastic glovebox, while 875954, 876289, and 876577 had the cardboard glovebox.

Sun Visors

Sun visors were fitted to the coupes only, and I am not aware of any design changes.

Console Frame, Trim, and Components

On a few of the prototype cars, the console was quite different from the early production cars. Some of the unusual features are square speaker grilles, no ashtray above the radio, less rivets on the chrome strip around the shift boot, and a rectangular ashtray (or perhaps cubby) on the lower part of the console next to the parking brake. These features tend to show up as a group. In *Jaguar E-Type: The Definitive History*, which pictures all these features together, Porter stated that they are of "the interior of one of the two Fixed Head prototypes with several curious features in evidence."

There were many changes in the console area after production began in earnest. Three types of ashtrays were used. The first of these was a chrome rotating type with a simple oblong shape. It was used in this form for the first few years of production, and then two "wings" were added to the top of the oblong shape. Porter includes a view of a winged ashtray on a car with a black center dash, so apparently the black dash covering came in before the winged ashtray was discontinued.

Sometime after the console was changed to the covered type with the armrest-storage box, the ashtray was changed again to the drawer type as used in the Series I 4.2-liter cars.

From research of surviving cars: Serial numbers 860084, 876052, 876577, and 879093 had the wingless ashtray, while 879325 and 889076 had the winged ashtray.

About May 1963, the ashtray was changed at chassis numbers 850695/6, 861149/50, 879291/2, and 888512/3. This is likely the addition of the wings to the oblong rotating ashtray. This change is listed only in *Jaguar E-Type: The Definitive History*.

About January 1964, the ashtray was changed again, at chassis numbers 850785/6, 861383/4, 880614/5, and 889503/4. The new one is not interchangeable with the old. This is likely the institution of the large, rectangular ashtray. This change is listed only by Porter.

Similar to the trim change of the dashboard center section, the front and bottom console trimming underwent two changes. The first change was in the pattern used on the aluminum. The circular pattern was replaced with the cross pattern, exactly as in the case of the first center-dashboard trim change.

In the second change, the trim on the front and bottom consoles was changed from aluminum to a material matching the interior color of the car. However, instead of the vinyl trim used on the later dashboard center sections, the trim was leather. The trim changes from aluminum to leather did not occur at the same time for both front and bottom console sections. The

The aluminum trim on the early consoles followed the progression of the center dash, coming first in the dot pattern and later in the cross pattern. This is the early dot-pattern material.

The later consoles were trimmed in leather, and had an armrest-storage area at the rear.

The plastic transmission covers came in both white and black.

lower console was trimmed in leather, and a storage area was added to it before the aluminum was replaced with leather on the front console.

Changes at chassis numbers 850609/10, 860912/3, 878301/2, and 887131/2: About October 1962, the patterns embossed on the aluminum finisher panels on the assembly above the gearbox and on the assembly over the gearbox and driveshaft cover were changed.

Changes at chassis numbers 850736/7, 861215/6, 879760/1, and 888858/9, except for 850725, 850727, 879531, 879543, 789545, 879546, 879553, 879556, 879562 (these cars come before the listed change, so I assume "except for" means the new consoles were fitted to these earlier cars before it was made standard): About August 1963, the console was changed to a new one that had an armrest with storage space. This change is listed only in *Jaguar E-Type: The Definitive History*.

Changes at chassis numbers 850751/2, 861253/4, 879802/3, and 889029/30: About September 1963, the front finisher panel was changed from embossed aluminum to leather. This change is listed only by Porter.

Changes at chassis numbers 850786/7, 861388/9, 880630/1, and 889525/6: About March 1964, the radio panel part of the console was changed. This change is listed only by Porter.

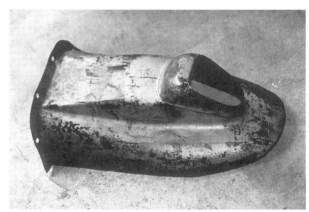

Metal transmission covers were also used.

Back view of the metal transmission cover

Under Console Area

The transmission cover over the large opening in the transmission tunnel came in different types. Typically, these pieces were made of molded plastic, and they came in black and white.

I am aware of one instance, serial number 875109, where the transmission cover was made of metal. It is a different style than those found on some 4.2-liter cars, and it differs from the plastic covers in several ways. Its mounting is affected at the rear by a tang that goes under the rear edge of the transmission tunnel aperture. Serial number 889076, a late coupe, had this same type of metal cover. The plastic covers, and the 4.2-liter covers, are affixed with sheet-metal screws all around.

The earliest transmission-tunnel inspection hole covers were made of steel. The disc was held in place by a spring riveted to the center of the plate. This is the cockpit-side view.

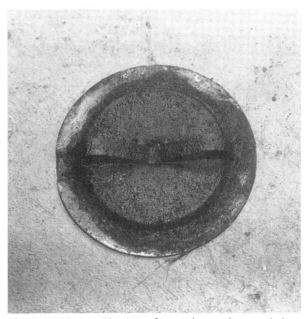

This transmission-side view of an early metal transmission-tunnel inspection-hole cover shows the three-piece construction, with a deflecting metal bow that retains it in the hole.

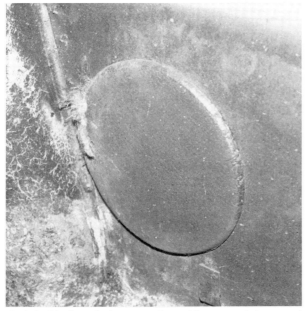

Cockpit-side view of a later one-piece rubber transmission-tunnel inspection hole cover.

Transmission-side view of a later one-piece rubber transmission-tunnel inspection hole cover. The deterioration seen here is typical.

An early car without an armrest on the door.

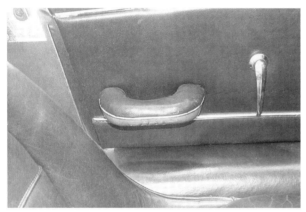

Door armrest on a later car. This is the sort of armrest used on the Series I 4.2-liter two-seater.

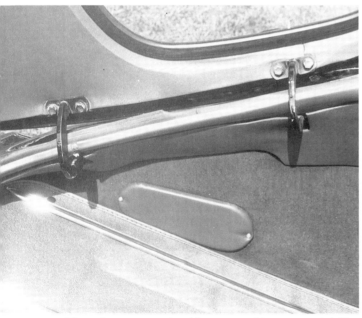

The early coupe rear-door hinges were without covers. It is likely these uncovered hinges often fowled against the contents of the luggage area.

The round plugs used to fill the gearbox inspection holes on the left side of the transmission tunnel came in at least two types. Some of the early cars had three-piece metal covers instead of the later rubber ones.

From research of surviving cars: Serial numbers 875026 and 875109 had the metal covers, while 860084, 889076, and 890061 had the rubber covers.

Carpets and Interior Trim

There are a few references about leather being employed for the trim, as well as the seats. For example, *The Autocar* magazine, March 17, 1961, states that "leather is used throughout for the trim. . . ." In *Jaguar Sports Cars*, Skilleter says, "Leather was employed for the trim, except for the carpeted areas and the headlining. . . ." I do not have any other evidence that this ever occurred. Leather was used for the seats, shift boot, and early heel pads.

The headliner color was grey or beige, for cars without a green interior, and green for cars with a green interior.

As with other areas of the car, there are numerous pictures of prototypes, or very early production cars, with unusual features. Unusual interior trim is shown running up the pillars on a prototype roadster in *Car and Driver*, May 1961. Chrome trim strips are absent on the doors of a very early car on that issue's cover. The lower chrome strip is absent on one of the prototype coupes in *Jaguar E-Type: The Definitive History*, and 9600HP is shown with both chrome strips.

Changes at chassis numbers 850723/4, 861188/9, 879495/6, and 888697/8: About June 1963, armrests were added to the doors. This change is listed only in *Jaguar E-Type: The Definitive History*.

Changes at chassis numbers 850357/8, 860175/6, 876581/2, and 885503/4: Flintkote was added to the front floor and the front carpets were changed.

Changes at chassis numbers 860478/9 and 886013/4: About May 1962, the headlining, including the cantrail and rear trim panels, the panel assembly for trimming the windscreen header rail, and the trim panel assembly for the windscreen header rail were all changed.

Changes at chassis numbers 850526/7, 860580/1, 877355/6, and 886092/3: About June 1962, changes were made to the mat assembly on the floor behind the seats, the mat assembly on the rear bulkhead panel, and the moquette face piece for the lower bulkhead panel, the casing assembly below the quarter light, the hinged extension for the luggage compartment floor, and the support rail assembly for the hinged extension in its lowered position.

The luggage compartment mat in the coupes was originally two pieces, but later it was changed to one piece. On a few very early cars, the small piece of the two-piece mat had a small tab on the forward end, presumably to lift it up.

Changes at chassis numbers 861092/3 and 888256/7: About August 1963, the mat assembly on the luggage compartment floor changed from a two-piece to a one-piece unit.

Changes at chassis numbers 861098/9 and 888301/2: About August 1963, the trim panel for the shut pillar, the casing assembly at the side of the luggage compartment floor, and the hinged extension assembly for the luggage compartment floor were all changed.

Changes at chassis numbers 850713/4, 861178/9, 879422/3, and 888657/8: About June 1963, a trim panel was fitted to the hinge face of the door and was retained by the door light-switch striker. This change is listed only in Porter's *Jaguar E-Type: The Definitive History*.

On early cars, the heel board sewn onto the floor mat had a wooden backing.

Changes at chassis numbers 850751/2, 861255/6, 879892/3, and 889053/4 (and some prior cars): About September 1963, the front carpets were changed to a type with a plastic heel pad. This change is listed only by Porter.

Changes at chassis numbers 850771/2, 861324/5, 880411/2, and 889346/7: About November 1963, the carpet fasteners were changed. This change is listed only by Porter.

Changes at chassis numbers 850808/9, 861445/6, 880839/40, and 889786/7: About March 1964, the

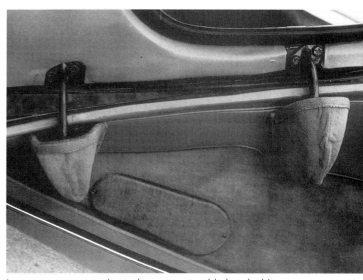

Later on, moquette-trimmed covers were added to the hinges.

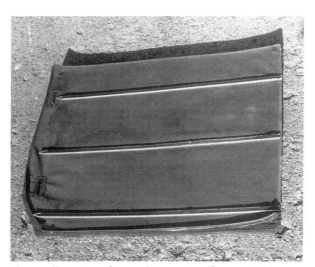

The small section of an early two-piece floor mat. The two brackets sticking through the left side of the mat were likely added after the car left the factory.

The early coupes had a two-piece mat in the luggage area. The large section was in an L shape, as seen on this very early RHD coupe.

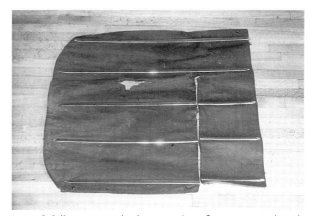

Later 3.8-liter coupes had a one-piece floor mat. A slot allowed it to be rolled back to access the spare tire area.

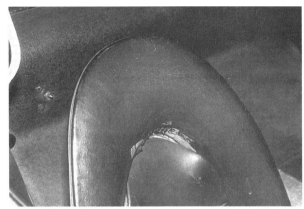

The seats used on roadsters had a small radius of curvature at the top.

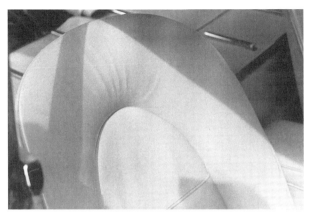

The coupe seats had a large radius of curvature at the top. Apparently, a few coupes were fitted with roadster seats.

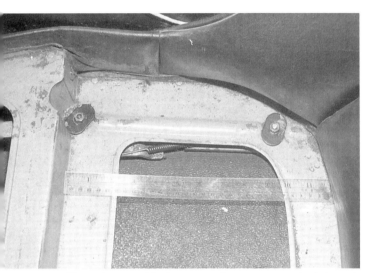

The early cars, with short seat-adjustment range, had the early mounts with mounting bolts close together.

After the range of seat adjustment was increased, the mounts were changed, and the mounting bolts were farther apart.

interior door trim was changed. This change is listed only by Porter.

One of these 3.8-liter interior trim changes was the introduction of covers over the coupe rear-door hinges. The early cars had bare hinges while the later cars had covers over the hinges.

Seats and Mounts

The seats on some prototype cars were different from those in production cars. They had flat, squared-off shape to the seat back, and, in some instances, different stitching arrangements.

After these few early cars, two seat types came to be standard: the small-radius or narrow-back seats, and the large-radius or wide-back seats. Typically, the narrow-back seats were used on roadsters, and the wide-back seats were used on the coupes. Roadster seats were narrower on the back, and some early seats had coarser grain leather. Some early coupes were fitted with roadster seats. Serial number 860005 is fitted with the narrow-back seats.

Seat cushions in 1961 cars had thin padding, which was improved for 1962.

In *The Jaguar E-Type: A Collector's Guide*, referring to a picture showing coarse-grained leather, Skilleter stated, "This 1961 roadster has the rather unusual large-grain-pattern leather, which was sometimes used in early cars."

In *Jaguar Sports Cars*, Skilleter stated that "pre-1962 cars had 'unfortunately placed' beading across the seat back which could become an annoyance on long journeys." In *The Jaguar E-Type: A Collector's Guide*, he also stated that "Trim shop messed around with different sorts of padding in different places. . . ."

The early seats had short mounts, allowing only a small adjustment range. For these early seats, the longitudinal spacing of the four bolts holding the seats to the slides is shorter than the spacing found on later cars.

Changes at chassis numbers 850526/7, 860580/1, 877355/6, and 886092/3: About June 1962, the seat slides were changed.

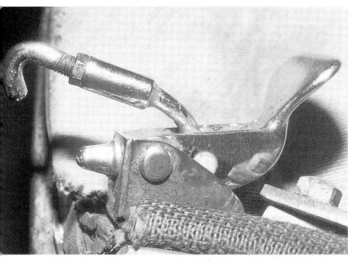

From the delicate appearance of the early necked-down convertible-top clasp, it is evident why not may survive.

The thick convertible-top clasps, as found on most Series I cars, were much more durable.

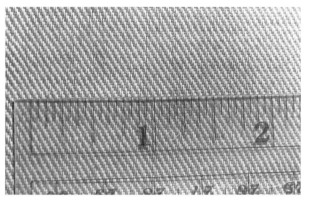

A close-up of the fabric used to cover the steel section at the front of the convertible-top frame.

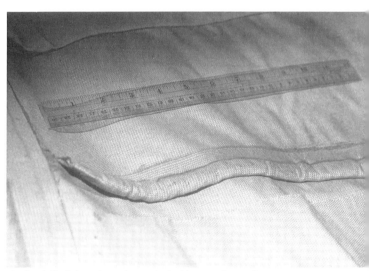

The lead-filled damping tube on the inside top of an early convertible top was provided to prevent drumming of the top at speed.

Convertible-Top Frame and Hardware

On the earliest cars, the outer two convertible-top clasps were necked-down. The later outer clasps had more uniform and thicker cross sections. I presume this change was made to increase the strength of the clasps, which must have broken easily.

From research of surviving cars: Serial numbers 875026, 875109, 875186, and 875251 had the necked-down clasps. Number 875407 had a single necked-down clasp (it may have come this way, or the other one may be a replacement).

Convertible-Top Cloth and Window

In the top of the convertible top, there is a long bag of lead shot in a damping tube.

Convertible-Top Cover

The convertible-top cover came in various color combinations. One combination I have seen illustrated in early photographs is a black cover with red piping on a white external-latch car with a red interior. I've also seen black-and-white pictures that illustrate dark covers with both light and dark piping.

Changes at chassis numbers 850934/5 and 881864/5: About October 1964, the convertible-top cover was changed. This change is listed only in *Jaguar E-Type: The Definitive History.*

On the early cars, three clasps on the bulkhead fastened the boot, instead of the later two.

Hardtop Mounting Equipment

The early roadsters were not fitted with hardtop mounting brackets, and could not take a hardtop without modification.

Changes at chassis numbers 850023/4 and 875026/7: The first type of detachable hardtop mounting assembly began.

The earliest roadsters did not come with mounting brackets for the hardtop. It became available as an option after a few cars were produced.

A hardtop mounting bracket on a later roadster.

The two spring clasps were used to store the T-key on a very early car. Pouches were also used.

An external view of an early convertible-top cover with three retaining straps.

An interior view of an early convertible-top cover.

Changes at chassis numbers 850091/2 and 875385/6: The hardtop fitting kit was changed.

Changes at chassis numbers 850356/7 and 877430/1: In about July 1962, the hardtop mounting brackets were changed. This change is listed only in *Jaguar E-Type: The Definitive History*.

Changes at chassis numbers 850455/6 and 876974/5: The hardtop fitting kit was changed.

T-Key Storage Mount

On at least some external-bonnet-latch cars, there were clip mounts to store the T-key when not in use. The mounting slips appear to be the same as those used to hold the jack rod in the trunk. In Porter's *Original Jaguar E-Type*, a T-key is shown on a restored car in the same position, but in a small bag. In Jenkinson's *Jaguar E-Type 3.8 & 4.2 6-cylinder; 5.3 V-12*, a T-key mount is shown on the right bulkhead just in front of the right-hand-side door in an *Autocar* line drawing.

From research of surviving cars: Serial number 875026 had the clip mount on the rear of the console. Numbers 875179, 875282, and 875340 have the bag mount.

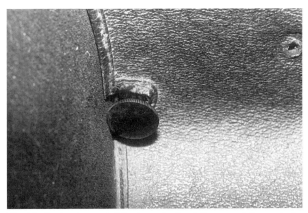

The black plastic trunk-lid release in the right rear of the cockpit.

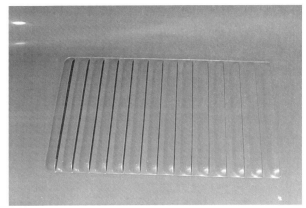

Welded-in hood louvers were characteristic of the early cars.

Interior Release

I am not aware of any design changes.

Trunk Release

The cable release that opens the roadster trunk is operated by pulling a black plastic knob in the right rear of the cockpit. I am not aware of any design changes.

Bodywork: Front Fenders

Changes at chassis numbers 850091/2, 860004/5, 875385/6, and 885020/1: About October 1961, the hood and front fenders assembly was changed and the bonnet latch was moved inside.

Hood Center Section

The welded-in louvers are a well-known feature of the early cars, and were only in production for a few months. Afterward, the louvers were pressed directly into the hood center section.

Some early cars show spot welds on the external surface of the hood where the wheelwells fasten to the internal surface of the hood.

Changes at chassis numbers 860478/9 and 886013/4: About June 1962, the hood and its hinges were changed. This change is listed only in *Jaguar E-Type: The Definitive History.*

From research of surviving cars: Serial numbers 860005, 875407, 875967, and 876052 had the welded-in louvers, while numbers 876577, 885576, 885733, and 885980 had the pressed-in louvers. The external hood-latch car, serial number 875186, had pressed-in louvers. This is an anomaly; likely the center section of the hood was replaced in the past. It is somewhat curious, though, as there is no apparent evidence of damage to the front fenders, which still have the external hood latches.

Hood Hinges and Lifts

Changes at chassis numbers 850238/9, 860138/9, 876457/8, and 885384/5: The hood hinge and front cross-member of the front frame were changed about February 1962.

Changes at chassis numbers 860138/9 and 885384/5: The hood hinge was changed on the coupe

Inside view of the welded-in louvers.

only. In spare parts catalog, June 1963 version, the later-type coupe hood hinge is listed for use on all roadsters.

Changes at chassis numbers 860478/9 and 886013/4: About June 1962, the front subframe assembly and hinge were changed.

Hood Latches

On the First 500 cars, the hood-latching mechanism was operated from outside the hood with a T-key.

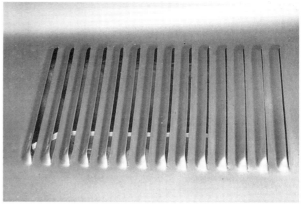

Later 3.8-liter cars had the hood louvers stamped into the center-hood section sheet metal.

Inside view of the stamped-in louvers.

While typically all E-Type hoods show signs of spot welding, it was particularly pronounced on the early cars. This external view of the hood of an outside-latch car clearly shows spot welds above the right-side wheelwell baffle.

A later hood hinge.

The hood hinge on an early car.

The early hood-latch mechanism was found on the inside of the front fender.

The catches for the early mechanism were bolted to the tops of the front sills.

The two retaining screws for the external hood-latch catch on the body were continued some time after the hood latches were moved inside.

With the introduction of the internal hood latches, the catch was mounted on the hood.

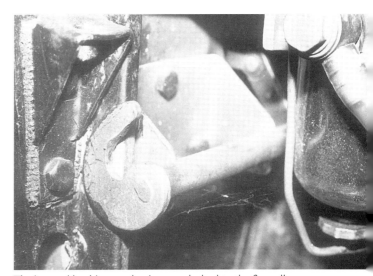

The internal latching mechanism was bolted to the firewall.

The latch control handle was mounted in front of the doors.

An internal view of the flat floor of an early car. The brake and clutch pedals can be seen on this RHD car.

The rubber hood bumpers of the external-latch cars were mounted on these brackets. This one shows the mount only as the rubber pad is missing.

Some very early cars were fitted with these metal patches pop-riveted on the front of the outer edges of the front bulkhead.

Subsequently, the mechanism was changed to one operated from inside the cockpit without a key.

Changes at chassis numbers 850091/2, 860004/5, 875385/6, and 885020/1: About September 1961, hood lock, escutcheon, and so on were changed to internal lock.

Three holes in the firewall to mount interior latches were introduced before the latches were actually changed to inside-operated types. They are plugged with white plugs.

For a period after the latches moved into the cockpit, the two screws used to retain the catch on the body on each side were continued. From research of surviving cars: Serial numbers 860084, 875427, 875954, and 876052 have these screws on each side.

What looks like an interior latch mechanism is shown in the interior of an early car on the cover of *Car and Driver*, May 1961. This car appears to be the same one discussed in Porter's *Jaguar E-Type: The Definitive History*, and identified there as serial number 850002. If so, it appears to have had external latches but no T-key hole covers.

Rubber Stops

As part of the exterior hood-latch setup, rubber stops were mounted on the firewall where the hood came up against it.

In Porter's book, there are two views of an early car (likely serial number 885002) that does not seem to have these stops.

Changes at chassis numbers 850091/2, 860004/5, 875385/6, and 885020/1: The rubber buffer cushioning the hood sides in the closed position was discontinued (incorporated as part of the new internal latch).

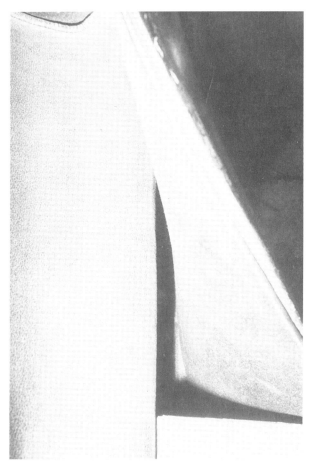

The straight rear bulkhead of an early car.

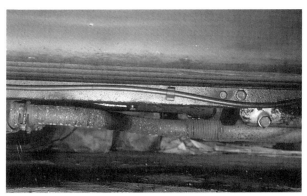

An external view of the flat floor of an early car.

Early in production, these sunken footwells were introduced to increase room in the cockpit.

External view of the sunken footwells of a later car.

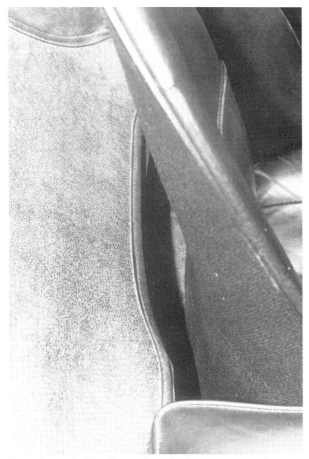

Later, the rear bulkhead was indented to increase seat travel.

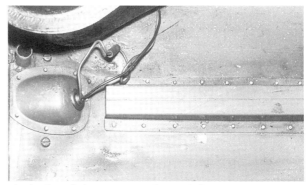

The back-up light recesses in the trunk floor were pop-riveted in on the very early cars. Note here that the center support rail is also pop-riveted in.

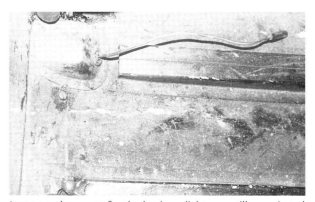

Later on, the recess for the back-up light was still pop-riveted in, but the center support rail was welded in.

In spite of this, however, in Martinez and Nory's *European Automobiles of the 50's and 60's*, there are two clear pictures of an early internal-latch car with the rubber stops of the external-latch setup. I suspect this is indicative of how the car left the factory because the car is a quite original example, and in any case this would be an unusual and difficult part to fit as a modification. From research of surviving cars: Serial number 860005 has these rubber stops, while 876052 does not have them.

Rear Tub Sheet Metal, Firewall, and Underside

Changes at chassis numbers 860478/9 and 886013/4: About May 1962, changes were made to the rear fender assembly, the tail panel below the trunk lid, the trunk gutters, the casing assembly at the rear side of the luggage compartment floor, the roof panel assembly, the windscreen header panel assembly, the scuttle top panel and windscreen pillars, the cantrail panel assembly, the drip bead on the cantrail panel assembly, the windscreen pillar assembly, the underframe, the closing panels under the screen pillars, the outer sills, the roof panel, the rear fenders, and the trunk lid.

Changes at chassis numbers 850526/7, 860580/1, 877355/6, and 886092/3: The body underframe assembly, floor assembly, and rear-end body shell were changed.

Changes at chassis numbers 850655/6 and 879023/4: The seal assemblies at the rear of the wheel arches were changed about March 1963.

Changes at chassis numbers 860580/1 and 886092/3: The body underframe assembly and floor assembly were changed.

Cockpit Sheet Metal

The best-known change in the cockpit sheet metal was the introduction of the sunken footwells and the recessed rear bulkheads, on both the driver's and passenger's sides. While the E-Type prototype E1A had sunken footwells, the footwells of the early production E-Types were flat. This, and the welded-in louvers, are two often-quoted features of early E-Types.

In *Jaguar Sports Cars*, Skilleter stated that "all the 1962 E-Types incorporated footwells in both driver's and passenger's side of the cockpit and an indentation made in the rear bulkhead on both models also allowed more rearward travel for the seats." This indicates that Skilleter considered all flat-floor cars as 1961 models.

Changes at chassis numbers 850357/8, 860175/6, 876581/2, and 885503/4: In late winter 1962, the floor assembly was changed to include heelwells. Note that the June 1963 version of the parts book lists chassis numbers 876381/2 instead of 876581/2, the numbers given in other sources. The Jaguar service bulletin lists the body numbers for the change as OTS: 2879/2889, FHC: 1635/1647.

Changes at chassis numbers 860478/9 and 886013/4: The retainers for the cantrail seals were changed.

Changes at chassis numbers 850526/7, 860580/1, 877355/6, and 886092/3: About June 1962, the body underframe assembly, floor assembly, and rear-end body shell were changed. This included modifying the rear bulkhead of the body shell to include recesses to allow the seats 1 1/2 inches more rearward travel.

In *Jaguar E-Type: A Collector's Guide*, Skilleter stated that a temporary modification had been carried out on the driver's side shortly after the introduction of the car.

Changes at chassis numbers 860580/1 and 886092/3: The body underframe assembly and floor assembly were changed.

Doors

Changes at chassis numbers 860478/9 and 886013/4: About May 1962, the door shells and hinges were changed. Skilleter cites this change with chassis numbers 860475/6 instead of 860478/9.

Changes at chassis numbers 850506/7 and 877201/2: About May 1962, the door shell assembly was changed. Some cars before these chassis numbers were also modified.

Door Hinges and Supports

Changes at chassis numbers 860478/9 and 886013/4: About May 1962, the door shells and hinges were changed. Skilleter cites this change with chassis numbers 860475/6 instead of 860478/9.

Door Latches

I am not aware of any design changes.

Trunk Sheet Metal

The recess for the back-up light in the rear inside of the trunk floor changed on the early cars. On early cars it was pop-riveted in, and on later cars it was welded in.

From research of surviving cars: Serial numbers 875026 and 875109 had the pop-riveted recesses, while 875254 and 876052 had the welded-in type.

A similar change occurred in the first support rail to the right of center on the trunk floor. On early cars, it is pop-riveted in, while on later cars it is welded in. The change for the support rail occurred before the change in the back-up-light recess.

From research of surviving cars: Serial number 875026 had the pop-riveted rail, while 875109 had the welded-in rail.

Changes at chassis numbers 860478/9 and 886013/4: The support panel for the trunk-lid aperture was changed.

There were variations in the drains in the trough around the trunk aperture on the early roadsters. The earliest cars had a single, centrally located drain, while the later cars had two drains, one at each rear corner. There was also a period when three drains were used, one in the middle and the two corner ones.

Changes at chassis numbers 850117/8, 860006/7, 875520/1, and 885032/3: About October 1961, the single center drain tube for the trunk-lid aperture was changed to two tubes on the right and left.

From research of surviving cars: Serial numbers 875026, 875109, 875251, 875254, and 875407 had a single center drain hole; numbers 875186 and 875223 had three drain holes; and numbers 875954, 875958, 876052, 876289, and 876577 had two holes.

The trunk mat for the three-drain-hole car, serial number 875223, has recesses for the three drains in it. It appears to be a factory-original mat.

Changes at chassis numbers 861615/6 and 890339/40: About May 1964, the rear casings at the side of the luggage compartment floor were changed. This change is listed only in *Jaguar E-Type: The Definitive History*.

Trunk Lid

Changes at chassis numbers 860478/9 and 886013/4: The casing assembly on the trunk lid was changed.

Trunk Hinges and Supports

The trunk-lid hinges came in three types. The earliest type is a single, thin-aluminum casting. The next type has dual, thin-aluminum sections that appear to be made by welding together two of the early, thin-walled hinges. Lastly, the conventional, thick-aluminum cast hinges were used.

From research of surviving cars: Serial number 875026 had thin hinges; numbers 875109, 875166, 875179, 875186, and 875407 had double hinges; and numbers 875254, 875954, 875958, 876052, 876289, and 876577 had thick hinges. Serial number 875254 seems out of place; perhaps the hinges were changed at some point.

In the last configuration, both the recess for back-up light and the support rail were welded in.

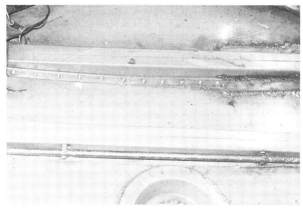

The pop-riveted center trunk support rail on a very early roadster. Note the handle for the early turret jack held by two clips on the welded-in rail.

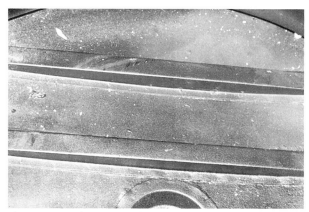

The center trunk support rails on most cars were welded in.

Single water-drain hole, far left.

The hinges for the coupe door were made in two varieties. The early-style hinges were fabricated and have sharp edges. The later hinges were cast and are rounded.

From research of surviving cars: Serial numbers 860084 had the early fabricated hinges, and 889076 had the late hinges.

An early coupe, probably a prototype, shown with unusual springs on the rear door and no trunk-lid prop, is pictured in *The Jaguar E-Type: The Collector's Guide* and in *Jaguar E-Type: The Definitive History*.

Changes at chassis numbers 860478/9 and 886013/4: The trunk-lid hinge assembly was changed. The prop supporting the trunk lid in the open position, the pivot bracket on the trunk lid for the prop, and the bracket on the body receiving the prop were all changed. The striker and safety catch for the trunk-lid lock were changed.

Changes at chassis numbers 861013/4 and 887316/7: About December 1962, the trunk-lid prop and its bracket were changed.

The prop is typically chromed, but one is seen in black on the Geneva car in *Jaguar E-Type: The Definitive History*.

Changes at chassis numbers 850767/8 and 880290/1: About January 1964, a hole was added to the number-plate panel at the rear to allow access to the trunk-lid latch in case the release cable should break, using a right-angle 3/16-inch diameter rod. A rubber seal was inserted in this hole.

Fuel Filler Recess, Lid, and Hinge

The 3.8-liter cars came with two types of gas caps. The early cap was fabricated from chromed steel, and was of the type fitted to many British cars of the period. The later cap was a casting with fluted edges. From research of surviving cars: Serial numbers 860084 and 875026 were fitted with the fabricated cap.

Changes at chassis numbers 860478/9 and 886013/4: The fuel filler box and its lid were changed about May 1962. *The Jaguar E-Type: A Collector's Guide* cites chassis numbers 860475/6 instead of 860478/9.

Changes at chassis numbers 850907/8, 861722/3, 881705/6, and 890721/2: About October 1964, the gas cap was changed. This may be the end of the reeded-edge chrome-steel fabricated cap and the beginning of the cast fluted cap. This change is listed only in *Jaguar E-Type: The Definitive History*.

Trunk Panels, Mat, and Flooring

The shape of the roadster trunk mat and the plywood flooring in both the coupes and roadsters were altered at the rear to accommodate the change in the water drain locations. Cars were produced with one, two, and three trunk drain holes.

Changes at chassis numbers 860580/1 and 886088/9: About July 1962, the strikers for the luggage-floor hinged extension latches, and the rubber buffers for the extension in its raised position, were changed. This change is listed only by Porter.

Trunk-Lid Sealing Rubber

The sealing rubber on the early cars was glued to the trunk lid itself, while on later cars it was fastened around the edge of the trunk aperture.

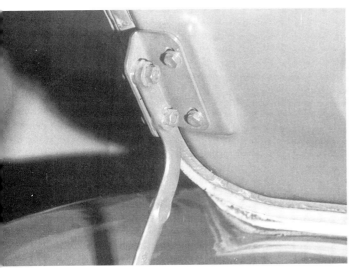

The very early roadsters had thin aluminum trunk-lid hinges. These probably did not hold up well, as they were quickly changed to a dual support arrangement.

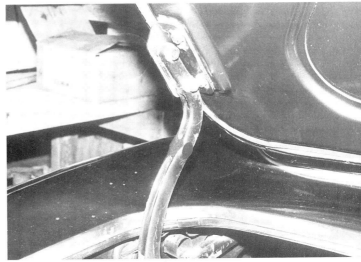

The dual, thin-aluminum roadster trunk-lid hinges were introduced early on, but were not used long.

Changes at chassis numbers 860478/9 and 886013/4: The sealing rubber around the trunk-lid aperture was changed from one piece to two pieces.

Jack Handle Mounts

In some early cars, the handle to the screw-type jack handle (a long steel rod) is stored in two clip mounts in the trunk. The mounts are screwed on the side of the first support rail to the right of center on the trunk floor. These appear to be the same type of clips used to mount the T-key to the back of the console on some early cars.

From research of surviving cars: Both serial numbers 875026 and 875109 had these clips.

Later, trunk apertures had dual drain holes.

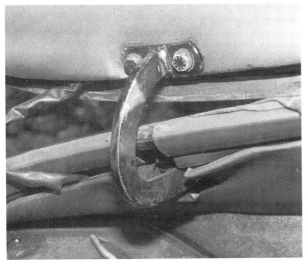

The rear-door hinges on the very early coupes were fabricated and had an angular look.

The final configuration of the roadster trunk-lid hinges was a fat aluminum casting. This type was used throughout the remaining production.

The rubber plug in the access hole in the number-plate panel. These were found on later 3.8-liter cars, but this illustration is from a 4.2-liter car.

Later on, the coupe rear-door hinges were cast, and had the appearance of the cast coupe rear-door hinge.

On the early cars, the trunk sealing rubber was mounted on the lid.

The number plate had chassis, body, engine, and transmission numbers stamped on it. It was pop-riveted on the right-hand side of the engine compartment.

On later cars, the sealing rubber was on the inner lip of the trunk aperture.

A plate added by the state of California. J-62 means 1962 Jaguar.

Exterior and Interior Colors

The following listing is compiled from several lists published in various literature. These lists were similar, but not identical, so I have combined them to form a central list. Other sources contain basically the same information.

Exterior and Interior Colors 1961 and 1962

Interior	Exterior
Black	Red, Grey, Light Tan, or Tan
British Racing Green	Suede Green, Beige, Light Tan, or Tan
Bronze	Beige, Red, or Tan
Carmen Red	Black, Biscuit, or Red
Claret	Beige
Cotswold Blue	Dark Blue
Cream	Black, Cream, or Red
Imperial Maroon	Tan
Indigo	Red or Light Blue
Mist Grey	Red
Opalescent Dark Blue	Dark Blue or Red
Opalescent Dark Green	Suede Green, Beige, Tan, or Light Tan
Opalescent Gunmetal	Dark Blue, Light Blue, Red, or Beige
Opalescent Silver Blue	Grey or Dark Blue
Opalescent Silver Grey	Red, Light Blue, Dark Blue, or Grey
Pearl	Dark Blue or Red
Sherwood Green	Suede Green, Light Tan, or Tan

Exterior and Interior Colors 1963 and 1964

Interior	Exterior
Black	Red, Grey, Light Tan, or Tan
British Racing Green	Suede Green, Beige, Tan, or Light Tan
Bronze	Beige, Red, or Tan
Carmen Red	Black or Red
Cotswold Blue	Dark Blue
Cream	Black
Mist Grey	Red
Opalescent Dark Blue	Dark Blue or Red
Opalescent Dark Green	Suede Green, Beige, Light Tan, or Tan
Opalescent Gunmetal	Dark Blue, Light Blue, Red, or Beige
Opalescent Maroon	Maroon or Beige
Opalescent Silver Blue	Grey or Dark Blue
Opalescent Silver Grey	Red, Light Blue, Dark Blue, or Grey
Pale Primrose	Black or Beige
Pearl	Dark Blue or Red
Sand	Black or Beige
Sherwood Green	Suede Green, Light Tan, or Tan

While these were the standard color combinations, there were variations.

Cans of touch-up paint may have been supplied with some cars. An example of this is seen in the December 1961 *Car and Driver*.

Serial-Number Markings

Serial numbers of different sorts are marked on the car in numerous places. A number plate, summarizing chassis, body, engine, and transmission numbers, is located on the horizontal area behind the right hood latch. There is evidence that a few very early cars had this summary plate mounted on the firewall.

The chassis number is stamped on the top of the right-hand side of the front frame member, just above the top shock-absorber mounting point, and on the number plate.

The engine number on 3.8-liter cars is stamped on the block above the oil filter, on the back of the cam chain area of the head, on the edge of the flywheel, and on the number plate.

The transmission number is stamped on the top of the aluminum transmission cover, on the iron transmission case, and on the number plate.

The body number is stamped on a pressed plate affixed to the firewall in the engine compartment on the right-hand side on early cars, on the left-hand-side bulkhead in the trunk on later cars, and on the number plate. From research of surviving cars: Serial numbers 875026 (body number R.1044), 875109 (body number R.1129), 875186 (body number R.1263), and 875251 (body number R.1362) had the body number on the firewall, while serial numbers 875340 (body number R.1460), 875954 (body number R.2210 or R.2202), 876052 (body number R.2301), and 885358 (body number V.1526) had the body number in the trunk.

An additional chassis-number plate mounted on the right-hand-side firewall of this French-specification car.

The chassis number was stamped on the front section of the front subframe, above the right shock-absorber mount.

The differential number is stamped on the bottom of the differential housing case.

The radiator number is stamped on an aluminum plate screwed to the top of the radiator.

In addition to these usual markings, there are others that sometimes show up. For example, serial number 875109 has its body number 1129 stamped on the right rear of its hood. But I do not think this was a completely standard practice, as 875026 has no such marking. The hood on serial number 875026 is the original, and carries the crayon marking 1044 USA inside the rear of the right fender. Similar crayon markings of body numbers are shown on the outside license-plate area. I have seen this practice used on various early E-Types. Body numbers are sometimes found on the inside of the coupe rear door.

Pictured in *Jaguar E-Type: The Definitive History* is one instance of an early car (likely serial number 885002) that does not have the number plate in its usual location behind the right hood latch.

"E-TYPE" and "J" were stamped on the front frame member, next to the chassis number, on this French-specification car. These were likely not factory stampings.

The engine number was stamped in several places. Here it is on the block above the oil filter.

The engine number was stamped on the head, behind the camshaft chain gallery.

The engine number was stamped on the outer edge of the flywheel.

The transmission number was stamped in two places. Here it is on the transmission cover.

The transmission number was also stamped on the side of the case.

The engine number is stamped on the head, on the rear side of the cam chain gallery. This is what is usually referred to as the head number.

Cars sold in California received an additional identification plate.

Labels and Decals

A run-in sticker was applied to the inside of the driver's side windshield.

On some differentials, metal tabs are bolted down under some of the cover retaining bolts.

The brakes and clutch master cylinders often carry aluminum straps with dates inscribed on them.

Some of the windshield-washer bottles come with a Lucas Screenjet sticker on them.

In the spare-tire well of the trunk, next to where the spark-arrester DC connections are made for the fuel pump, an aluminum warning label is pop-riveted to the sheet metal. I believe this is present on virtually all 3.8-liter cars. In addition to the warning label pop-riveted to the sheet metal, the plastic lid of the spark arrester itself has a warning message on it.

On some cars, a small paper label is affixed to the windshield-washer-fluid motor, under the spade terminals.

Some very early cars had a rectangular decal on the rear of the right cam cover.

Dated Components

The Lucas electrical components used on the car were, for the most part, dated with a month and year designation, such as 6 60.

Another component that carries a date is the engine block. On its lower left-hand side, in front of and below the dipstick location, is a designation such as 27-2-61, cast into the block. I have been told that this is the casting date of the block at the foundry, and this seems likely from the dates I have seen.

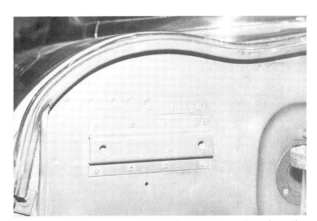

On early cars, the body-number plate was pop-riveted on the right-hand side of the firewall.

Later on, the body-number plate was pop-riveted on the left-hand side of the trunk. The cardboard trim has been removed to show this plate.

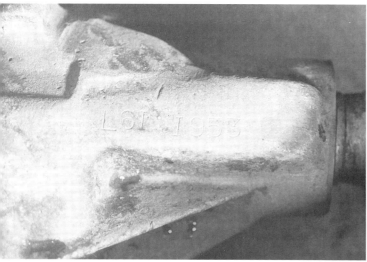

The differential number was stamped on the bottom of its case.

The aluminum radiators had a serial-number plate screwed on top.

The body number marked in crayon on the inside of a coupe rear door.

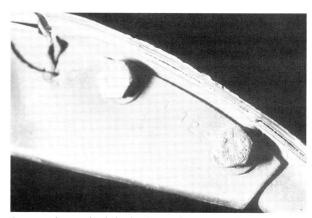

Some early cars had the body number stamped on the upper right rear of the hood.

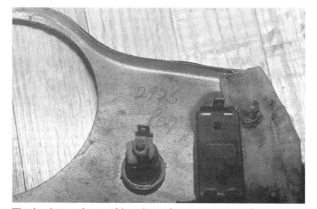

The body number and interior color were crayoned on numerous pieces of the interior trim. Here they are found inside the instrument-cluster dash panel.

The body number was marked in crayon on the inside right fender of the bonnet of some early hoods. This one also denotes the destination of the car as the United States.

The 43/13 tab on this differential cover denotes a 3.31:1 axle ratio.

A fuel-pump connection warning plaque was mounted in the spare-tire well. Note above it the label on the lid of the spark arrester for the fuel-pump DC power connection.

The Lucas Screenjet sticker from an early windshield washer bottle.

Another type of windshield-washer motor label on an early RHD coupe.

A windshield-washer motor label on an early LHD roadster.

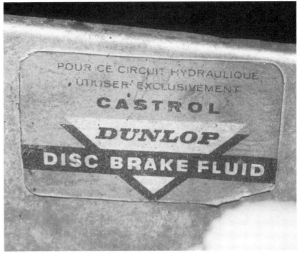

A Castrol-Dunlop sticker on the brake-fluid heatshield of a French-specification car.

This metallic label was affixed to a later-type metal-topped reservoir cap that was fitted as a replacement part some time after six-cylinder E-Type production ceased. It is marked "Manufactured and Tested 27 MAR 1974." I have seen no evidence of such labels being fitted to caps supplied new with the cars.

This illustration of the inside of the central instrument cluster shows a strip of masking tape marked with the body number, yet another form of unofficial marking applied to facilitate with assembly of the cars. Also note the handwritten date "3-61" marked on the ammeter case.

The engine blocks also carry dates. A date of September 6, 1961, is cast into this 3.8-liter block, just in front of the dipstick entry hole.

Dated aluminum straps were found on the brake master cylinders.

Most electrical components were dated. Here, a June 1962 date is scratched on the back of a horn button.

A June 1963 date stamped on a submerged fuel pump.

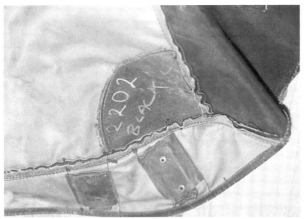

The body number and interior color written in crayon inside an early convertible-top cover.

An August 1961 date stamped on a screen-washer motor.

A May 1961 date stamped on a coil.

Tools

A listing of the tool kit items is given in spare parts catalog, June 1963 edition:

    Jack and handle
    Hammer (copper and rawhide)
    Budget lock key
    Bleeder tube
    Valve timing gauge
    Grease gun
    Feeler gauge
    Screwdriver for contact breaker points
    Tire valve extractor
    Tire pressure gauge
    Adjustable spanner
    Pliers
    Tommy bar (short)
    Box spanner [wrench]
        (sparking plugs and cylinder head nuts)
    Box spanner (9/16x5/8 inch SAE)
    Box spanner (7/16x 1/2 inch SAE)
    Box spanner (3/4x7/8 inch SAE)
    Open-ended spanner (11/32x3/8 inch AF)
    Open-ended spanner (9/16x5/8 inch AF)
    Open-ended spanner (1/2x7/16 inchAF)
    Open-ended spanner (3/4x7/8 inch AF)
    Tommy bar (long)
    Screwdriver
    Special wrench (for handbrake adjustment)

A fan belt is included in this list. It is not included, however, in the tool list found in the June 1963 parts catalog. Also, a paper-wrapped grease gun is included in the kit, but is not listed here.

Hand Tools and Roll Case

I am aware of two tool-case varieties. On a few early cars, the tools were kept in the round sedan-type case that stores in the spare tire. Later cars had the usual roll-type case that is usually associated with E-Types.

This March 1965 date on a windshield wiper motor indicates that it is a replacement unit; it is too late to be an original 3.8-liter part.

A typical tool kit from a 3.8-liter car. The brake-bleeder hose and can are missing.

The back view of the hubcap wrench.

The sedan-type kit was likely delivered with only a handful of extremely early cars.

The roll-type case was introduced quite early. One is shown on a car claimed to be 875012 in the December 1961 *Car and Driver*. Car 875026 came with a roll-type case.

The open-ended wrenches came from different manufacturers. On various Jaguars I have seen them marked with a T over a W in a circle: "GARRINGTON," "SSP," "SNAIL BRAND," and "EAGLE," instead of "JAGUAR" with "CHROME VANDIUM" on the opposite side, and "SHEFFIELD ENGLAND" on either sides of "EAGLE." I have seen the pliers marked "SHEFFIELD-MADE IN ENGLAND."

There seems to be a lot of variety in the tools, and I am not sure if any particular wrench is correct for any particular year of car. On serial number 875026, the

Some tire gauges were marked "DUNLOP."

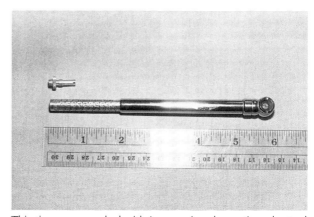

This tire gauge marked with Jaguar wings has a tire-valve tool screwed into its base.

original wrenches are of the T over a W in a circle and "GARRINGTON" type.

I have seen two types of tire gauges in E-Type tool kits: those marked "DUNLOP" and those marked with the Jaguar wings symbol. I am not sure which, if either, of these is correct for a specific year car. I believe the Dunlop is the correct gauge for the earliest cars, as I have seen these in tool kits for older sedans.

Changes at chassis numbers 850647/8, 861070/1, 878936/7, and 888138/9: A combination screwdriver (Phillips head and conventional) was introduced.

For European cars fitted with earless hubcaps, the tool kit included a large brass wrench that fitted around the hubcap and allowed hammer-blows to tighten or loosen the cap. This is a different tool from the one used on late 4.2-liter cars.

Another specialty tool found in only the early kits was the Allen wrench used to adjust the early, manually adjusted parking brakes.

Jack

On the early cars, the jack was originally an iron and aluminum cast screw-type. In later cars, this was changed to a steel fabricated type. I am not aware of any

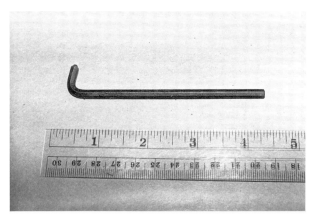

An Allen wrench for adjusting the parking brake was included in the early tool kits.

The early screw jacks were typically painted a light grey.

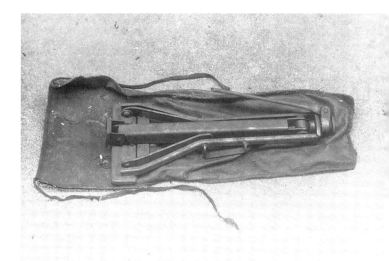

Later on, a fabricated steel jack was introduced. These were typically painted a dark grey. For 3.8-liter cars, these jacks had the handle permanently attached. During 4.2-liter production, the jacks were changed to a type with detached handles.

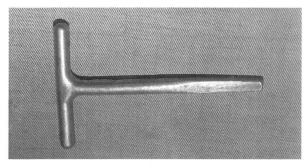

The original bonnet T-keys had a cylindrical top.

These T-keys with the teardrop-shaped top are often found with early cars, but were not likely ever supplied by the factory.

other jack variations. An unusual looking screw-type jack with an angular top section is pictured in *Jaguar E-Type: The Definitive History*. I believe this is a machined replacement top. The design of the original rounded tops was weak where the turning rod went in and often cracked, and I suspect this angular top is an improved replacement made outside the factory. Other than this instance, I am aware of no variations in the screw-type jack during the time it was used.

An early jack appears to be shown in a storage bag in *Car and Driver* magazine, December 1961. I have not seen any other evidence for storage bags for the early jacks.

As with many early features, sometimes the existence of the early jack is not acknowledged.

Changes at chassis numbers 850548/9, 860660/1, 877518/9, and 886246/7: About June 1962, the jack was changed to the cantilever type with integral handle, and the container for the jack was introduced.

T-Key

The T-key is listed, without any change notes, as part of the tool kit in the June 1963 spare parts catalog. It probably came only in the kits for the 500 cars with outside bonnet latches.

The correct T-key is cast steel with a cylindrical cross section. A key that is now frequently seen with early cars is the one with a teardrop cross section (of the sort often seen on Triumph cars), but I have seen no evidence it ever came with the early cars.

The question of T-key location, whether it was part of the kit or carried in mounts, is discussed earlier in this chapter.

Literature

In this section I'll discuss various items of literature issued by the factory or by factory dealers. I have broken the section into five subcategories: driver's handbooks and dust jackets; pouches and service vouchers; service manuals; spare parts catalogs; and service bulletin books.

Driver's Handbooks

The 3.8-liter E-Type driver's handbook comes in several varieties. The version is denoted on the first page of the handbook, where E/122/X is printed, with X being a number from 1 to at least 6. In the E/122/1 handbook, the earliest version, the only way listed to open the bonnet is with a T-key. Thus E/122/1 seems correct for the very early cars. From research of surviving cars: Serial number 875026 came with handbook E/122/1.

E/122/1 sometimes came with an insert, "Amendments and Additions to the Jaguar 'E' Type Operating, Maintenance and Service Handbook." This publication is only a few pages long, and carries no publication number. It gives revised information on serial numbers, timing, capacities, hood lock, lowering the convertible top, and so on.

In handbook E/122/5, the hood opening is indicated as internal only, although the cars are illustrated with external hood latches. E/122/6 shows only the internal

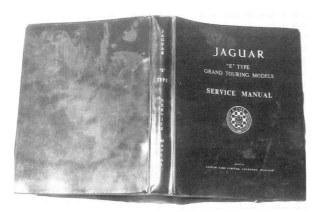

There were variations in the literature package that came with the car, but this is a typical grouping. The list of distributors is in the lower center, the handbook with red vinyl jacket is on the lower right, the vinyl packet is in the upper left, and the lube chart is in the upper right.

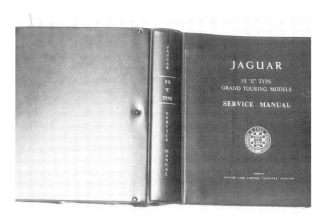

The cover of this later manual has 3.8 markings.

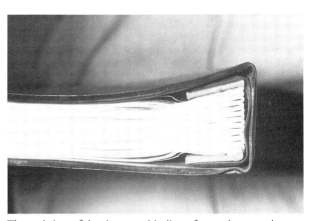

The end view of the signature binding of an early manual.

This cover of an early manual does not have 3.8 markings. It is bound in signatures held together by two brass bolts.

The brass bolt retainers on an early signature-bound manual.

hood opening, and the illustrations show 4.2-liter Series I cars in the coupe and roadster models.

The handbook is reproduced in E/122/5 form. The reproductions are not marked as such, but the photographic reproductions in the front are more grainy.

A dark-red vinyl dust jacket with a gold Jaguar wings crest was sometimes supplied with the handbook.

A red and black lubrication chart was folded and put in the driver's handbook. An early one was marked 5M.3/61 in the right lower corner.

Pouches and Service Vouchers

In addition to the driver's handbook, the purchaser of a new E-Type received other papers and pouches. Included were a service voucher book, a warranty booklet, a listing of Jaguar dealers, and a pouch.

Service voucher books came with the car. These have dark burgundy covers with a yellow Jaguar wings crest, the name "JAGUAR," and "PERIODIC MAINTENANCE VOUCHERS" in white letters and "Issued by THE SERVICE DEPARTMENT, JAGUAR CARS LIMITED, COVENTRY, ENGLAND" in yellow at the bottom. One version of the book is marked E/119/2 in the lower right of the inside cover, and I assume the 2 is a postscript that changed.

Another book contained listings of Jaguar dealers. The cover on one example is white with a globe, the Jaguar wings crest, "JAGUAR OVERSEAS DISTRIBUTORS AND DEALERS" printed in blue, and "20th EDITION, SEPTEMBER 1960." The date is on the lower left outside cover, and there is no apparent printing number. The dates may vary.

A break-in windshield sticker was stuck to the inside corner of the windshield, on the steering wheel side. It had the Jaguar head and "JAGUAR" in silver letters on black on the front, and break-in instructions on the back.

A warranty booklet was also included.

Service Manuals

The service manual was an option; it did not automatically come with a new car.

The 3.8-liter E-Type service manual comes in several varieties. The version is denoted on the title page, where E/123/X is printed, with X being a number from 1 to at least 5.

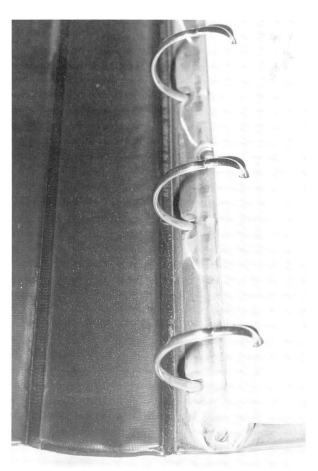

The retaining rings on a later, ring-bound manual.

The cover of early parts catalog. Many features are in relief.

This close-up of the cover of an early parts catalog shows the Jaguar wings symbol and the lettering in relief.

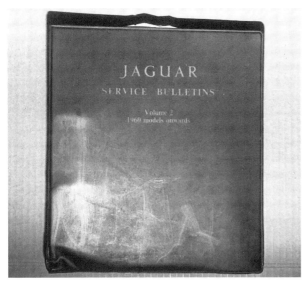

The cover of a service bulletin.

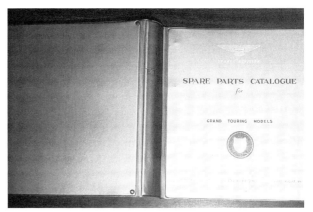

The cover of a later parts catalog.

The early printing series of the service manuals were bound in signatures held in place by two brass screws, while later versions were bound in a four-ring looseleaf notebook that allowed pages to be added at any place.

On the earliest printing of the manual, the numbers 3.8 do not proceed the name E-Type on the spine, cover, title page, or introductory pages to the various sections. In addition, there is no designation of printing series at all in this book; the lower left-hand corner of the front page is blank.

I have seen a manual with E/123/3 that was bound with brass screws. This was with a 1965 4.2-liter roadster.

I am not aware of any reproductions of the service manual that try to duplicate the original in overall appearance. The reprints I have seen of the manual are easily distinguishable from the original. In particular, there is the perfectly bound reprint by Robert Bentley, Inc., Cambridge, Massachusetts, that is comprised of the 4.2-liter E-Type driver's handbook, the 3.8-liter service manual with the 4.2-liter supplement, and the special tuning handbook. This book has two pages reduced and printed side-by-side on a page, and is easily distinguishable from an original.

Similar to the service manual, there was a special-tuning manual that gave recommended modifications to prepare the cars for racing.

Spare Parts Catalogs

The spare parts catalog was an option; it did not automatically come with a new car.

The 3.8-liter E-Type spare parts catalog comes in at least two varieties, both designated as publication J.30. The first was published in August 1961, and the second was an updated reprint published in June 1963. This reprint is designated as AL1.

These two books are outwardly similar, but are quite different internally. The June 1963 reprint contains many more notes on production changes than does the original printing of J.30. Consequently, the June 1963 book is longer, at 322 pages, than the August 1961 book, at 307 pages.

Both versions have a similar cover, depicting the August 1961 date. The reprint designation is found on page ii where the June 1963 reprint note is shown in the lower right-hand corner. Another obvious difference between these two versions of the books is seen on the title page, where the August 1961 version reads: "ENGINE NUMBERS R.1001 Onwards." The June 1963 version reads "ENGINE NUMBERS R.1001 Onwards, RA.1001 Onwards." This reflects the RA continuation of the engine numbering system.

There are many other differences between the two catalogs. The cover on the August 1961 version has the Jaguar wings and crest, as well as the words "SPARES DIVISION" AND "JAGUAR 'E' TYPE" embossed into the vinyl cover. On the June 1963 version, the words are flat-printed on the vinyl. On the August 1961 version, the name "A.E. WALKER, LTD., LONDON, N.1." is embossed on the inside of the back cover in the lower left. On the June 1963 version, the words "PRODUCT OF ENGLAND A.E. WALKER LTD. LONDON. N.1 (1968)" are embossed under the lip of the chromed-steel bracket that the rings are mounted in. The chromed-steel mount for the four binding rings in the August 1961 version is embossed with a pattern of small, parallel lines, and "Combi" in script. The June 1963 version has no lines, and "Combi" is in block letters.

There are instances where tentative indications of changes were put in the August 1961 version. For example, space was left on page 40 of the August 1961 version to accommodate changes that were upcoming. After part number C.17540, the base assembly for the air-intake box, it says "Fitted From Engine No. R.1001 to R.   ," the ending engine number omitted. In fact, when the information was put in the June 1963 version, it was done by chassis number, not by engine number.

I am not aware of any reproductions of the spare parts catalog that try to duplicate the original in overall appearance.

Service Bulletin Books

Jaguar supplied ringed notebooks containing their service bulletins. These were not assigned to a particular model, but covered all Jaguar models over a given period.

Options and Variations: Axle Ratios

In the August 1961 spare parts catalog, the standard ratio is referred to as 3.31:1, and the alternates are shown as well. This is in contrast to the June 1963 version, where the standard ratio is referred to as 3.07:1, with the alternates again included.

In *Jaguar Sports Cars*, Skilleter stated that the early standard axle ratio was 3.31:1, and that 2.9:1, 3.07:1, and 3.54:1 were options.

About October 1962, 3.07:1 became the standard rear-axle ratio for all cars except those going to the United States or Canada, for which the standard ratio was 3.31:1; 3.54:1 was the alternate ratio.

Changes at chassis numbers 879758/9 and 888966/7: About September 1963, the 3.07:1 rear-end ratio was made standard for Italy, France, Germany, Belgium, and the Netherlands.

Changes at chassis numbers 850736/7, 861225/6, 879820/1, and 889002/3: About September 1963, the 3.31:1 rear-end ratio was made standard for all countries except Italy, France, Germany, Belgium, the Netherlands, the United States, Canada, and Newfoundland.

Changes at chassis numbers 879751 to 879808, 880025/6, 888952 to 888994, and 889123/4: About September 1963, the 3.54:1 rear-end ratio was made standard for the United States, Canada, and Newfoundland.

Wheels

A racing rear wheel, painted in stoved aluminum, was offered.

Tires and Tubes

Dunlop R.5 6.00x15-inch racing tires and tubes were offered for the front wheels, and Dunlop R.5 6.50x15-inch tubes for the rear wheels.

Mirrors

Wing mirror part number C.19909 was available as an option for front fender mounting from 1961 on.

Seatbelts

Changes at chassis numbers 850300/1, 860112/3, 876358/9, and 885317/8: Seatbelts were introduced as an option, and seatbelt attachment points were introduced about January 1962. *The Jaguar E-Type: A Collector's Guide* quotes chassis numbers 875358/9 instead of 876358/9. *Jaguar International Magazine*, March 1986, cites chassis numbers 850200/1 instead of 850300/1.

By 1964, the coupes were fitted with shoulder-harness fixing points on the lower frame of the rear vent windows.

Radio, Suppressor Capacitor, and Blanking Plate

A variety of radios was used. I have seen Motorola Radiomobiles (made in England), but also radios

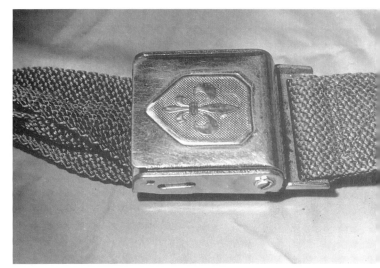

Hickok seatbelts on an early U.S.-specification car. Likely, these were fitted in the United States.

Back view of the Hickok seatbelts.

A shoulder-harness mount on the lower edge of the vent-window frame of a 1964 coupe.

A Motorola radio with "MOTOROLA" markings.

A Motorola radio with "JAGUAR" markings.

A Motorola radio with "PLAYMATE" markings.

A Motorola radio with "Signature Custom Line" script markings.

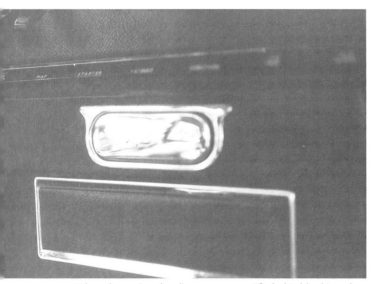

When the optional radio was not specified, this blanking plate was fitted in the radio aperture in the center console. It was trimmed in the same color as the interior.

marked World Radio, Ltd., Made in England. The same radio may carry various names on the front. Some of these are: Jaguar, Signature Custom Line (in script), and Playmate.

The radio is described as "H.M.V. Radiomobile (optional extra)" in the specifications section of the road test in *The Motor* magazine, May 22, 1961. Three radios of different bands are discussed as optional in the June 1963 parts catalog. A Playmate Radiomobile is shown on the cover of *The E-Jag News Magazine*, August 1976, and in *The E-Jag News Magazine*, March 1982. A Radiomobile radio and two speakers were described as the standard option in *Jaguar Sports Cars. The Autocar*, March 17, 1961, also stated that twin speakers were used. I suspect that actually one speaker was standard. There are two grilles, and this may have led to the two-speaker idea. On serial number 875026 there is only one speaker, and it is on the left side. It could be that there was always one speaker, and it was put on the driver's side. The two grilles would accommodate RHD and LHD cars.

An AM Blaupunkt radio in a car shipped to the United States.

An AM/FM Blaupunkt radio in a car shipped to France.

The optional locking gas cap

A firewall-mounted suppressor capacitor on an early E-Type.

Changes at chassis numbers 850786/7, 861388/9, 880630/1, and 889525/6: About March 1964, the radio was changed to one with only one speaker. As mentioned, I am not certain the early radios had two speakers. This change is listed only in *Jaguar E-Type: The Definitive History*.

While the front appearance of these radios is often the same, some have small trim plates over a large front plate, while others don't. The trim plates come in flat black and frosted silver with horizontal lines. Sometimes only the large trim plate is fitted.

Locking Gas Cap

A locking gas cap is listed in the June 1963 parts book as part number C.12816, WB.718653.

Key Fob

A key fob was an option, either number 5194, fob (part number 11/721) with Jaguar wings, or number 9036, fob (part number 11/723) with Jaguar badge. Both are listed in the June 1963 parts book.

Tinted Glass

Changes at chassis numbers 860478/9 and 886013/4: The tinted Sundym glass became an option for the rear window on the coupe.

The key fob and keys supplied new with an early U.S.-specification car. I believe this is key fob number 11/723.

Back view of the key fob and key. Notice the name of the dealership embossed on the leather.

Back view of the Jaguar medallion on the fob. The CUD lettering is in a different style from the block-style letters used in the early 1970s.

An external view of the optional fiberglass removable hardtop. The very early roadsters were not equipped to take these.

Anti-Mist Element: Coupe

The anti-mist element for the rear window of the coupe was offered as an option soon after the introduction of the car, in late 1961 or early 1962.

Air Conditioning

In *The Jaguar E-Type: A Collector's Guide,* Skilleter stated that air conditioning was offered on later LHD 3.8-liter cars: "Later offered (at a cost of £100), but few 3.8 E-Types seem to have had this extra fitted. . . ." However, no mention is made of this in the June 1963 parts catalog, and I have never seem a 3.8-liter E-Type with factory-installed air conditioning.

Hardtop

The hardtop was first available as of May 1962.

Changes at chassis numbers 850023/4 and 875026/7: The first type of detachable hardtop mounting assembly began.

In *Car and Driver,* May 1961, an unusual hardtop is shown on an early car, and the caption says it's aluminum. In *The Jaguar E-Type: A Collector's Guide,* Skilleter stated that a light alloy hardtop was used on competitions Es instead of the fiberglass hardtop of the standard road cars.

Transmissions

An optional close-ratio gearbox was available.

Flywheel

A lightened flywheel was available.

Clutch

A competition clutch was available.

Bumper Guards

Both front and rear bumper guards are commonly found on E-Types. While this is generally regarded as an aftermarket item, there is some evidence it may have at times been fitted by the factory. This is in agreement with the statements made in *Road Test* magazine, May 1965, that suggest the 4.2-liter cars were delivered with the guards.

An unusual lower-section-only front bumper guard was fitted to an early RHD coupe. A similar guard is seen on a French car in *European Automobiles of the 50's and 60's.*

Luggage

According to Porter in *Original Jaguar E-Type,* fitted luggage is said to have been available for the E-Type, and a case is shown. I have seen no other evidence of this.

An internal view of the optional fiberglass removable hardtop.

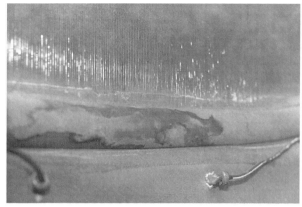

This heated rear window is in RHD coupe serial number 860084. The wires powering the heater can be seen coming through the trim. I am not sure if this is a factory installation, or if it was done later. In other respects, this car is quite original.

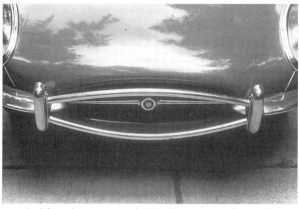

A typical front bumper guard. This illustration is from a Series I 4.2-liter car, but these guards were available throughout Series I production.

A typical rear bumper guard. This illustration is from a Series I 4.2-liter car.

This unusual lower-section-only front bumper guard was fitted to a very early RHS coupe.

Chapter 6

3.8-LITER ENGINE, DRIVETRAIN, AND CHASSIS COMPONENT CHANGES

This chapter covers changes made to the 3.8-liter E-Type's engine, drivetrain, chassis, and other mechanical parts.

Engine: Cylinder Block

The cylinder blocks carry dates cast into them. This is discussed in the previous chapter.

Changes at engine numbers R.7194/5: About October 1962, the dowels between the bearing caps and the cylinder block were enlarged.

Changes at engine numbers RA.6024/5: About April 1964, the cylinder block was changed to mount the new lower-timing-chain intermediate damper; two tapped bosses were added about May 1964.

Cylinder Head and Camshaft Covers

On early cars, the color of the gold paint used on the heads of the 9.0:1 compression-ratio engines was different from that seen on later 3.8-liter cars. It was not the bronzelike metallic gold of the later cars, but rather an orangish pumpkin color. The Winter 1974 issue of *The Milestone Car* contains a black-and-white photo of an early cylinder head with what is likely the pumpkin-colored head, as the glossy finish of the paint is that of the pumpkin-colored paint and not that of the metallic paint.

From research of surviving cars: Serial numbers 860005 (engine R.1522-9), 875026 (engine R.1037-9), 875186 (engine R.1289-9), 875283, and 876052 (engine R.2447-9) had this pumpkin-colored paint. Engine numbers RA.5516-9 had the later metallic paint.

Factory correspondence with the owner of serial number 876052 on September 30, 1987, states that there was only one type of gold paint used on the cylinder heads: "With regard to cylinder head color for your vehicle, our records quite clearly indicate only one specification for the 3.8-liter model: Bradite Old Gold paint—2991 Air Drying." However, in light of the above evidence, it is likely their records are incomplete.

Changes at engine numbers R.2599/600: About December 1961, the sealing port at the left rear of the cylinder head was changed.

Changes at engine numbers R.2599/600: About December 1961, the cover for the left-hand (exhaust) camshaft was changed.

Changes at engine numbers R.3690/1: About March 1962, the head stud holes in the cylinder head gasket were enlarged.

Changes at engine numbers R.6723/4: About September 1962, the inlet valve guides were lengthened.

Changes at engine numbers RA.2971/2: About September 1963, the material of the exhaust valves was changed.

Changes at engine numbers RA.5648/9: About March 1964, the pistons were changed to have chamfer and oil drain holes below the control ring (to reduce oil use). This change is listed only in *The Jaguar E-Type: A Collector's Guide.*

Changes at engine numbers RA.5736/7: About April 1964, the cylinder heads on E-Types and Mk X cars were made the same. I'm not sure if this means the E-Type head was changed or not. This change is listed only in *Jaguar E-Type: The Definitive History.*

Changes at engine numbers RA.7323/4: About August 1964, engine-lifting brackets were added to the cylinder head. Some head studs had to be made longer. This change is listed only by Porter.

Oil Pan and Plug

The oil pans on the early cars were smooth. This is in contrast to the pans on later cars, which had cooling fins on them. Factory parts catalog, June 1963 version, does not designate a change for this part.

From research of surviving cars: Serial numbers 860084 (engine number R.3137-9), 875026 (engine number R.1037-9), and 885748 (engine number R.4276-9) had smooth sumps, while 876289 had the finned sump.

Changes at engine numbers R.5399/400: About June 1962, the oil-pan filter basket was changed to have four semicircular cutouts. This change is listed only in *The Jaguar E-Type: A Collector's Guide.*

Changes at engine numbers R.6417/8: The oil-pan drain plug was changed to steel about September 1962.

The right side of an early oil pan.

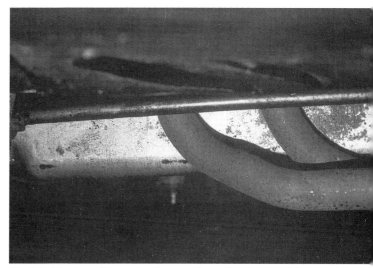

The left-side view of an early oil pan without fins. Some original black paint is still showing here.

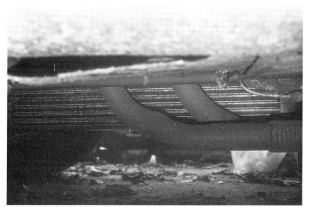

This left-side view of a later oil pan shows the cooling fins that were adopted.

The right-side view of a later oil pan with fins. The drain plug is not original, nor is the clamp on the hose.

This change is listed only in Porter's *Jaguar E-Type: The Definitive History*.

Changes at engine numbers RA.4573/4: About March 1964, the oil-pan drain plug was changed. This change was listed only by Porter.

Some of the early sumps were painted black. This was the case on serial number 875026 (engine numbers R1037-9).

Starter Motor

I am not aware of any design changes.

Engine Mounts

Changes at chassis numbers 850168/9, 860009/10, 875590/1, and 885050/1: About December 1961, the support bracket for the rear engine mount was changed.

Crankcase Breather

The corrugated aluminum breather pipe venting the crankcase fumes out the bottom of the engine compartment, a holdover from the XK series, is a feature of the First 500 E-Types.

At least one car was made with the breather venting in D-Type fashion, from the camshaft covers themselves.

Classic and Sportscar magazine, April 1986, stated that this was "a special D-Type breathing arrangement" on chassis number 885002, and that it, along with other modifications, was used to make this press car a better performer. Thus it is not a typical feature of the early cars.

Changes at chassis numbers 850091/2, 860004/5, 875385/6, and 885020/1: About October 1961, the front cover and breather assembly and flexible breather pipe to open the vent changed to vent into the air-intake box.

Oil Filter Assembly

Changes at engine numbers RA.4974/5: About March 1964, the oil filter was changed. This change is listed only in Porter's *Jaguar E-Type: The Definitive History*.

Changes at engine numbers RA.6833/4: About August 1964, a plastic ring impregnated with magnetized metal particles replaced the metal magnetic ring in the oil filter assembly. This change is listed only by Porter.

This corrugated crankcase breather pipe from one of the First 500 cars is of the same type used on the XK Jaguars, attaching at the front of the cam chain gallery. It vented crankcase fumes out the lower left side of the engine compartment.

As with the earlier vent, the through-the-air-cleaner crankcase breather pipe originated at the front of the camshaft chain gallery. However, it came out the right side of the engine, and was routed through this upright cylindrical casting.

After the First 500 cars, the through-the-air-cleaner crankcase breather was adopted. This is where the vent attaches to the air cleaner.

Timing Chain Cover

Changes at engine numbers R.1509/10: The bolts securing the timing cover to the cylinder block were changed.

Changes at engine numbers R.1845/6: The bolts securing the timing cover to the cylinder block were changed.

Changes at engine numbers RA.6419/20: About August 1964, the front timing cover was changed so that the oil seal could be changed without removing the cover. This change is listed only in *Jaguar E-Type: The Definitive History*.

Crankshaft Damper and Pulley

Changes at engine numbers R.1458/9: The crankshaft pulley was changed. The new crankshaft pulley was cast iron instead of alloy, and was introduced in October 1961.

Changes at engine numbers R.5249/50: About June 1962, the crankshaft pulley for the fan belt, and the dynamo and jockey pulley assemblies were changed to accept the new duplex belt.

Changes at engine numbers RA.6453/4: About May 1964, the crankshaft damper was changed. This change is listed only in *Jaguar E-Type: The Definitive History*.

Oil Dipstick

Changes at engine numbers R.9699/700: About February 1963, the dipstick was changed.

Crankshaft, Connecting Rods, Bearings, Caps, Pistons, and Rings

Changes at engine numbers R.2563/4: About December 1961, the rear-end crankshaft cover was changed, an asbestos oil seal was added, and the crankshaft was codified accordingly.

Changes at engine numbers R.2563/4: The cover assembly for the rear of the cylinder block, and the associated hardware, were changed.

Changes at engine numbers R.3161/2: About February 1962, the big-end connecting-rod bearing clearances were reduced.

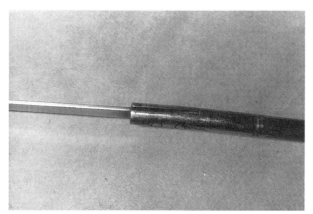

The early flat dipstick. The flat stick is inserted into a slot in the handle, and retained with two rivets.

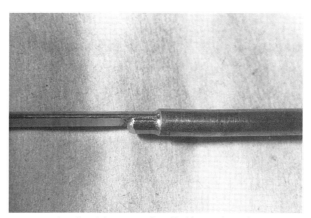

Later on, the dipstick was made of half-round stock. It was inserted into a hole in the end of the handle, next to a second short piece of half-round stock, and soldered in.

Changes at engine numbers R.7103/4: About September 1962, the connecting rods and pistons were changed. The upper pressure ring was chamfered on its inner edge, and a two-part scraper ring was introduced. The connecting rods had an oil-spray hole added near the small end, and were marked with yellow paint near the rib.

Changes at engine numbers R.7194/5: About October 1962, the dowels between the bearing caps and the cylinder block were enlarged.

Changes at engine numbers R.7308/9: The crankshaft was changed about October 1962. This change is listed only in Porter's *Jaguar E-Type: The Definitive History*.

Changes at engine numbers R.9520/1: In about February 1963, the main-bearing cap bolt lock washers were changed. This change is listed only by Porter.

Changes at engine numbers RA.6745/6: About August 1964, the scraper rings on the pistons were changed for 8.0:1 and 9.0:1 compression-ratio engines. The new rings are Maxiflex 50. This change is listed only by Porter.

In late 1963, new oil control rings were introduced which reduced oil burning.

Valves, Valve Gear, Camshafts, Chains, and Sprockets

Changes at engine numbers R.1075/6: The separate intermediate timing-chain sprockets were replaced by a single-piece unit about October 1961. This change is listed only in *Jaguar E-Type: The Definitive History*.

Changes at engine numbers R.1216/7: About August 1961, a hole was added to the base of the inlet camshaft.

Changes at engine numbers R.2599/600: The oil thrower at the rear of the exhaust camshaft was changed.

Changes at engine numbers R.5000/1: About May 1962, the inlet camshaft was drilled to reduce cold-starting noise.

Changes at engine numbers R.5532/3: About June 1962, the intermediate damper assembly for the upper timing chain was changed.

Changes at engine numbers R.8138/9: About November 1962, the vibration damper for the lower timing chain was changed.

Changes at engine numbers RA.6024/5: About May 1964, the lower timing chain intermediate damper was changed; the new damper was positioned differently and was attached to two tapped bosses on the cylinder block.

Oil Pump and Oil Delivery System

Changes at engine numbers R.1008/9: The size of the oil pump was increased in June 1961. This change is listed only in *The Jaguar E-Type: A Collector's Guide*.

Changes at engine numbers RA.2077/8: About June 1963, the oil pump was changed and the oil suction pipe was changed to 3/4 inch instead of 11/16 inch.

Changes at engine numbers RA.6603/4: About May 1964, a support was added to the first intermediate bearing cap to support the oil delivery pipe. This support replaced a lockwasher that was on the cap before. This change is listed only in *Jaguar E-Type: The Definitive History*.

Fuel System: Carburetors and Manifolds

The cap on the dash-pot piston was changed from copper to black plastic around 1963. From research of surviving cars: Serial number 876577 (engine R.3653-9) had the brass carburetor tops, while numbers 879325 (engine RA.1769-9) and 887576 (engine R.8910-9) had the plastic carburetor tops.

From looking at serial number 875026 (engine R.1037-9), which I believe has never had its intake manifold apart, the chrome hex nuts holding the manifolds to the head, holding the air and water manifolds to the intake manifolds, and holding the carburetors to the intake manifolds are all oriented so that the beveled edges of the nuts face outward, and the sharp edges face inward.

The water-outlet pipe connecting the three intake manifolds changed very early in production. On the early cars, the area behind the blanking plate is dipped in, while on later cars it is flat.

From research of surviving cars: Serial numbers 875026 (engine R.1037-9) and 860005 (engine R.1522-9) have the dipped-in pipe, while number 876577 (engine R.3653-9) had the pipe without a dip.

The early carburetor dash-pot caps were made of plated copper.

Later on, the dash-pot caps were made of black plastic. These sometimes failed, and let the damper rod protrude out the top of the cap.

This view of the top of the SU HD8 of an XK-150S shows the early long-neck suction chamber design used in SU HD8 carburetors prior to the E-Type. Contrast the length of the top of the suction chamber, where damper assembly screws in, to the same section of the suction chambers on the other pictures in this chapter, which are much lower.

Sometimes the plastic damper assembly caps are found in this light tone. This tone may be the result of the plastic resin fading with time. As with the black plastic caps, the "AUC" marking is molded into the cap.

Changes at engine numbers R.2933/4: About January 1962, the air-balance pipe was changed to accommodate the simplified throttle linkage, and the air-balance pipe was changed from three bosses to two.

Changes at engine numbers RA.2463/4: The needle valve and seat in the carburetor float chamber was changed to Delrin, and changes were made in the lid and hinged lever. In *The Jaguar E-Type: A Collector's Guide*, Skilleter cites a date of about June 1963 for this change. Porter, in *Jaguar E-Type: The Definitive History*, cites about April 1964 for the change. Based on these dates I suspect the engine numbers of this change are really RA.5463/4 instead of RA.2463/4.

Changes at engine numbers RA.4115/6: About January 1964, the throttle spring bearings in the carburetors were changed to an impregnated plastic material. This change is listed only by Porter.

Changes at engine numbers RA.7175/6: About October 1964, the intake manifold gasket was changed from cupronickel to a tin-plate material. This change is listed only by Porter.

The early water-inlet pipe on the intake manifolds had a dipped-in region just in front of the blanking plate. The knurled nut on the temperature sensor is also a feature of the early cars.

This later replacement damper assembly cap has the "AUC" marking in white letters. I believe these were never originally fitted to the cars during their production run, but were fitted as replacements at a later date.

The throttle linkage on the early cars was a complex arrangement, having many redundant adjustments. Each of the three carburetor control arms was separately clamped to one of two round rods, allowing separate angle adjustments for each arm. In addition, the relation between the two rods could be set using the corrugated clamp connecting them.

Later water-inlet pipes were flat in front of the blanking plate. On this later car, a hex nut is used to retain the temperature sensor wire.

Early fuel filter bracket was turned downward.

Later fuel filter brackets faced upward.

The later throttle linkage was greatly simplified, with the three control arms permanently fixed to a single rod. The center pivot was discontinued.

Throttle Linkage

Changes at chassis numbers 850248/9, 860020/1, 875910/1, and 885124/5: About January 1962, changes were made to the spacing collar and washer on the accelerator pedal assembly, and to the accelerator-pedal lever assembly itself.

Changes at engine numbers R.2933/4: About January 1962, the slave-shaft assembly for throttle operation was changed from three to two slave-shafts using a flexible coupling.

Fuel Filter and Lines

Changed at chassis numbers 850091/2, 860004/5, 875385/6, and 885020/1: About October 1961, the bracket for mounting the fuel filter to the frame changed.

Air Filter

Very early in production, the seam flange running around the outside edge of the triangular fiberglass air-cleaner plenum was decreased in size. From research of surviving cars: Serial number 875026 had the wide flange, while 875235 had the narrow flange.

Changes at chassis numbers 850091/2, 860004/5, 875385/6, and 885020/1: About October 1961, the base assembly for the air-intake box was changed to accept the new vent.

Gas Tank

The cylindrical drain plug or sump seen on the bottom of the gas tanks of later E-Types is absent on some of the prototype or early cars.

When the cylindrical drain plug first appeared, it was a multipiece unit.

Changes at chassis numbers 850091/2, 860004/5, 875385/6, and 885020/1: About October 1961, the gas-tank assembly was changed to adopt the one-piece sump. When the early sump was fitted, the gas tank had female threads and the sump had the male. This was reversed for cars fitted with the later sump.

Fuel Pump, Mount, and Lines

All 3.8-liter cars had submerged fuel pumps. However, the fuel pump and its bracket in the gas tank on the First 500 cars were different in many ways from later pumps.

The early air-cleaner plenums were supplied with a wide sealing flange.

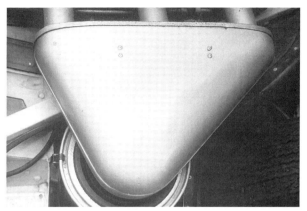

The later air-cleaner plenums had narrow flanges.

An early multipiece gas-tank sump removed from the car. Note the male threads.

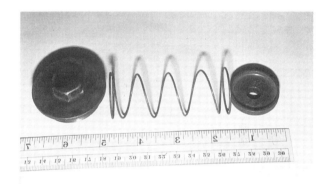

This disassembled view of the internal assembly of the early multipiece sump shows the bottom cap on the left, the spring in the middle, and the sealing cap on the top. The filter is not shown.

This view of a later sump removed from the car shows the increased length, and the seams on either end where it was brazed together. Though not visible here, the left-hand side has female threads. On these later cars, the filter was attached to the bottom of the fuel-pump intake pipe.

Left
The gas tanks on the early cars had female threads to retain the sumps. The intake pipe on the bottom of the fuel pump is showing here.

The gas tanks for the later cars had male threads to retain the sumps.

The gas caps on the early cars were fabricated from chromed steel. They were the same caps used on many other British cars of the era.

Later on, the gas caps were changed to cast alloy with a fluted edge.

Right
The front view of the fuel pump and bracket assembly of the First 500 cars.

This top view of the fuel pump used in First 500 cars shows the characteristic rounded cap.

The top view of a later fuel pump. Notice the lead-sealed wire.

The back view of a later fuel pump and bracket.

Changes at chassis numbers 850091/2, 860004/5, 875385/6, and 885020/1: About October 1961, the fuel pump, bracket, pipe, and filter bracket were changed.

Changes at chassis numbers 850254/5, 860026/7, 876030/1, and 885160/1: About January 1962, the fuel pipe from the pump and its bracket were changed, with the attachment of the line to the pump by a banjo fitting. This change is listed only in *Jaguar E-Type: The Definitive History*.

Changes at chassis numbers 850526/7, 860583/4, 877354/5, and 886094/5: In summer or early fall of 1962, the fuel line from the pump to the gas-tank outlet connection was changed from the Vulkollan material to nylon.

Changes at chassis numbers 850785/6, 861385/6, 880618/9, and 889509/10: About January 1964, the fuel pump was changed. The operating pressure went up. This change is listed only by Porter.

Changes at chassis numbers 850934/5, 861780/1, 881863/4, and 890847/8: About October 1964, the feed pipe filter to the fuel pump was changed. This change is listed only by Porter.

Fuel-Level Sender Unit
The fuel-level sender unit mounted in the top of the gas tank came in at least two types. The later type had small holes in the top, and the early type had no hole.

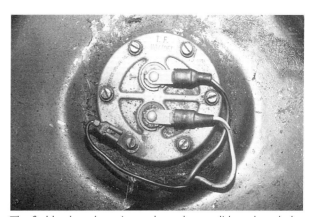

The fuel-level sender units on the early cars did not have holes cast into them.

From research of surviving cars: Serial numbers 875026 and 875109 had the early sender, without holes, and 879325 had the later type with holes.

Ignition System: Coil and Bracket
Changes at chassis numbers 850091/2, 860004/5, 875385/6, and 885020/1: An extension assembly for the coil bracket was added about October 1961.

Later fuel-level sender units had blind holes cast in them.

Two styles of wire-retainer caps were used on the coil. While the retainers used on the distributor caps were slightly shorter, they are found in both varieties.

Distributor

Changes at engine numbers RA.1381/2: The distributor and vacuum suction pipe were changed about April 1963.

Changes at engine numbers RA.6833/4: About July 1964, the distributor was changed on 9.0:1 compression-ratio engines.

Changes at engine numbers RA.7201/2: About October 1964, the distributor was changed on 8.0:1 compression-ratio engines. This change is listed only in *Jaguar E-Type: The Definitive History*.

Distributor Rotor, Cap, and Wire Retainers

The seven spark-plug wire retainers on the top of the distributor cap and the one on the coil came in at least two types. On the early cars these retainers came with tightly spaced grooves. Later cars had retainers with widely spaced grooves.

The standard coils originally fitted were produced by Lucas and had black plastic insulating caps.

This later replacement coil was also produced by Lucas, but it uses a white plastic insulation cap.

As with all Lucas electrical components, the month and date of manufacture ("1 59") of this original Lucas coil were stamped on the case.

This later replacement Lucas coil also has the manufacture date stamped on it ("6 89"), but the other markings are different.

Changes at engine numbers RA.2289/90: About August 1963, rubber sleeves were fitted to the spark-plug wires where they enter the distributor cap. This change is listed only by Porter.

Spark-Plug Wires and Organizers

The spark-plug cable organizers on the early cars were comprised of a chromed steel ring and black plastic discs, and a rigid, black plastic sleeve. In later cars the wires were housed in a flexible, black plastic sheath (the discs and rings were no longer present), and a single narrow organizer was used.

The wire and retainer routing and configuration vary on early cars. Sometimes the wires were routed over the surge tank hose, and sometimes under it. In addition, the chrome retaining ring was seen fastened

The early distributor had a squared-off appearance to both the cap and body.

The later distributor had a rounded shape to both the cap and the body. This one has rubber sealing boots.

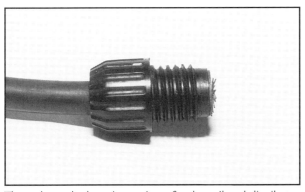

The early spark-plug wire retainers for the coil and distributor cap had small slots and an abrupt taper at the end.

The later spark-plug wire retainers had wide slots and a more gradual taper.

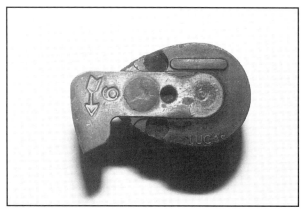

A typical rotor, as originally supplied with the cars.

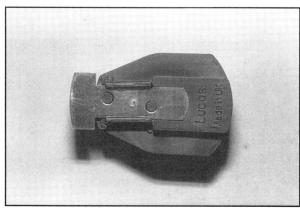

This modern rotor is a replacement now being found in many cars. It functions, but is not of the original design.

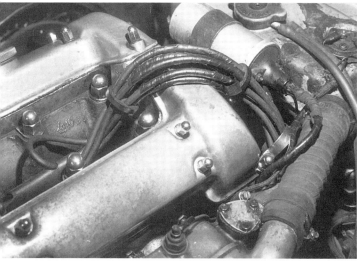

The early spark-plug cable organizers consisted of a chrome ring and black plastic discs with six holes in them.

This spark-plug wire guide was used on the later engines.

Later on, a flexible black-plastic sleeve was used to organize the wires.

The earliest cars had spark-plug caps with circular "CHAMPI-ON" lettering on the top and a dot in the center.

112

to different right-front cam cover bolts.

Changes at engine numbers R.3854/5: The spacers for the spark-plug leads were changed.

Changes at engine numbers R.3854/5: About March 1962, the spark-plug cables were increased in length, and rerouted.

Changes at engine numbers RA.5633/4: About April 1964, the spark-plug cables were changed. This change is listed only in Porter's *Jaguar E-Type: The Definitive History.*

Changes at engine numbers RA.7323/4: About August 1964, the spark-plug cables had to be lengthened to accommodate the new engine-lifting brackets. This change is listed only by Porter.

Spark-Plug Caps

The spark-plug caps on early cars are round, with the word "CHAMPION" written in a circular fashion. This same cap was also supplied to other British cars, for example, late 1950s or early 1960s BMC Minis. On most later cars, "CHAMPION" is molded across the top, inside a bow-tie shape. Some later cars have the oval-top type, with "CHAMPION" written in a straight line across the top. From research of surviving cars: Serial numbers 875026 (engine numbers R.1037-9) and 876052 (engine numbers R.2447-9) had the circular caps, and 876577 (engine numbers R.3653-9) had the later bow-tie types.

Spark Plugs

The spark plugs are Champion N.5, according to the specification sheet in *The Motor*, May 22, 1961, and in the August 1961 spare parts catalog. However, in the June 1963 catalog, the part number UN.12Y is given. Also, *Car and Driver*, December 1961, commented about using N.5 plugs for the street, and N.3 for racing. The service manual E.123/5 lists UN.12Y, with N.3 for racing.

Changes at engine numbers R.9527/8: In about December 1962, the spark plugs were changed to Champion UN.12Y. This change is listed only in *Jaguar E-Type: The Definitive History.*

These bow-tie spark-plug caps were found on the later cars. Typically, the raised section was painted white.

The contacts on the tops of the original Champion spark plugs were machined.

These oval-top spark-plug caps were also found on the 3.8-liter cars.

The Champion N.11Y plugs available now are not identical to the ones available earlier. The older-type plugs have machined top contacts that are fixed to the plug, while the currently available plugs have molded top contacts that are screwed to the top of the plug. The parting line from the mold is visible on the modern contacts.

The modern replacement Champion spark-plug top contacts are cast, and the parting line is evident.

This is the back view of an early aluminum radiator. The fiberglass shroud has been removed.

Cooling System: Radiator and Fan Shroud

I am not aware of any design changes to the aluminum crossflow radiator during the time it was used. These radiators were serially numbered on a plate screwed on the top.

Later cars had a brass radiator.

Header Tank

The header tank was changed, and the flow was modified internally. The inlet was at the corner for the early cars, and at the side for later cars. From research of surviving cars: Serial numbers 875026 and 875186 had the early tanks, while 876052 had the later tank.

Changes at chassis numbers 850656/7, 861090/1, 879043/4, and 888240/1: About March 1963, the radiator header-tank assembly was changed; the 4-pound pressure cap was changed to a 9-pound one.

Pictured in Porter's *Jaguar E-Type: The Definitive History* is an unusual header tank with a wide sealing flange on an early prototype E-Type coupe.

The back view of the brass radiator from a late 3.8-liter car. I have seen several such radiators in later cars, but I am not certain this was fitted at the factory; it may be a replacement unit.

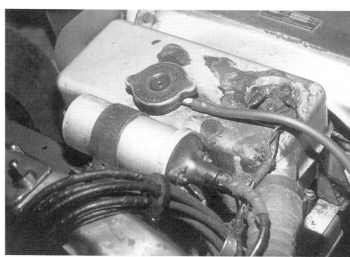

The early header tanks had the right-hand connection on the rear corner.

Water Pump and Pulley

Changes at engine numbers R.5249/50: About June 1962, the pulley for the water pump and the belt were changed to accept the new duplex belt, and the material of the pulley was changed from aluminum to cast iron.

Changes at engine numbers RA.3289/90: About September 1963, the water pump impeller was changed. This change is listed only by Porter.

Hoses and Clamps

There were several different manufacturers of the hose clamps. Among these are Regent and Cheney.

Changes at chassis numbers 850656/7, 861090/1, 879043/4, and 888240/1: The water hose between the engine water outlet and the header tank was changed about March 1963. This change is listed only by Porter. At some point the header-tank hose was changed from convoluted to straight, and perhaps this is what is being referred to here.

The later header tanks had the right-hand connection in the side of the tank.

There were several types of radiator hose clamps. This is a "REGENT" clamp. Note that the longitudinal slots do not go all the way through the strap.

A "CHENEY" radiator hose clamp.

The early fan belts were the single-grooved type.

The later belts were double-grooved, and were wider than the early belts.

This manual-adjust fan belt system was used only on a few very early cars.

Later on, this auto-adjust fan belt system was introduced.

The aluminum cover immediately identifies the early RB.310 voltage regulator.

Thermostat

Changes at engine numbers R.8299/300: About November 1962, a quick-lift thermostat was fitted with a higher opening temperature.

Charging System: Generator and Bracket

Changes at chassis numbers 850091/2, 860004/5, 875385/6, and 885020/1: About October 1961, the generator was changed (part number 22531/A-C45.PV5/6 changed to 22902/A-C42).

Changes at engine numbers R.1509/10: The dynamo mounting bracket, pulley, and fan for the dynamo pulley were changed.

Pulleys and Belt

Changes at engine numbers R.1509/10: The dynamo adjusting link was changed.

Changes at engine numbers R.1844/5: About October 1961, the dynamo adjusting link was changed and a jockey pulley assembly was added. Apparently, these were retrofitted to some early engines by Jaguar.

Changes at engine numbers R.5249/50: About June 1962, the fan belt was changed to the duplex type, and the dynamo pulley was changed. The early fan belts were of the single-grooved type, and the later belts were of the wide, double-grooved type.

Changes at engine numbers RA.1099/100: About March 1963, the automatic fan-belt tensioning system was changed. This change is listed only in Porter's *Jaguar E-Type: The Definitive History*.

Changes at engine numbers RA.1100/1: The carrier for the jockey pulley was changed.

Changes at engine numbers RA.5885/6: About April 1964, the jockey pulley bracket was changed to have impregnated plastic bushes instead of the brass bushes that were used earlier. This change is listed only by Porter.

The RB.340 voltage regulator has a black plastic cover. It was used on most 3.8-liter cars.

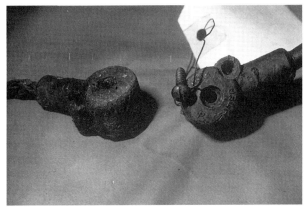

The original battery cable connectors were the lead-cup type. They were retained by a screw on the top.

Serial number 875026 (engine numbers R.1037-9) has an idler pulley mounted between the generator and water-pump pulleys, apparently used for tensioning the belt. This is not the usual spring-loaded jockey pulley of the later 3.8-liter cars. Given the history of this car, it is likely this was the way it left the factory. However, I have found no instances of this pulley in the literature.

Voltage Regulator and Bracket

Changes at chassis numbers 850091/2, 860004/5, 875385/6, and 885020/1: About October 1961, the control box and bracket were changed (part number 37304A-RB.310 changed to 37331A/RB.340).

Battery, Cables, Tray, and Mounts

The battery was a Lucas tar-topped unit with six separate filler caps.

An interesting pair of battery photos are seen on page 243 of *Jaguar E-Type: The Definitive History*. The upper photograph shows an early prototype car with a battery with the "LUCAS" letters on the side highlighted in white. The lower picture shows a later 3.8-liter car with a non-highlighted battery.

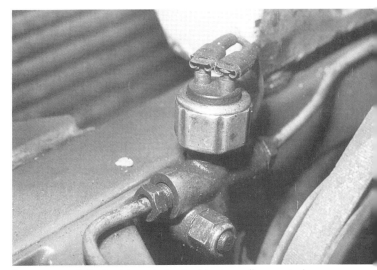

Some very early brake-light switches had horizontally mounted spade connectors.

A typical brake-light switch with vertically mounted spade connectors.

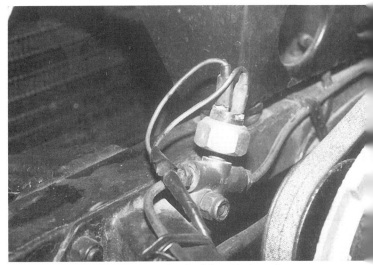

Some of the later brake-light switches had flat-sided nut faces. Contrast this illustration to the earlier two.

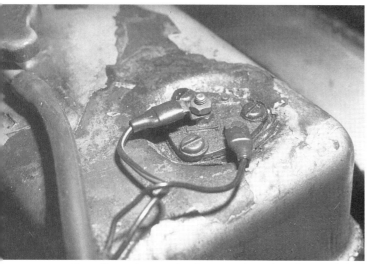

On a few early cars, the thermostatic cooling fan switch had the spade connector bolted on.

Changes at chassis numbers 850209/10, 860012/3, 875760/1, and 885085/6: Two more rubber corner pads were added to the battery clamp in about November 1961. This change is listed only in *Jaguar E-Type: The Definitive History*.

Changes at chassis numbers 850572/3, 860722/3, 877660/1, and 886381/2: About August 1962, the rubber pads under the corners and end of the battery clamp were changed to a single pad.

Electric: Wiring Harness

Changes at chassis numbers 850273/4, 861186/7,

Most cars had this later thermostatic cooling fan switch with the spade connector molded in. These have "Otter" molded in the plastic in script.

878020/1, and 886748/9: About November 1962, the forward wiring harness was changed.

Changes at chassis numbers 850499/500, 860435/6, 877154/5, and 885970/1: About May 1962, the cable to the front lamp connector was changed.

Changes at chassis numbers 850723/4 and 861186/7: About June 1963, the front wiring harness was changed. This change is listed only by Porter.

Windshield Washer

I am not aware of any design changes.

Brake-Light Switch

Some of the very early brake-light switches deviated from the standard configuration in that the spade connectors connected horizontally instead of vertically.

The earliest cars had cylindrical brake and clutch fluid reservoirs with vertical spade connectors in the caps.

The second style of brake and clutch reservoirs still had cylindrical reservoirs, but had horizontal spade connectors in the caps.

Cooling Fan, Relay, and Switch

The thermostatic switches operating the radiator cooling fan came in at least two types. The first type has a nut and bolt contact, with a spade-type connector bolted to it. The second type has a spade-type connector molded in the top. The second type is molded from red plastic (at least sometimes) and has the word Otter in stylized print molded in it.

From research of surviving cars: Serial numbers 860005, 875026, and 876052 have the early switch.

Changes at chassis numbers 850273/4, 861186/7, 878020/1, and 886748/9: The relay for the fan motor was changed in late 1962 or early 1963.

Horn and Relay

Changes at chassis numbers 850499/500, 860435/6, 877154/5, and 885970/1: The horns were changed about May 1962.

Starter Solenoid

Changes at chassis numbers 850839/40, 861549/50, 881202/3, and 890234/5: About April 1964, the starter solenoid was changed to reduce water leakage. This change is listed only by Porter.

Tachometer, Pressure, and Temperature Senders

I am not aware of any design changes.

Brakes and Hydraulics: Brake and Clutch Fluid Reservoirs and Mounts

The brake reservoirs on 3.8-liter cars came in at least three types. On the earliest cars the reservoirs were round with large, black plastic tops. These caps were later replaced by hybrid caps, made of aluminum with black or white plastic tops. Lastly, the round reservoirs were replaced by rectangular ones, with the same hybrid tops.

The floats on the reservoir caps came in at least two types. On some early caps, the fluid-lever sensor float was a hollow nylon unit. On later caps, the float was cork.

The clutch fluid reservoirs follow the pattern of the brake fluid reservoirs, going from round to square, but the

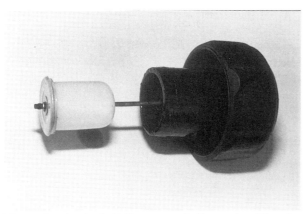

The earliest brake-fluid floats were hollow nylon. The aluminum damping covers have been removed to show the float.

The second-style caps also came in white.

The third style of reservoirs was rectangular, but still had the second-style caps. Here they are fitted with the rubber covers.

A similar progression occurred for the RHD cars, but the reservoirs were mounted on the firewall on the opposite side of the engine compartment. Here the round reservoirs are shown.

Very early on, the floats were changed to cork. The aluminum damping covers have been removed.

A late 3.8-liter car with the heat shield bend toward the front.

The early heater-box ends were held in by three screws on the top and sides.

cap on the early round type was metal. On later reservoirs, the cap was made of plastic. In neither case did the clutch reservoir cap have electric sensors. From research of surviving cars: Serial number 875026 has round reservoirs with the black plastic caps, and numbers 875109 and 875235 have round reservoirs with black plastic and metal caps.

In Jaguar publication number E/123/5, there is a line drawing of an early clutch reservoir with a cap like the earliest large black plastic ones. It appears identical, with the exception of the electric sensors, which are absent. I have seen no other evidence for such a clutch reservoir cap. There are also drawings illustrating the metal clutch reservoir cap.

Changes at chassis numbers 850555/6, 860677/8, 877556/7, and 886282/3: About July 1962, the brake and clutch reservoir assemblies, including their mounting brackets, were changed.

Changes at chassis numbers 877556/7 and 886282/3: The brake reservoir assembly, and its bracket, were changed.

Changes at chassis numbers 850565/6 and 860677/8: About July 1962, the mounting bracket for the fluid reservoirs changed. This change is listed only in the March 1986 *Jaguar International* magazine.

Changes at chassis numbers 850654/5, 861085/6, 878979/80, and 888184/5: About March 1963, the brake-fluid reservoir caps were changed. The addition of a level indicator is also cited, but this must be an error, as the level indicators had been fitted before this time. This change is listed only by Porter.

Changes at chassis numbers 850656/7, 861426/7, 888759/60, and 889696/7: About January 1964, a cover was introduced for the brake-fluid reservoir cap. Due to the date and the nature of the change, I think the RHD coupe and LHD chassis numbers 850656/7 here should be 850806/7. This change is listed only in *The Jaguar E-Type: A Collector's Guide.*

Changes at chassis numbers 850729/30, 861203/4, 879576/7, and 888790/1: About June 1963, the filter in the clutch fluid reservoir was changed. This change is listed only in *Jaguar E-Type: The Definitive History.*

Changes at chassis numbers 850806/7, 861426/7, 880759/60, and 889696/7: About March 1964, the protective caps for the brake-fluid level indicators were changed. This change is listed only by Porter.

Brake and Clutch Fluid Reservoir Heat Shield

The heat shield for the brake and clutch reservoirs in LHD cars has a bend in it. The early cars were assembled with this bend at both the back and the front.

Jaguar E-Type: The Definitive History pictures an unusual "tall" shield, bent forward at the top, on an early car, presumed to be chassis number 885002.

Changes at chassis numbers 877556/7 and 886282/3: The shield for the reservoirs was changed.

Hydraulic Lines, Switch, Cylinders, and Activation Mechanism

The early cars had at least two types of brake-light switch: those with horizontally mounted spade connectors, and those with vertically mounted spade connectors.

Changes at chassis numbers 850232/3, 860020/1, 875858/9, and 885104/5: About December 1961, the clutch pedal, the bushing in the boss of the clutch pedal, and the housing for the clutch pedal and brake pedal were changed. The brass bush in the brake and clutch pedal housing was changed to impregnated plastic.

Changes at chassis numbers 876014/5 and 885155/6: The brake master-cylinder assembly was changed.

Changes at chassis numbers 850254/5, 860026/7, 876014/5, and 885155/6: About February 1962, the front and rear brake master-cylinder assemblies were changed. The modification gave a more positive location of the rear spring support to the piston.

Changes at chassis numbers 850376/7, 860192/3, 876638/9, and 885571/2: The balance link for operation of the master cylinders was changed about March 1962.

Changes at chassis numbers 850474/5, 860374/5, 876998/9, and 885870/1 (including 860365): About May 1962, the brake connecting lever was changed to increase the mechanical advantage; an eccentric barrel nut was installed to adjust the servo arm.

Changes at chassis numbers 850547/8, 860646/7, 877488/9, and 886218/9: About June 1962, the clutch master cylinder was changed to give more positive location for the main spring support to the piston.

Changes at chassis numbers 850649/50, 861079/80, 878963/4, and 888168/9 (including 860365): The brake connecting lever between the pedal shaft and the plate of servo bellow was changed.

Miscellaneous: Steering

Changes at chassis numbers 850403/4, 860231/2, 876846/7, and 885735/6: About March 1962, changes were made to the spring, covers, plunger, and so forth on the rack and pinion housing, and the rack friction damper.

Changes at chassis numbers 850499/500, 860425/6, 877275/6, and 886045/6: About May 1962, the hardware for the rack and pinion assembly was changed; a two-stud mount was introduced for the rack thrust plate, and the studs with self-locking nuts replaced the two hexagon-headed setscrews.

Changes at chassis numbers 850558/9, 860691/2, 877578/9, and 886305/6: About July 1962, the three studs on the thrust plate and the mounting rubber for the rack and pinion were changed.

Heater

The screen filter on the top of the heater box seems to have come painted (or plated) both light and dark.

The endplates on the early heaters are held on by more screws than on later cars.

From research of surviving cars: Serial numbers 860005, 875026, 875109, 875186, 875251, 875325, 875954, 875958, 876052, 876733, and 885733 have the early heater box, and number 876289 has the later heater box.

Later heater-box ends were retained by one screw on the top and two on the sides.

Brake Vacuum System

At least some of the vacuum reservoirs were marked with "TRICO" markings in white paint. I am not sure how prevalent this might have been, as I have seen the paint used for the lettering readily dissolve and wash off when wiped with gasoline, and many may have been lost during cleanings.

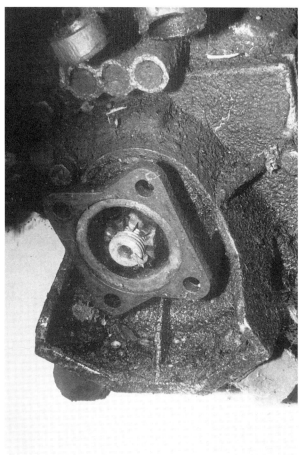

The first style of transmission mount had two cylindrical rubber mounts affixed to a metal plate. The plate is not present here.

The second-style transmission mount had a single central post with a spring around it. The post on the end of the transmission is seen here.

The lower plate of the first type of transmission mount.

The lower plate and spring of the second type of transmission mount.

Left-side view of the typical 3.8-liter transmission with a nonsynchromesh first gear.

Splash Shields

Changes at chassis numbers 850712/3, 861177/8, 879372/3, and 888611/2: About June 1963, the engine compartment undershields were increased in size and a cover was placed over the hole in the right-hand-side shield (under the oil filter). This change is listed only by Porter.

Drivetrain: Bellhousing, Flywheel, Clutch, and Slave Cylinder

On the early cars, the washers on the bolts retaining the clutch plate assembly to the flywheel were changed to nylon locknuts. There is no indication in the June 1963 factory parts catalog of this occurring or when it may have occurred.

Changes at engine numbers RA.5800/1: About May 1964, the clutch was changed to the Laycock diaphragm type. About March 1964, the flywheel was changed to accept either Borg and Beck or the diaphragm clutch.

Transmission and Mounts

Changes at chassis numbers 850648/9, 861061/2, 878888/9, and 888081/2: About January 1963, the rubber mounts at the rear of the gearbox were changed to a

Left-side view of an all-synchromesh transmission of the sort probably used in a few late 3.8-liter cars.

spring mount, except for the following serial numbers: 850653, 850654, 861087, 878895, 878900, 878907, 878908, 878913, 878914, 878915, 878926, 878936, 878937, 878939, 878958, 878986, 879005, 879024, 879049, 888086, 888096, 888101, 888103, 888109,

888113, 888117, 888118, 888120, 888134, 888157, 888178, and 888238.

Changes at gearbox numbers EB.245/6 JS: The rear-end transmission cover and the speedometer driver gear were changed.

Changes at gearbox numbers EB.1653/4: The dowel screws in the transmission gear-selection mechanism were changed. This change is listed only in *Jaguar E-Type: The Definitive History*.

Changes at gearbox numbers EB.8858/9 JS: The rear-end cover of the transmission was changed. This change took place about February 1963, and was related to the change in the rear engine mounting.

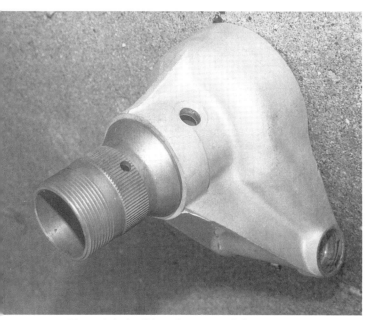

The early hubs did not have water deflectors.

A water deflector on a later hub. This illustration is from a Series I 1/2 car, but it depicts the water throwers used on the late 3.8-liter cars.

Changes at chassis numbers 850653, 850654, 861087, 878895, 878900, 878907, 878908, 878913, 878914, 878915, 878926, 878936, 878937, 878939, 878958, 878986, 879005, 879024, 879049, 888086, 888096, 888101, 888103, 888109, 888113, 888117, 888118, 888120, 888134, 888157, 888178, and 888238: These cars were equipped with the transmission rear-end cover fitted to transmissions just prior to gearbox number EB.8858 JS.

In *Jaguar E-Type: The Definitive History*, Porter stated that the late 3.8-liter cars were fitted with the fully synchromesh gearbox. *Autocar* magazine, May 14, 1965, stated that the 4.2-liter E-Type with synchromesh gearbox was originally announced as an alternate model to the still-produced 3.8-liter E-Type with the old gearbox. Thus, if late 3.8-liter cars were fitted with fully synchromesh gearboxes, it would have been very late in production.

Driveshaft

Changes at chassis numbers 850103/4, 860005/6, 875495/6, and 885025/6: About October 1961, the driveshaft was changed, and its universal joints were enlarged.

Changes at chassis numbers 850479/80, 860386/7, 877044/5, and 885887/8: About May 1962, the driveshaft was changed, and sealed-for-life universal joints were introduced. A gaiter was fitted to the sliding joint, and the grease nipples on the universal joints and sliding joint were deleted.

Differential

Pictured in *The Jaguar E-Type: A Collector's Guide* is a temperature sensing unit on an early car's differential drain plug. The car was said to be part of the experimental test fleet, and the sensor certainly does not represent a production feature.

In the August 1961 parts book, the housing for the driveshaft bearings is shown without the O-ring seal, while in the June 1963 parts book, the housing is shown with an O-ring seal. However, in the June 1963 parts book, there is no indication of it having ever been there, as if it was included in all E-Types from the beginning.

In addition, in the June 1963 parts book illustration, the housing for the driveshaft bearings is shown with a notch recessed into it to take the oil seal, while this same item in the August 1961 parts book has no notch. Yet no mention of a change is made in the June 1963 parts book.

In *Jaguar E-Type: The Definitive History*, Porter noted the addition of an O-ring on the housings for the driveshafts in the rear end about November 1961. From research of surviving cars: Serial number 875109 has no O-ring, nor any groove for one.

Another difference between the two catalogs is that June 1963 parts book shows the small pin going in the center of the two shafts for the pinion mate gears. This pin is not shown at all in the August 1961 parts book. This seems to suggest that early cars were not fitted with a pin, while later ones were. But there is no serial number information in either publication about when this took place.

On some early cars metal tabs were bolted to the differential housing.

The four self-locking nuts holding the halfshafts and brake discs to the output flanges of the differential are found in different styles.

Changes at chassis numbers 879440/1 and 888672/3: About June 1963, for cars with 3.54:1 rear ends, the rear end was changed.

Changes at chassis numbers 879460/1 and 888694/5: About June 1963, for cars with 3.31:1 rear ends, the rear end was changed.

Changes at chassis numbers 850721/2, 861184/5, 879493/4, and 888705/6: About June 1963, for cars with 3.07:1 rear ends, the rear end was changed.

Changes at chassis numbers 850736/7, 861225/6, 879820/1, and 889002/3: About September 1963, the 3.31:1 rear-end ratio was made standard for all countries except Italy, France, Germany, Belgium, the Netherlands, the United States, Canada, and Newfoundland.

Changes at chassis numbers 879758/9 and 888966/7: About September 1963, the 3.07:1 rear-end ratio was made standard for Italy, France, Germany, Belgium, and the Netherlands.

Changes at chassis numbers 879751 to 879808, 880025/6, 888952 to 888994, and 889123/4: About September 1963, the 3.54:1 rear-end ratio was made standard for the United States, Canada, and Newfoundland.

Changes at chassis numbers 850784/5, 861363/4, 880561/2, and 889451/2: About December 1963, the differential breather was changed to one with an extension tube on the differential cover.

Chassis: Front Wheel Hubs

Changes at chassis numbers 850047/8, 860001, 875132/3, and 885001: About August 1961, the stub axle carrier on the right-hand and left-hand front hubs was changed, and a water deflector was added.

A-Arms and Pivots

The A-arms came in two colors: silver and black. It seems that both types were intermixed, at least on early cars.

Changes at chassis numbers 850253/4, 860022/3, 875963/4, and 885142/3: The front suspension assembly was changed about February 1962.

Changes at chassis numbers 850290/1, 860032/3, 876129/30, and 885209/10: The front suspension assembly was changed about February 1962.

Front Torsion Bars

I am not aware of any design changes. These were finished in black.

Front Shock Absorbers

Changes at chassis numbers 850321/2, 860121/2, 876394/5, and 885334/5: The front shock absorbers were changed about February 1962.

Front Antiroll Bar

Changes at chassis numbers 850707/8, 861171/2,

879331/2, and 888559/60: About May 1963, a keeper plate was added to the antiroll bar bushes. I am not sure if this reference is to the front or rear antiroll bar. This change is listed only in Porter's *Jaguar E-Type: The Definitive History.*

Rear Wheel Hubs and Carriers

The aluminum hub carriers have been shown painted in a dark color in various publications. Typically, though, these were bare aluminum.

Changes at chassis numbers 850091/2, 860004/5, 875385/6, and 885020/1: The outer rear hub bearings

On the very early cars, the rear springs had spacers at the top, and thick retainers at the bottom.

This is a typical later rear-spring assembly. It has the thin spring retainer, and there is no upper spacer (although this cannot be seen here).

were enlarged about October 1961. This change does not appear in the June 1963 parts book.

Changes at chassis numbers 850503/4, 860450/1, 877182/3, and 885984/5: About June 1962, the oil seals in the hub carriers, for the fulcrum shafts, were changed.

Changes at chassis numbers 850583/4, 860832/3, 877963/4, and 886685/6: About September 1962, the rear hubs and hub carriers were changed, and water throwers were added.

Radius Arms, Trailing Arms, and Halfshafts

The halfshafts were changed from a large-diameter, hollow-tube construction to a small-diameter, solid-tube construction.

Changes at chassis numbers 850549/50, 850552/3, 850554/5, 860657/8, 877534/5, 877544/5, 877549/50, and 886246/7: About July 1962, the rear-end halfshafts were changed from a tubular construction to solid forgings.

About December 1962, the grease nipples on the halfshaft universal joints were discontinued. The fitting hole was fitted with a plug. This change is listed only by Porter.

Changes at chassis numbers 850678/9, 861105/6, 879131/2, and 888326/7: About April 1963, various

parts in the rear suspension, such as the wishbones, mountings at inner fulcrum shafts, and the bracing plate, were changed.

The rear shafts were given water shields in 1963 to protect the universal joints. This change is listed only in Skilleter's *Jaguar Sports Cars*.

Changes at chassis numbers 850805/6, 861423/4, 880754/5, and 889688/9: The roller-bearing seals in the halfshaft universal joints were changed, and covers for the journal assemblies were added. This change occurred in late winter or early spring of 1964.

Changes at chassis numbers 850824/5, 861520/1, 881152/3, and 890170/1: About April 1964, the front bush in the rear suspension radius arms was changed. This change is listed only by Porter.

Rear Springs, Seats, and Spacers

Some of the early springs, spacers, and retainers differed from the standard early configuration that had packing rings at the top and the thick spring retainers at the bottom. For example, there are illustrations of early rear ends with very wide spring retainers on the bottom only in *Motor Racing*, April 1961, and in the May 15, 1961, *The Motor*. There is also a line drawing in *Motor Magazine*, March 15, 1961. In these illustrations, there are apparently no packing ring spacers on the top, as was used on the early cars.

Changes at chassis numbers 850136/7, 860007/8, 875541/2, and 885038/9: About October 1961, the rear suspension coil springs and seats for the springs were changed, and the aluminum packing piece at the top was dropped and the springs were lengthened.

From research of surviving cars: Serial numbers 875026 and 875109 had upper spacers and thick spring retainers, and on 875109 the rear springs appeared original and unaltered and were painted in a glossy black.

Changes at chassis numbers 850907/8, 861719/20, 881696/7, and 890714/5: About October 1964, packing rings were added to the top of the rear springs. This change is listed only by Porter.

Rear Shock Absorbers

From research of surviving cars: On serial number 875109, there were four very old and apparently original shocks labeled "GIRLING" and 64054324. These were painted a glossy grey color (which is standard for these shock absorbers).

Changes at chassis numbers 850321/2, 860121/2, 876394/5, and 885334/5: The rear shock absorbers were changed.

Rear Antiroll Bar

From research of surviving cars: On serial number 875109, the rear antiroll bar and the two steel sheet-metal brackets securing it to the rear tub appeared original and unaltered and were painted in glossy black.

Changes at chassis numbers 850707/8, 861171/2, 879331/2, and 888559/60: About May 1963, a keeper plate was added to the antiroll bar bushes. But I am not sure if this reference is to the front or rear antiroll bar. This change is listed only by Porter.

Brakes

While typically the brake calipers were plated in a silver color, some early ones may have been black (perhaps painted). From research of surviving cars: The rear calipers and cylinders of serial number 875109 were plated with a silver-colored coating.

Changes at chassis numbers 850253/4, 860022/3, 875963/4, and 885142/3: About December 1961, the front and rear brake caliper assemblies were changed from malleable iron to cast iron, and the pistons were changed to have an integral backing plate.

Changes at chassis numbers 850290/1, 860032/3, 876129/30, and 885209/10: The brake pad material was changed. This change is listed only in *Jaguar E-Type: The Definitive History*.

Changes at chassis numbers 850577/8, 860740/1, 877735/6, and 886455/6: About September 1962, the setscrew and tab washer holding the rear calipers to the final drive unit were changed.

Changes at chassis numbers 879440/1 and 888672/3: About June 1963, for cars with 3.54:1 rear ends, the rear brake discs were increased in thickness to 1/2 inch, the brake pad material was changed to Mintex M.59, and the rear calipers were mounted on adapter plates (as opposed to bolted direct).

Changes at chassis numbers 879460/1 and 888694/5: About June 1963, for cars with 3.31:1 rear ends, the rear brake discs were increased in thickness to 1/2 inch, the brake pad material was changed to Mintex M.59, and the rear calipers were mounted on adapter plates (as opposed to bolted direct).

Changes at chassis numbers 850721/2, 861184/5, 879493/4, and 888705/6: About June 1963, for cars with 3.07:1 rear ends, the rear brake discs were increased in thickness to 1/2 inch, the brake pad material was changed to Mintex M.59, and the rear calipers were mounted on adapter plates (as opposed to bolted direct).

The early brake-caliper cylinders had a large retaining plate in the center for the adjustment rod. This is a rear cylinder.

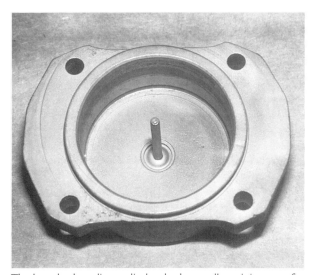

The later brake-caliper cylinders had a small retaining area for the adjusting rod. This is a front cylinder.

The side view of an early multipiece brake piston.

The inside view of an early multipiece brake piston.

A disassembled early multipiece brake piston. The inner, brass center section is on the left, and the steel section facing the pad is on the right.

The later brake pistons had a larger inner circumference than the early ones, and required a different sealing rubber.

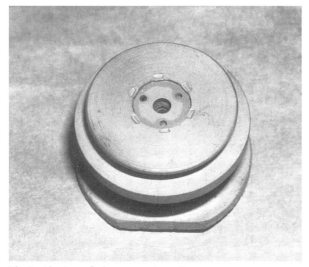

The inside view of a later one-piece piston.

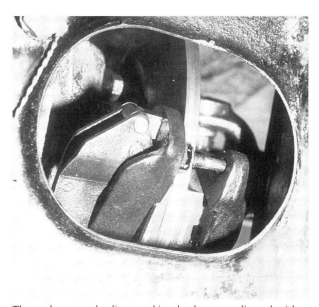

The early manual-adjust parking brake was adjusted with a small Allen key that was contained in the tool kit.

In *Jaguar Sports Cars*, Skilleter stated that in 1963 the brake pad material went from Mintex M.33 to Mintex M.59.

Parking Brake

Changes at chassis numbers 850089/90, 860003/4, 875331/2, and 885014/5: The handbrake assembly was changed to the auto-adjust type about October 1961.

In *Jaguar Sports Cars*, Skilleter stated, "The handbrake operated on an extra caliper on one rear disc, which suggests there was only one rear handbrake, but I think this must be an error. I have never seen any evidence for any car with a parking brake on only one rear disc.

Changes at chassis numbers 850550/1, 850552/3, 850554/5, 860663/4, 877534/5, 877539/40, 877566/7,

and 886262/3: About July 1962, the handbrake assembly on the rear brakes was changed.

Changes at chassis numbers 850554/5, 860663/4, 877566/7, and 886262/3: The handbrake cable assembly was changed.

Changes at chassis numbers 850722/3, 861202/3, 879550/1, and 888759/60: About August 1963, two fork ends replaced the compensator inner-lever link in the handbrake. Some sources cite chassis numbers 850727/8 rather than 850722/3.

Front Wheelwells and Engine Compartment Undershields

The aluminum sheet-metal shield mounted on the bottom of the left side of the engine compartment was

Later parking brakes were of the automatic-adjusting type. As the pads wore, a ratchet compensated for it. The mechanism is encased in the housing here, and cannot be seen.

The early left-hand-side engine compartment shield had a cutout on one corner to allow the crankcase breather pipe to pass through. This type of shield continued in use after the crankcase breather was changed to the later type.

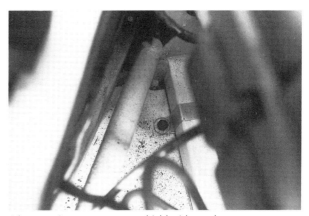

A later engine compartment shield without the vent cut out.

changed during 3.8-liter production. The early shields had a large cutout on the front to accommodate the crankcase-breather vent pipe that passed through on its way to the bottom of the car. While this type of crankcase vent was only used on the First 500 cars, the early style shields were used well beyond the First 500. Late in production, the shield was changed and the cutout was reduced to a size only big enough to allow the plate to fit in the frame aperture.

What appear to be aluminum wheelwells are shown on an early car on the cover of *Car and Driver*, May 1961, but this is the only case I know of where the wheelwells appear to be of a different material or different design than the usual steel ones.

Changes at chassis numbers 850680/1, 861120/1, 879159/60, and 888352/3: About April 1963, a canvas and rubber seal for the left-hand front frame under-shield was introduced.

Wheels, Weights, and Hubcaps

Wheels typically came painted silver, or chromed. In the June 1963 spare parts catalog, both chromium

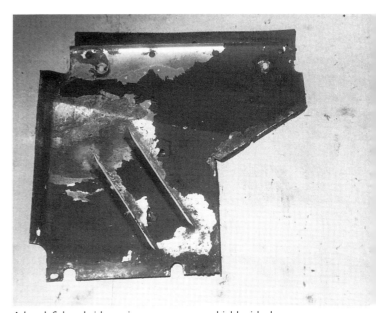

A late left-hand-side engine compartment shield with the canvas seal.

The standard eared hubcap used on most 3.8-liter cars.

The earless hubcap used on cars shipped to Germany. This is a different cap than those used on the late 4.2-liters, which had three lobes rather than the two rectangular tabs seen here.

An original three-ounce wheel weight is on the right.

wheels and wheels painted in stoved aluminum are listed, and the chromium wheels are indicated as special order. For later U.S.-specification cars, however, the chrome wheels were standard.

There are a few cases of early cars with dark painted wheels.

Wheel weights are listed as available in the June 1963 parts book, but no changes are denoted. The original wheel weights were rectangular in shape. I believe these weights were used throughout the 3.8-liter production run, as I have seen similar weights on a Series I 4.2-liter car.

Cars shipped to Germany had earless hubcaps that required a special wrench for removal.

Tires and Tubes

The 3.8-liter cars came with the then-new Dunlop RS.5 tires. These tires came in three types: blackwalls, and wide and narrow whitewalls. All were 6.40x15-inch Dunlop RS.5 tires.

U.S. cars tended to have whitewalls, and the English cars had blackwalls.

One source, *Sports Car World* magazine, October 1963, cites the tires as Pirelli Rolle. I believe this is an error, as I have seen no other evidence for this.

Front Subframe

In the June 1963 spare parts catalog, it is stated that a different front subframe assembly is listed as used on all roadsters.

Changes at chassis numbers 850238/9, 860138/9, 876457/8, and 885384/5: About February 1962, the bonnet hinge was changed with an associated change in the cross-member of the front subframe.

Changes at chassis numbers 860138/9 and 885384/5: The front subframe assembly was changed on the coupes. In the June 1963 parts book, a different front subframe assembly is listed as used on all roadsters, and no changes are listed.

An original equipment Dunlop RS.5 blackwall tire.

Changes at chassis numbers 860478/9 and 886013/4: The front subframe assembly and hinge were changed about June 1962.

There has been controversy about the nuts and bolts holding the front subframe together and onto the car. It is questioned whether or not they are sometimes painted along with the subframe, or whether they are always installed after the subframe was painted, and thus are bare.

Numerous assembly-line pictures of cars show the bolts as unpainted. Engine compartment pictures of many cars also show unpainted bolts. I found no instances of original pictures with painted subframe bolts.

Rear Subframe, Mounts, and Stops

The brace plate on the bottom of the subframe came in two types. The early type had a large aperture, and the later type had a small aperture.

Changes at chassis numbers 850678/9, 861105/6, 879131/2, and 888326/7: About April 1963, the mountings for the inner fulcrum shafts changed, along with other parts in the rear end, such as wishbones, mountings at inner fulcrum shafts, and the bracing plate.

Tubing and Cables

I am not aware of any changes.

Exhaust System

Changes at chassis numbers 850178/9, 860011/2, 875607/8, and 885058/9: The welded-together exhaust tailpipe assembly was changed to a two-piece assembly about December 1961.

Changes at chassis numbers 860175/6 and 885503/4: The bracket for the muffler was discontinued.

Changes at chassis numbers 850754/5, 861270/1, 879989/90, and 889095/6: About September 1963, the mufflers and their mounts were changed. This change is listed only in *Jaguar E-Type: The Definitive History*.

An unusual muffler mount, a sort of horizontal tang, is shown on an early car in *The Jaguar E-Type: A Collector's Guide*.

Rear Pipes and Resonators

The rear part of the exhaust system was a welded-together unit on the early cars, while on later cars it was made up of separate pieces bolted together. The early welded-together resonator unit is shown in Jaguar publication E/123/5.

The resonators on the early cars had longer large-diameter sections than the later resonators. Within the early long large-diameter section resonators, there are at least two varieties: flat ends and pointed ends. Resonators with long, turned-down tips were also used on some very early cars.

The early resonators were welded together, not bolted as on later cars, and they were larger than the later ones.

I am not certain that any 3.8-liter cars were fitted with the short large-diameter section resonators (as fitted

A Dunlop RS.5 wide-whitewall tire. These were optional, but were typically fitted to U.S.-specification cars. Later on, narrower whitewalls were adopted.

An early rear-end assembly brace plate with the large hole.

A later rear-end assembly brace plate with the small hole.

to Series I 4.2-liter cars). *Jaguar International Magazine*, March 1986, seems to suggest they were, and in *Jaguar E-Type: The Definitive History*, a picture appears to be illustrating such a late 3.8-liter car. However, this might illustrate a nonoriginal car.

Apparently, the length was modified to cut resonance. This may also be the reason for the various resonator types.

Changes at chassis numbers 850178/9, 860011/2, 875607/8, and 885058/9: The welded-together exhaust tailpipe assembly was changed to a two-piece assembly in December 1961.

Exhaust Heat Shield

Changes at chassis numbers 850648/9, 861061/2, 878888/9, and 888081/2: About January 1963, the heat shield assembly was changed, probably to accommodate the new gearbox mount. The June 1963 spare parts catalog also states that the following chassis were fitted with the early shield: 850653, 850654, 861087, 878895, 878900, 878907, 878908, 878913, 878914, 878915, 878926, 878936, 878937, 878938, 878958, 878986, 879005, 879024, 879049, 888086, 888096, 888101, 888103, 888109, 888113, 888117, 888118, 888120, 888134, 888157, 888178, and 888238.

The resonators on the early 3.8-liter cars had long large-diameter sections. Most had the squared-off tips seen here.

A fabricated exhaust system clamp. The clamping bolt is not shown here.

The later resonators had short large-diameter sections and squared-off tips.

Chapter 7

4.2-LITER BODYWORK AND INTERIOR COMPONENT CHANGES

As in chapters 5 and 6, this chapter lists the production changes by component classification rather than by order of serial number. The introductory comments of chapter 5 apply here as well.

In addition, while the Series I, Series I 1/2, and Series II cars are well covered in this chapter, their differences are not the subject of this chapter. These changes are reviewed briefly in chapter 1. Occasionally, a model-change difference is discussed or illustrated. This occurs whenever there is doubt as to whether they occurred exactly at a model-change boundary, and occasionally in other cases to help define the different 4.2-liter models.

As in chapters 5 and 6, each figure illustrates the single, specific feature discussed in its caption. Any other features in the illustrations are incidental, and may or may not represent the original state of the car. I will not always cite unoriginal features when they appear.

Exterior: Headlights and Trim

I am not aware of any changes to the headlight covers or trim before the headlight covers were done away with in 1967. The markings on the original headlight covers, as well as the markings on some later replacements, can be seen on page 49.

There are several references in the literature to the headlight covers being plastic, for example in *Autosport* magazine, August 5, 1966. I think these references are in error, however, as I stated in chapter 5 regarding the 3.8-liter cars.

The first version of uncovered headlights (the low-set type, as used throughout the Series I 1/2 production) came in late 1967, slightly before the Series I was discontinued.

Changes at chassis numbers 1E.1863/4, 1E.15888/9, 1E.21583/4, 1E.34249/50, 1E.50974/5, and 1E.77644/5: About July 1967, the headlight covers were discontinued. In *Jaguar E-Type: The Definitive History*, Porter stated that about January 1968, the hood was changed to give direct access to the headlights, only chassis numbers 1ED.34549/50 were cited instead of 1E.34249/50. This note may be referring to the introduction of the first

style of open headlights, commonly thought of as Series I 1/2 headlights. As is noted in chapter 1, Skilleter cites these same chassis numbers as the beginning of the Series I 1/2 cars. Some late Series I cars had open headlights, chassis number 1E.15267 for example. So perhaps what is being referred to here is the introduction of the Series I 1/2 production, and not just the introduction of the open-headlight cars.

For RHD Series I roadsters, the covered headlights were discontinued about October 1967.

Lights of 75-60 watt (versus the 60-60 watt of the 3.8-liter cars) were fitted to some early 4.2-liter cars.

Changes at chassis numbers 1R.14065/6 and 1R.28294/5: The headlights were changed for cars exported to Belgium, Czechoslovakia, the Netherlands, Germany, Poland, Rumania, and Switzerland.

It is stated in *Original Jaguar E-Type* that the headlight trim finisher behind the headlight on the Series II cars was painted on cars exported to Australia.

All but the few last Series I cars had covered headlights of the sort fitted to the 3.8-liter cars.

The first version of open headlights was fitted to the Series I 1/2 cars, as well as some very late Series Is. The headlight itself was raised above the level of the hood, and the chrome trim was changed. In addition, the small strip of chrome trim running from the front of the headlight recess to the top of the front bumper was discontinued.

With the introduction of the Series II cars, the headlight assemblies were changed again. The lights were moved farther forward, and the chrome trim was changed.

The front side lights of the U.S.-specification Series II cars were not fitted to home-market cars.

A rear side light on a U.S.-specification Series II car.

Parking, Brake, and Side Lights and Trim

The stop-tail-flasher lights were red for Series I cars exported to the United States, and red and amber for other cars.

The stop-tail-flasher lights were red for Series II cars exported to Canada, Greece, Portugal, and the United States, and were red and amber for all other countries.

With the introduction of the Series II, side lights were included on export cars. Apparently, some early home-market cars were also fitted with these light units, but they were not operable. Typically, however, home-market cars did not have side lights.

The side-flasher lights for Series II cars were different for cars exported to Belgium and Japan; Canada, Greece, Portugal, and the United States; and all other countries. The side-flasher lights used a white lens for cars exported to Italy, Greece, and Japan. The side-flasher lights were different for cars exported to France, although the lens colors were the standard amber and white.

Changes at chassis numbers 1R.1392/3, 1R.11051/2, 1R.20485/6, 1R.27050, and 1R.35652/3: The side-marker lights were changed, but their colors remained the same.

Changes at chassis numbers 1R.11973/4 and 1R.27480/1: The stop-tail-flasher lights were changed for cars exported to Canada, Greece, Portugal, and the United States only, but the color of the lens remained red.

Changes at chassis numbers 1R.13427/8 and 1R.28054/5: The side-flasher lights changed for cars exported to Canada and the United States only.

Side-marker lights are shown on one early Series II, but are absent on another in *The Jaguar E-Type: A Collector's Guide*. Skilleter stated that these "were fitted to many export cars and some of the early home-market deliveries." Side lights are shown on an early LHD Series II roadster pictured in *Road Test* magazine, February

The Series I cars had polished-chrome wiper arms and trim.

This view of a combination frosted-chrome wiper arm with polished-chrome nut and cowl is from a late Series I 1/2 car.

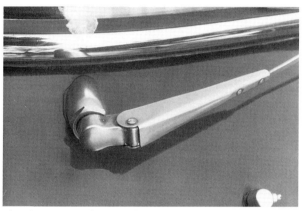

The wiper arms and trim on the late Series I 1/2 and Series II cars had frosted chrome trim. This was required by U.S. specifications.

As on the 3.8-liter cars, dual cowl-mounted squirter nozzles were fitted to all two-seater and steep-screen 2+2 cars.

1969, but are absent on a late RHD Series II coupe (Australian specification) in *Modern Motor*, March 1971.

License-Plate Lights and Trim

I am not aware of any changes.

Back-up Light and Trim

I am not aware of any changes.

Wiper Arms, Blades, and Windshield Squirter Nozzles

The 2+2 wiper blades are longer than the blades for the two-seaters, even on the early steep-screen cars. The outer pair of wiper blades are longer on the early 2+2 cars.

On the late steep-windscreen 2+2 cars, the dual, cowl-mounted squirter nozzles were replaced by a single dual-head nozzle mounted on the bonnet. In addition, these units had a frosted finish on the Series II cars.

Other than this, I am not aware of any changes to the squirter nozzles within the basic model groups.

Motor magazine, January 13, 1968, claimed that the matte finish of the wiper arms and spindles was a result of complying with U.S. safety regulations which

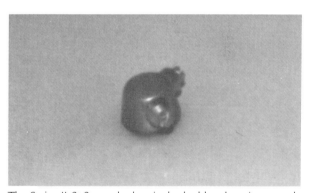

The Series II 2+2 cars had a single dual-head squirter nozzle mounted on the hood.

prohibited a polished reflecting surface. It is indicated there that this change came in with the Series I 1/2, but no specific serial numbers are cited. I have seen one instance of a late Series I 1/2 car with a frosted wiper arm and a chrome nut and cowl. I am not sure if this hybrid is original or not. Pictured in *Jaguar E-Type: The Definitive History* is what may be an early Series I 1/2 with this hybrid combination. Two close-up views

The early bumpers had internal mounts, and could only be removed from inside the bodywork. This is a front bumper.

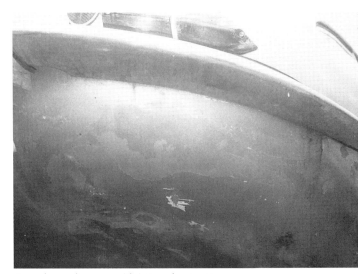

An early rear bumper with internal mounts.

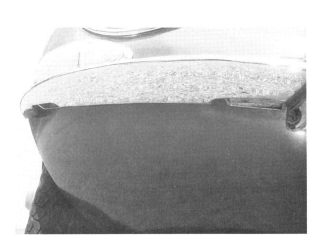

Later on, the bumpers and mounts were modified to allow removal of the bumpers from outside the car. The mounting bolts are accessible through the openings on the bottom of this front bumper.

A late rear bumper with external mounts.

show a frosted arm, cowl, and nut. Frosted wiper arms are shown on a late RHD, Series II coupe in *Modern Motor*, March 1971.

Bumpers

Changes at chassis numbers 1E.1412/3, 1E.11740/1, 1E.20999/1000, and 1E.32009/10: About March 1966, the rear bumper fittings were changed so that the bumpers could be removed from outside the car. This change is listed only in *Jaguar E-Type: The Definitive History*.

Vent Trim

The vent trim at the rear of the hood was changed at the introduction of the Series II cars. I am not aware of any changes.

Door Handles

I am not aware of any variations. On the Series I two-seater cars, the lock was in the pushbutton, while in the Series I 2+2s, the lock was in a separate position below.

Top Door Trim

Changes at chassis numbers 1E.50121/2 and 1E.75862/3: About December 1966, the screws retaining the chrome beads at the top of the doors were changed to retainers and rivets.

Convertible-Top Trim

The retaining hooks for the convertible-top cover (as mentioned in chapter 5 for the 3.8-liter roadsters) seem to have been present on all 4.2-liter roadsters.

External Markings and Decorative Trim

The Series I and Series I 1/2 4.2-liter cars have the same grille bar as the 3.8-liter cars, while the Series II cars had a bar with an elongated escutcheon.

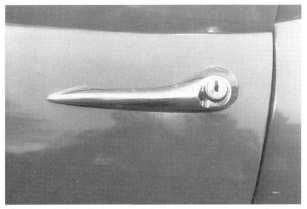

The door-lock keyholes on all the two-seater cars were located in the pushbutton in the door handle. This is the same arrangement used on all 3.8-liters.

The Series I 2+2s had the keyhole located below the door handle.

The pre-Series II 4.2-liter cars had a round grille medallion, as used on the 3.8-liter cars.

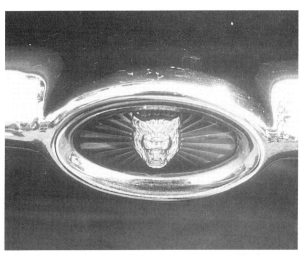

With the introduction of the Series II, the grille bar was changed, and an oval medallion was adopted.

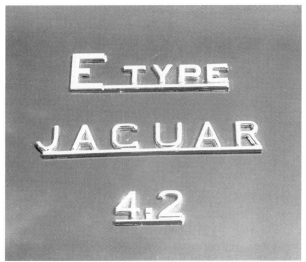

The 4.2-liter trunk-lid markings included the model name and engine displacement.

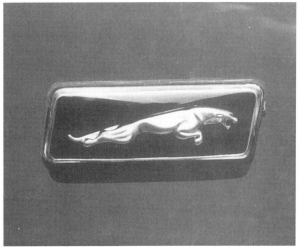

This plastic leaping-cat emblem from a 1971 car is located in approximately the same location as the external-latch mechanism had been ten years earlier.

The trunk-lid markings of the 4.2-liter cars had, in addition to the "JAGUAR" nameplate, a "4.2 LITER" plate below, and an "E-TYPE" nameplate above.

Possibly some very early 4.2-liter cars only had the "4.2" and "JAGUAR" plates, as pictured in *The Jaguar E-Type: A Collector's Guide*. In addition, *Motor Sport* magazine, April 1966, stated that the 4.2-liter E-Types have "4.2-LITER JAGUAR" on the trunk lid, and no mention is made of "E-TYPE" showing there.

In one instance, as illustrated in *Motor* magazine, October 31, 1964, a very early 4.2-liter coupe is fitted with only the "JAGUAR" nameplate on the rear door. In the January 1965 issue of *Motor Sport*, an early 4.2-liter coupe is shown with all three plates on its rear door.

On the last year's production of Series II cars, a plastic leaping Jaguar medallion was attached to the hood in approximately the same location as the exterior hood latches on the First 500 cars. This feature was not continued when the V-12 cars came out the following year.

Another feature of the last Series II cars was the introduction of chrome trim around the air-intake aperture.

Changes at chassis numbers 1E.1711/2, 1E.14582/3, 1E.21472/3, 1E.34146/7, 1E.50709/10, and 1E.77046/7: About January 1968, the motif bar and its rubber mountings were changed. This change is listed only in *Jaguar E-Type: The Definitive History*.

Windshield and Pillars

The inclination of the windshield of the 2+2 cars changed with the introduction of the Series II cars.

Changes at chassis numbers 1E.1657/8, 1E.13386/7, 1E.21388/9, and 1E.33139/40: About March 1967, the windshield glass was changed. This is a different change than for the 2+2 glass. This change is listed only by Porter.

As with all previous E-Types, the early Series II air intakes had no chrome trim around the outside. This car has an aftermarket bumper guard fitted.

The very late Series II air intakes had a narrow strip of chrome trim running around the edge. This was a precursor of the more elaborate Series III V-12 trim, which included an egg-crate grille.

The early 2+2 cars had a steep angle to the windshield. This was a result of increasing the height of the roof.

The later 2+2 cars had an increased slope to the windshield. This was achieved by moving the leading edge of the windshield forward on the cowl.

Side Windows, Trim, Frames, Winding Mechanisms, and Sealing Rubber

Changes at chassis numbers 1E.20952/3 and 1E.31919/20: About February 1966, the coupe window-frame seals were changed from felt to a flocked runner.

Changes at chassis numbers 1E.21311/2 and 1E.32765/6: About September 1966, the regulator channel for the wind-up windows was changed. This change is listed only by Porter.

Wing Vents

I am not aware of any changes.

Rear Window

I am not aware of any changes.

Front License-Plate Mount

The U.S.-specification 4.2-liter Series I cars had the same connecting-rod-actuated front license-plate mount as the later 3.8-liter cars.

As in the case of the later 3.8-liter cars, those without the front license-plate holder were still fitted with the connecting-rod hole in the area beneath the air intake.

License-Plate Holder

I am not aware of any changes.

Interior: Instruments and Controls

During Series I 1/2 production, the bezels of the instruments changed in cross section from angular to hemicircular.

The speedometers were different for 2.88:1, 3.07:1, 3.31:1, and 3.54:1 rear ends, and were offered in mile and kilometer calibrations.

Changes at chassis numbers 1E.1103/4, 1E.10045/6, 1E.20207/8, and 1E.30033/4: About June 1965, the speedometer cable was changed. This change is listed only in *Jaguar E-Type: The Definitive History*.

Changes at chassis numbers 1E.1408/9, 1E.11714/5, 1E.20977/8, and 1E.32008/9: About March 1966, the speedometers were changed to reflect the Dunlop tire change. This change is listed only by Porter.

Changes at chassis numbers 1E.16537/8, 1E.34944/5, and 1E.77837/8: About July 1968, the water temperature gauge was changed to one with only zones marked on it, as opposed to the earlier calibrations. This change is listed only in *The Jaguar E-Type: A Collector's Guide*.

Changes at chassis numbers 1R.1351/2, 1R.10536/7, 1R.20424/5, 1R.26834/5, 1R.35563/4, and 1R.42676/7: About October 1969, the clock was changed from a mercury-cell type to one operated by the car's battery. Some references cite chassis numbers 1R.1350/1 instead of 1R.1351/2, and numbers 1R.24424/5 instead of 1R.20425/6.

The change of the clock from the tachometer-mounted unit to the center-dash-mounted unit took place when the dash went over to toggle switches. This occurred during the Series I 1/2 production, and an early

The instrument bezels on the Series I and early Series I 1/2 cars had the same triangular cross section bezels used on the 3.8-liter cars.

The late Series I 1/2 and Series II cars had hemicircular cross section instrument bezels.

The late Series I 1/2 and early Series II cars did not have the choke control label.

Later in Series II production, a nonilluminated choke control label was introduced.

As in the case of the choke control labels, the late Series II heater control labels were illuminated from behind.

The late Series II choke control labels were raised and illuminated from behind.

The early four-way flasher switches did not have a cover on the back.

The late Series I 1/2 and early Series II cars had a nonilluminated heater control label. These labels came in with the upgraded rocker switch dash, unlike the choke control labels, which were introduced after the new dash had been in production a while.

Later four-way flasher switches had a cover on the back. Note the off-on label added to the front.

illustration of this is seen and discussed in *Motor* magazine, January 13, 1968.

Switches and Controls

A Series I 1/2 roadster is shown with toggle switches and starter button in *The Jaguar E-Type: A Collector's Guide*, and Skilleter stated there that later Series I 1/2 cars had the tumbler switches.

The choke control assembly was different for Series II cars exported to Canada (including Newfoundland) and the United States (including Hawaii).

All Jaguar models could be supplied in the United States with hazard lights.

Changes at chassis numbers 1E.12024/5 and 1E.32193/4: About December 1965, a hazard warning light (or four-way flasher) was fitted as standard. Porter cites this change as occurring for U.S. cars in about July 1967.

Changes at chassis numbers 1E.13804/5, 1E.33688/9, and 1E.76921/2: About July 1967, a cover was added to the four-way-flasher switch panel (for those cars with four-way flashers). This change is listed only by Porter.

Series II cars had the four-way-flasher switch as part of the central row of switches, and the indicator light between the tachometer and speedometer.

With the introduction of the rocker switch dash during Series I 1/2 production, the four-way flasher switch was located on the end of the central switch row.

When the four-way flasher switch moved to the central row of switches, the indicator light was moved to a position between the tachometer and speedometer.

The early Series II switch housings were flat. This is actually a view from a late Series I 1/2 car.

The later Series II switch housing had two raised buttresses on either side of the headlight switches.

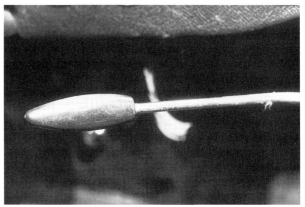

The early Series I turn-signal stalk was of the sort used on the 3.8-liter cars.

The cable for the headlight flasher was different for cars exported to Italy.

Changes at chassis numbers 1E.1457/8, 1E.12033/4, 1E.21206/7, and 1E.32200/1: About September 1966, the turn signal-headlight flasher switch was changed. This change is listed only by Porter.

Changes at chassis numbers 1E.1497/8, 1E.12716/7, 1E.21265/6, and 1E.32691/2: About September 1966, the illumination color of the instruments and switch label strip was changed from blue to green. This change is listed only by Porter.

Changes at chassis numbers 1E.2038/9 and 1E.21783/4: About April 1968, the dashboard was revised. The heater controls, choke, and switches were changed. A lid was added to the glovebox, and the heater box was changed. I think this is also the introduction of the rocker switches, which I believe was simultaneous with the addition of the glovebox lid (except for the 2+2 cars, which had it earlier). This change is listed only in *Jaguar E-Type: A Collector's Guide*.

Changes at chassis numbers 1R.7747/8 and 1R.25430/1: The choke assembly was changed.

Changes at chassis numbers 1R.1775/6, 1R.14120/1, 1R.20952/3, and 1R.28319/20: The headlight dip-switch was changed.

The movement of the horn button to the turn-signal stalk came in with the Series I 1/2.

Illumination was added for the heater and choke controls in 1970. Before this, the heater was marked with a metal label, and the choke was labeled with a similar metal label, or, in the early Series II cars, had no label at all.

The plastic housing for the row of tumbler switches in the Series II cars changed during Series II production. On the early Series II cars, this piece was flat in the center, while on later cars it had two buttresses on either side of the light switches.

Indicator Lights

I am not aware of any changes.

Cigar Lighter

I am not aware of any changes.

Ignition Switch and Key

Changes at chassis numbers 1R.1084/5, 1R.20094/5, and 1R.35098/9: About December 1968, a steering column lock was fitted to RHD cars.

On some RHD Series I 1/2, cars this resulted in there being two ignition switches, one in the center of the dash and one on the steering column.

Changes at chassis numbers 1R.9859/60, 1R.26532/3, and 1R.42381/2: About April 1969, the starter switch was changed to one that isolated some auxiliaries while the starter is cranking.

A key warning buzzer (that sounds when the key is in the ignition and the driver's door is closed) was new in 1970.

Grab Handle

I am not aware of any changes.

Steering Wheel and Column

At least two types of steering wheels were used in the 4.2-liter cars: the polished wheel (with the scooped-out rim, as found on later 3.8-liter cars) found on Series I 4.2-liter cars, and the brushed-finish wheel found on Series I 1/2 and Series II cars.

In *Motor* magazine, January 13, 1968, and in Porter's *Jaguar E-Type: The Definitive History*, it is claimed that the brushed-finish steering wheel was a result of complying with U.S. safety regulations, which prohibited a polished reflecting surface. It is indicated that this change came in with the Series I 1/2.

All 4.2-liter steering wheels had the thumb-groove cut in the wood trim, as on later 3.8-liter cars.

As in the 3.8-liter cars, a locking steering column was available for some export Series I cars. Such a column was fitted to cars exported to Denmark, Germany, and Sweden, and also by special order.

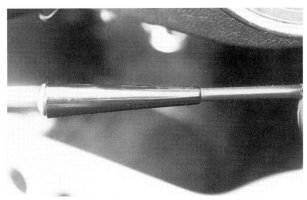

The later turn-signal stalks had a tapered handle. The horn was now actuated by pushing on the end of the stalk, and not by pushing on the medallion in the center of the steering wheel.

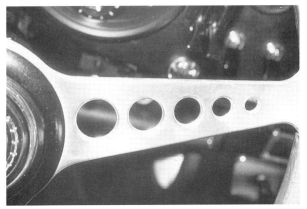

Early 4.2-liter cars had a polished finish on the aluminum of the steering wheel.

Later steering wheels had a brushed finish.

Series I cars had a chrome center trim ring.

In the Series I cars, the horn was actuated by pressing the escutcheon in the center of the steering wheel. These escutcheons had a chrome trim ring. For Series II cars, the horn was actuated on the turn-signal stalk, and the trim ring in the center of the steering wheel was black. I am not sure exactly when these two changes took place, or if the chrome-and-black trim-ring change occurred simultaneously.

The energy-absorbing steering column came in with the Series I 1/2 cars.

Changes at chassis numbers 1E.1457/8, 1E.12033/4, 1E.21206/7, and 1E.32200/1: About March 1966, the upper steering column was changed. This change is listed only by Porter.

Changes at chassis numbers 1R.1057/8, 1R.20094/5, and 1R.35098/9: The steering column lock and ignition switch assembly was fitted to RHD cars.

Changes at chassis numbers 1R.1084/5, 1R.20094/5, and 1R.35098/9: About December 1968, a steering column lock was fitted to RHD cars.

Changes at chassis numbers 1R.1184/5 and 1R.20263/4: The upper-steering-column assembly was changed.

Pedals

I am not aware of any changes.

Mirror and Mounts

Series I cars had mirrors similar to those fitted to the 3.8-liter cars. I am not aware of the changes to the mirror within the 4.2-liter Series I cars. With the introduction of the Series I 1/2, the mirror changed.

The interior mirror was different for cars exported to the United States and Canada.

Some Series II roadsters came with a mirror mounted on the sliding rod. It was similar to those found on the Series I cars, but with a different mirror mount.

Interior Lights

I am aware of any changes.

With the introduction of the brushed-finish steering wheel, the center trim ring was changed from chrome to black.

The Series I coupes, and some early Series I 1/2 coupes, had the roof-mounted rearview mirror, of the sort used on the 3.8-liter coupes.

The Series I roadsters, and some early Series I 1/2 roadsters, had a rod-mounted rearview mirror, of the sort used on the 3.8-liter roadsters.

During Series I 1/2 production, a break-away rearview mirror was introduced. It was glued to the inside surface of the windshield. This mirror was also used on early Series II cars.

Some late Series II roadsters had a rod-mounted mirror. The mirror and mount were different from those used on the Series I cars.

Handbrake Lever

Changes at chassis numbers 1R.35018/9 and 1R.42038/9: The handbrake lever assembly was changed.

Dash Top

Changes at chassis numbers 1R.1057/8, 1R.7795/6, 1R.20087/8, and 1R.25430/1: The screen rail fascia and the defrosting equipment were changed.

Defroster Ducts

Changes at chassis numbers 1R.35649/50 and 1R.42551/2: About October 1969, a defroster-tube extension was fitted.

Dash Materials and Trim

Changes at chassis numbers 1E.1606/7, 1E.13205/6, 1E.21387/8, and 1E.33149/50: About March 1967, the right-hand-side scuttle top casing (under dash panel) was changed from Rexine-trimmed aluminum to fiberboard. This change is listed only in Porter's *Jaguar E-Type: The Definitive History*.

Changes at chassis numbers 1E.1685/6, 1E.13724/5, 1E.21442/3 and 1E.33643/4: About March 1967, the center scuttle top casing was changed from Rexine-covered aluminum to fiberboard. This change is listed only by Porter.

Changes at chassis numbers 1R.1392/3, 1R.11051/2, 1R.20485/6, and 1R.27050/1: The fascia panel assemblies were changed.

Glovebox

The glovebox lid came in with the 2+2 cars. On the two-seater cars, it came in during Series I 1/2 production, along with the rocker switches and other dash changes.

Changes at chassis numbers 1E.2038/9 and 1E.21783/4: About April 1968, the dashboard was revised. The heater controls, choke, and switches were changed. A lid was added to the glovebox, and the heater box was changed. I think this is also the introduction of the rocker switches, which I believe was simultaneous with the addition of the glovebox lid (except for the 2+2 cars, which had it earlier). This change is listed only in the *Jaguar E-Type: A Collector's Guide*.

Sun Visors

Changes at chassis numbers 1E.20938/8 and 1E.31787/8: About March 1966, a vanity mirror was added to the passenger's sun visor on the coupes. This change is listed only in Porter's *Jaguar E-Type: The Definitive History*.

Changes at chassis numbers 1E.1489/90 and 1E.12687/8: About September 1966, sun visors were added to the roadsters. This change is listed only by Porter.

Changes at chassis numbers 1R.1348/9 and 1R.10522/3: The sun-visor mechanism was changed.

The early Series I roadsters did not have sun visors. I could find no evidence of Series I 1/2 cars or Series II cars without them.

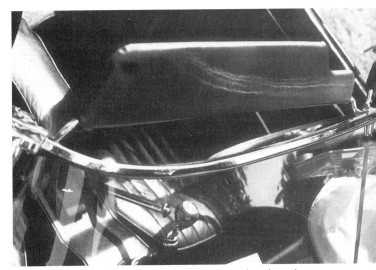
During Series I production, sun visors were introduced on the roadsters.

An outer mount for a roadster sun visor. Note how the sun visors merely bolted to existing hardware.

Under Dash Trays

Changes at chassis numbers 1E.50680/1 and 1E.77376/7: About July 1968, the package trays were changed. This change is listed only by Porter.

Console Frame, Trim, and Components

During Series I 4.2-liter construction, the boot on the shift lever changed. Initially it was of leather, in the same color as the seats, with a chromed-steel trim ring fastened with small rivets in the style of the 3.8-liter cars. About 1966, this was changed to an arrangement where the gearshift lever opening was reduced to a small circular aperture, and a rubber boot was used in place of the leather to cover the hole. This arrangement

was used for about a year, then the vinyl boot arrangement (of the Series I 1/2 and Series II) was introduced.

Changes at chassis numbers 1E.1060/1, 1E.10359/60, 1E.20102/3, and 1E.30349/50: The leather shift boot was changed to a rubber shift boot. In *The Jaguar E-Type: A Collector's Guide*, Skilleter stated that about November 1964, the finisher panel on the gearbox was changed and the chrome bezel and chrome ferrel for

Later Series I 4.2-liter cars had a small aperture for the shift lever, and a rubber shift boot.

An inner mount for a roadster sun visor.

Early 4.2-liter cars had a leather shift boot with a riveted retainer, in the manner of this boot from a 3.8-liter car.

Series II cars had a vinyl shift boot with a large aperture. This was similar in appearance to the early leather boots, but the edge trimming was pressed-on plastic.

the boot were deleted. But the only chassis numbers cited for this change are 1E.1060/1 and 1E.10359/60.

Changes at chassis numbers 1E.1201/2, 1E.10847/8, 1E.20501/2, and 1E.30889/90: About June 1965, the console was changed. This may be when the vinyl shift boot was introduced. I recall seeing some late Series I 4.2-liter cars with the leather shift boot of the early Series I 4.2-liters. However, I could find no evidence for this in the literature or in currently existing cars.

Changes at chassis numbers 1E.1685/6, 1E.13588/9, 1E.21441/2, 1E.33548/9, 1E.50585/6, and 1E.76910/1: About March 1967, the shift lever boot was changed to Ambla from the grommet that was used previously. I presume this was the introduction of the third style of shift lever boot, as found on late Series I and early Series II cars.

The Series I cars had a front, console-mounted ashtray, in the manner of the late 3.8-liter cars.

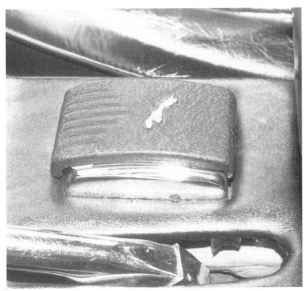

The Series II cars had an ashtray mounted on the lower part of the console, in front of the storage-armrest area.

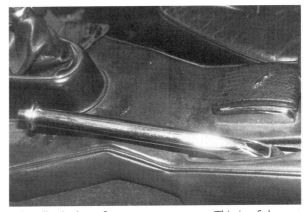

A handbrake lever from a two-seater car. This is of the sort used on 3.8-liters.

The thin-walled console storage compartment from a two-seater car.

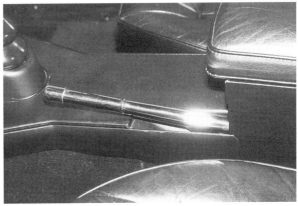

Handbrake lever from a 2+2 car. Notice the rib in the center, and the cup-type release cap.

The Series II cars had a vinyl shift boot with a smaller silver ring around it.

The handbrake levers were different on the 2+2 from those fitted to the two-seater cars.

Changes at chassis numbers 1R.35421/2 and 1R.42400/1: About March 1970, the handbrake lever was changed to one with a different material in the pivot pin and lever. This change is listed only in Porter's *Jaguar E-Type: The Definitive History*.

The shift knob on the automatic transmission was changed from spherical to elliptical on the Series I 1/2 cars to increase its surface area and meet U.S. specifications.

Changes at chassis numbers 1R.35656/7 and 1R.43164/5: About January 1970, the automatic transmission selector lever was changed. This is listed only by Porter.

With the change in the dash during the Series I 1/2 production, the front section of the console also changed to the more padded version of the Series II.

About the time of the front console change that occurred during Series I 1/2 production, the ashtray was changed and moved from the front console to a location in front of the armrest-storage area.

The storage area on the console was different on the 2+2s from the two-seater cars. The sidewalls were thicker on the 2+2 storage areas.

Under Console Area

Changes at chassis numbers 1E.1225/6, 1E.10957/8, 1E.20611/2, and 1E.30981/2: A rubber sealing plug was added to seal the gearbox apertures.

Changes at chassis numbers 1R.35815/6 and 1R.43923/4: About May 1970, the handbrake lever assembly was changed. The new one was longer and angled upward.

Carpets and Interior Trim

The door armrests changed several times during the 4.2-liter production. All the Series I cars had armrests, with different types for the two-seaters and 2+2s. During the production of Series I 1/2 cars, the armrests

The thick-walled console storage compartment from a 2+2.

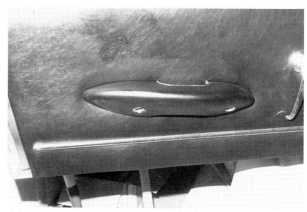

A Series I armrest from a 2+2. Note the longer, tapered shape.

This 4.2-liter Series I armrest from a two-seater is of the sort used on late 3.8-liter cars.

Early Series II cars did not have door armrests.

148

were discontinued. Then, shortly after the introduction of the Series II, the armrests were reintroduced. The newer armrests were of a simpler and more pointed design than the earlier ones.

Changes at chassis numbers 1R.1325/6, 1R.10334/5 (perhaps this should be 1R.10534/5), 1R.20390/1, and 1R.26755/6: Armrests were added to the doors.

The front of the doors, in the area where the door-light-switch striker is located, was trimmed in the 4.2-liter cars, whereas it was bare in the 3.8-liter cars.

In *The Jaguar E-Type: A Collector's Guide*, when speaking of a Series I coupe, Skilleter stated that the moquette was replaced with vinyl, and the rear mat was made into one piece. Later, this mat was replaced by trimming the panels in vinyl. Also, the moquette was used on early 4.2-liter cars.

The 4.2-liter cars were fitted with false toe boards on the passenger's side. I suspect this was a feature of all 4.2-liter cars.

Changes at chassis numbers 1E.20116/7 and 1E.30401/2: About February 1965, the casing assembly below the quarter lights was changed and the pocket assembly

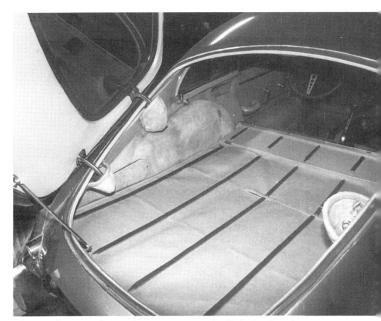

This 3.8-liter car shows the moquette and oil-cloth trimming as used in early 4.2-liter coupes.

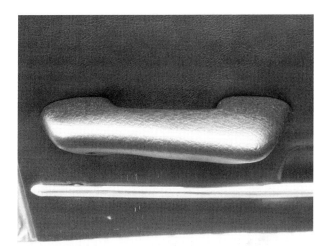

Late Series II armrests were molded in a single piece.

A general view of late 4.2-liter coupe vinyl trimming. This is a 2+2.

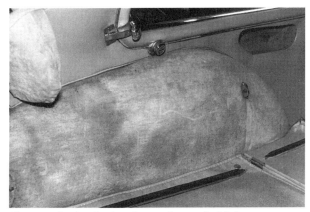

The rear-wheel arch trimming used on early 4.2-liter coupes.

Front view of a false toe board from a Series I car.

in the casing below the quarter lights was deleted. The cover assembly over the spare wheel and fuel tank and forward luggage floor area were trimmed, and the old luggage floor mat was done away with. The rear wheel-arch covers were changed from moquette trimmed to PVC trimmed. The hinged extension board and its support rail assembly were changed. Some carpets and hardura mats and insulating felts and interior trimming were changed.

The smooth leather on a Series II seat.

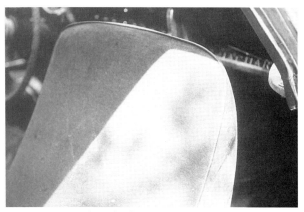

Moquette-covered seatbacks were used on early 4.2-liter cars.

Changes at chassis numbers 1E.21133/4 and 1E.32267/8: About September 1966, the hinged extension board in the luggage area was changed. This change is listed only in *Jaguar E-Type: The Definitive History.*

Changes at chassis numbers 1E.50422/3 and 1E.76663/4: The trim panels above the rear door aperture were changed, and the headlining was changed.

Seats and Mounts

In the Series II cars, the early seats had smooth leather and the later seats had perforated leather.

Changes at chassis numbers 1R.1137/8, 1R.8868/9, 1R.20211/2, and 1R.26004/5: About May 1969, the perforated leather trim was introduced for the seats, and the headrests were changed. The following cars were also fitted with the early seats: Chassis numbers 1R.8870, 1R.8871, 1R.8873, 1R.8874, 1R.8875, 1R.8876, 1R.8877, 1R.8878, 1R.8879, 1R.8880, 1R.8881, 1R.8882, 1R.8883, 1R.9029, 1R.9042, 1R.9069, 1R.9070, 1R.9077, 1R.9147, 1R.9169, 1R.9172, 1R.9174, 1R.9185, 1R.9195, 1R.9255, 1R.9328, 1R.9244 (perhaps this should be 9344), 1R.9350, 1R.9396, 1R.9419, 1R.26002, 1R.26007, 1R.26010, 1R.26022, 1R.26023, 1R.26025,

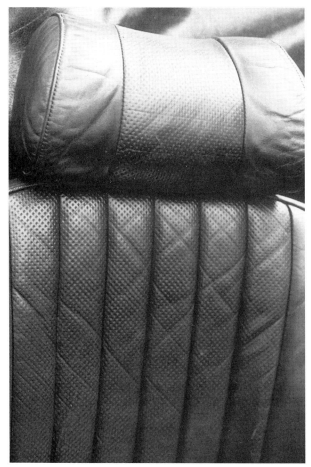

Later Series II seats had perforated leather trimming.

1R.26028, 1R.26033, 1R.26051, 1R.26053, 1R.26057, 1R.26069, 1R.26078.

Changes at chassis numbers 1R.1301/2 (and some cars after 1R.1277), 1R.10151/2 (and some cars after 1R.10114), 1R.20365/6 (and some cars after 1R.20354), 1R.26683/4 (and some cars after 1R.26649), 1R.35457/8 (and some cars after 1R.35440), and 1R.42559/60 (and some cars after 1R.42539): About August 1969, the seat assemblies were adapted to take headrests as an optional extra, but chassis numbers 1R.35457/8 and 1R.42559/60 were not mentioned in the factory parts catalog.

Changes at chassis numbers 1E.1011/2, 1E.10312/3, 1E.20079/80, and 1E.30251/2: About January 1965, spacers were introduced at the front mounts of the seat slides where they attach to the floor. This change is listed only by Porter.

Changes at chassis numbers 1E.1039/40, 1E.10337/8, 1E.20097/8, and 1E.30292/3: About January 1965, the fittings between the seat slides and the seat were changed. This change is listed only by Porter.

Changes at chassis numbers 1E.1418/9, 1E.11802/3, 1E.21037/8, and 1E.32039/40: The trimmed base assembly of the seats, and the screws and washers mounting them to the slides, were changed.

Changes at chassis numbers 1E.50660/1 and 1E.76949/50: About July 1967, the upper squab of the back seat was changed. This change is listed only by Porter.

The trim on the seatbacks changed during 4.2-liter production. The early seats had moquette covering, and the later seats had vinyl covering.

Convertible-Top Frame and Hardware

The trim on most of the convertible-top boards was a light-brown fabric. However, some Series II cars had black vinyl trimming.

A vinyl-covered seatback on a later car.

On some 4.2-liter roadsters, a warning label on the inner front area of the convertible top said to move the seats forward before raising the top. This was apparently not fitted to all 4.2-liter cars, as is evidenced by its absence in the illustration in *The Jaguar E-Type: A Collector's Guide*.

The convertible-top clasps of the late Series I 1/2 and Series II cars were different from the later 3.8-liter type. They had a thicker yolk, and the central clasp was changed. The thicker-type clasps came in an early, sharp-edged style and a later, smooth-edged style. The second style is the common one.

Convertible-Top Cloth and Window

The convertible-top material changed from the early mohair cloth material to a plastic material.

The plastic convertible-top material was introduced the same year as the open headlights.

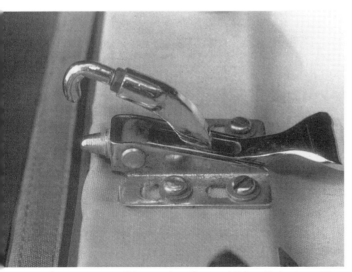

A center convertible-top clasp from a 4.2-liter Series I car. Note the thin handle and neck section, as used in later 3.8-liters.

A side convertible-top clasp from a Series I car.

An early version of a thick center clasp from a Series I 1/2 car. Note the sharp edges on the fat section of the handle.

An early thick side clasp from a Series I 1/2.

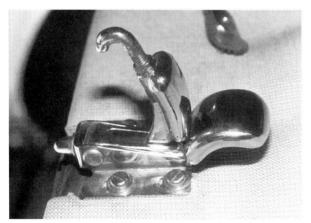

A late thick center clasp from a Series II car. Note the rounded edges and pronounced curvature of the handle.

Convertible-Top Cover

I am not aware of any changes. I believe the convertible-top cover was vinyl throughout 4.2-liter production.

Hardtop Mounting Equipment

I am not aware of any design changes.

Hood Release

I am not aware of any design changes to the interior release.

Trunk Release

With the introduction of the 4.2-liter cars, a lock was added to the trunk release on the roadsters. I am not aware of any changes.

Bodywork: Front Fenders

Changes at chassis numbers 1E.1478/9, 1E.12579/80, 1E.21227/8, and 1E.32631/2: About September 1966, the hood, front fenders, front bumpers, and heater air-intake plenum were changed to the type as used on the 2+2s. This change is listed only in *Jaguar E-Type: The Definitive History*.

Hood Center Section

Changes at chassis numbers 1E.1478/9, 1E.21227/8, and 1E.32631/2: About September 1966, the

A late thick side clasp from a Series II.

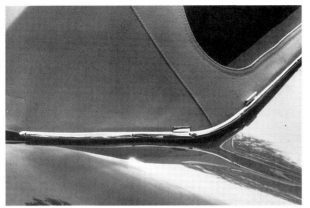

Early convertible tops were made of mohair.

Later convertible tops were made of vinyl.

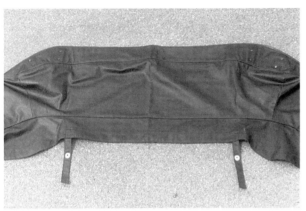

An outside view of the vinyl convertible-top cover used throughout 4.2-liter production.

This interior view of a late vinyl convertible top shows the lead-filled damping bag between the rear two bows.

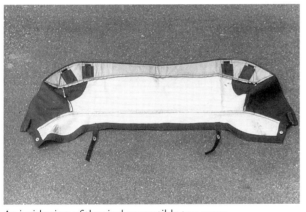

An inside view of the vinyl convertible-top cover.

The lockable trunk-lid release in the right rear of the cockpit.

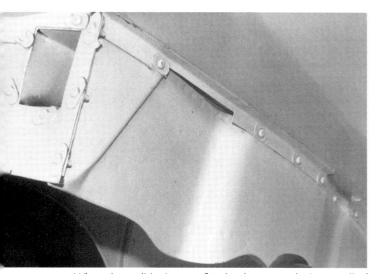

When air conditioning was fitted to later cars, the inner wall of the heater intake plenum was recessed. This is a late Series II roadster.

An early spring-loaded bonnet lift. Note, on this particular car, the mount on the front bulkhead of the hood for mounting the gas strut. This may be here because this is a late car, and near the transition to the new lift.

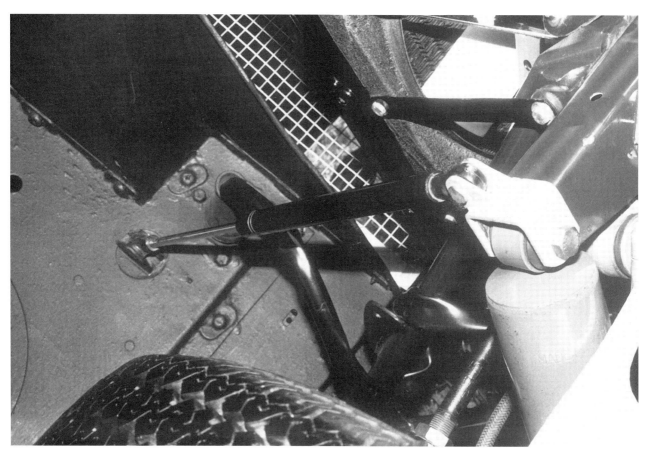

A later gas-strut hood lift. These were used on the left side only, unlike the earlier spring lifts, which were found on both sides.

hood, front fenders, front bumpers, and heater air-intake plenum were changed to the type as used on the 2+2s. This change is listed only by Porter.

Autocar magazine, October 12, 1967, stated that the air-intake aperture in the hood is "now single skinned." I am not sure exactly what is being referred to here. Other than this cryptic entry, I am not aware of any design changes.

When air conditioning was fitted, a portion of the inner wall of the heater plenum was recessed.

Hood Hinges and Lifts
Changes at chassis numbers 1R.1187/8, 1R.9569/70, 1R.20269/70, 1R.26386/7, 1R.35352/3, and 1R.42117/8: About June 1969, the hood-lifting springs were replaced by a gas-filled cylinder.

Hood Latches
Changes at chassis numbers 1E.1423/4, 1E.11885/6, 1E.21075/6, and 1E.32089/90: An O-ring was placed on the hood lock-operating rod to prevent vibration of the rod.

The safety catch on the Series II hoods was found both in the center of the hood and on the right-hand side.

The centrally mounted hood safety catch on a late Series II roadster. Note the provision on this car for a right-mounted safety catch. These extra bolts are not found on earlier cars.

The Series II 2+2s had a right-mounted hood safety catch.

Rubber Stops
I am not aware of any design changes.

Rear Tub Sheet Metal, Firewall, and Underside
Changes at chassis numbers 1E.1069/70, 1E.10425/6, 1E.20116/7, and 1E.30401/2: The bodyshell underframe and rear-end assembly were changed.

Changes at chassis numbers 1E.20116/7 and 1E.30401/2: About March 1965, bodyshell changes took place. This change is listed only by Porter.

Changes at chassis numbers 1E.1285/6, 1E.11117/8, 1E.20752/3, and 1E.31170/1: The front closing panel assemblies for the cockpit and sills were changed about September 1965.

Changes at chassis numbers 1E.1333/4 and 1E.11157/8: About November 1965, sealing panels were

The early 4.2-liter coupes had a post-type trunk-lid prop. The one shown here is actually from a late 3.8-liter car.

Later in Series I production, the trunk-lid prop was changed to a hinged type.

added between the rear bulkhead panel and wheel arch valances. This change is listed only by Porter.

Changes at chassis numbers 1E.1411/2, 1E.11727/8, 1E.20995/6, and 1E.32008/9: An attachment bracket assembly for the rear bumpers was introduced.

Autocar magazine, October 12, 1967, mentions that the rustproofing is said to be improved.

Cockpit Sheet Metal

Changes at chassis numbers 1E.1060/1, 1E.10359/60, 1E.20102/3, and 1E.30349/50: The cockpit panel assembly at the side of the gearbox was changed.

Changes at chassis numbers 1E.1201/2, 1E.10847/8, 1E.20501/2, 1E.30889/90: About June 1965, the drive shaft tunnel changed. This change is listed only in Porter's *Jaguar E-Type: The Definitive History*.

Changes at chassis numbers 1E.1225/6, 1E.10957/8, 1E.20611/2, and 1E.30911/2 (and some previous chassis): About June 1965, a speedometer-drive access aperture, with cover, was added to the right-hand-side gearbox side panel. This change is listed only by Porter.

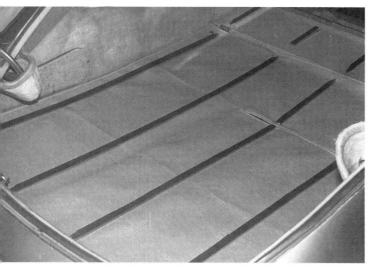
The trunk mat used on early 4.2-liter coupes.

In June 1968 the U.S. federal specifications for doors, casings, and linings were adapted to RHD cars. This change is listed only in *Jaguar E-Type: A Collector's Guide*.

Doors

Changes at chassis numbers 1E.1692/3, 1E.13951/2, 1E.21450/1, 1E.33774/5: About July 1967, the drain tray on the doors was changed. This change is listed only by Porter.

Door Hinges and Supports

I am not aware of any design changes.

Door Latches

I am not aware of any design changes.

Trunk Sheet Metal

I am not aware of any design changes.

In the October 12, 1967, issue of *Autocar*, the trunk floor of an RHD Series I roadster is shown without the brake inspection plate found on the 3.8-liter cars.

Trunk Lid

I am not aware of any design changes.

Trunk Hinges and Supports

Both the 3.8-liter type stick prop and the later hinge-type prop were used on 4.2-liter coupes.

Changes at chassis numbers 1E.20851/2 and 1E.31412/3: About November 1965, the coupe rear door support went from post-type prop to hinged-type prop.

Fuel Filler Recess, Lid, and Hinge

Changes at chassis numbers 1R.1392/3, 1R.11051/2, 1R.20485/6, 1R.27050/1, 1R.35642/3, and 1R.42849/50: The gas tank and cap were changed.

Trunk Panels, Mat, and Flooring

Changes at chassis numbers 1E.21133/4 and 1E.32267/8: About September 1966, the hinged extension board in the luggage area was changed. This change is listed only in *Jaguar E-Type: The Definitive History*.

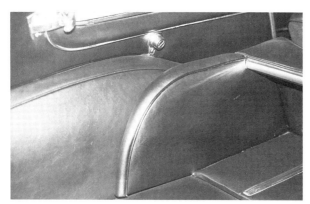
The rear-wheel arch trimming used on later 4.2-liter coupes.

The trunk floor area of a late 4.2-liter coupe. Note that the vinyl trimming is affixed to the floorboards.

Trunk-Lid Sealing Rubber

The trunk-lid sealing rubber for all 4.2-liter cars was on the edge of the trunk aperture, not on the lid.

Exterior and Interior Colors

As in the 3.8-liter section, the following listing is compiled from several lists published in various literature. These lists were similar, but not identical, so I have combined them to form a central list. Other sources contain basically the same information.

Exterior and Interior Colors 1965 to September 1967

Interior	Exterior
Black	Red, Grey, Light Tan, or Tan
Carmen Red	Black
Cream	Black
Dark Blue	Red, Light Blue, or Grey
Golden Sand	Red or Light Tan
Opalescent Dark Green	Suede Green, Beige, Light Tan, or Tan
Opalescent Maroon	Maroon or Beige
Opalescent Silver Blue	Grey or Dark Blue
Opalescent Silver Grey	Red, Light Blue, Dark Blue, or Grey
Pale Primrose	Black or Beige
Sherwood Green	Suede Green, Light Tan, or Tan
Warwick Grey	Red, Light Tan, or Dark Blue

Exterior and Interior Colors September 1967 to July 1968

Exterior	Interior
Beige	Red, Suede Green, Light Tan, or Tan
Black	Red, Grey, Tan, or Light Tan
British Racing Green	Suede Green, Beige, Light Tan, or Tan
Carmen Red	Black, Beige, or Red
Cream	Black
Dark Blue	Red, Light Blue, or Grey
Golden Sand	Red or Light Tan
Opalescent Maroon	Maroon or Beige
Opalescent Silver Blue	Grey or Dark Blue
Opalescent Silver Grey	Red, Light Blue, Dark Blue, or Grey
Pale Primrose	Black or Beige
Warwick Grey	Red, Light Tan, or Dark Blue
Willow Green	Grey, Suede Green, Light Tan, Tan, or Beige

Exterior and Interior Colors August 1968 to 1969

Interior	Exterior
Ascot Fawn	Red, Beige, or Cinnamon
Black	Red, Grey, Light Tan, Tan, or Cinnamon
British Racing Green	Suede Green, Beige, Cinnamon, or Tan
Cream	Black
Dark Blue	Red, Light Blue, or Grey
Light Blue	Dark Blue, Grey, or Light Blue
Pale Primrose	Black or Beige
Regency Red	Beige or Grey
Sable	Beige, Grey, or Cinnamon
Signal Red	Black, Biscuit, Dark Blue, Red, Beige, or Cinnamon
Warwick Grey	Red, Light Tan, Dark Blue, Beige, Cinnamon, or Black
Willow Green	Suede Green, Grey, Light Tan, Beige, or Cinnamon

Exterior and Interior Colors 1970 to March 1971

Interior	Exterior
Ascot Fawn	Red, Beige, or Cinnamon
Black	Red, Grey, Tan, Light Tan, or Cinnamon
British Racing Green	Suede Green, Beige, Tan, Light Tan, or Cinnamon
Dark Blue	Red, Light Blue, or Grey
Light Blue	Dark Blue, Grey, or Light Blue
Old English White	Black
Pale Primrose	Black or Beige
Regency Red	Beige or Grey
Sable	Beige, Grey, or Cinnamon
Warwick Grey	Red, Light Tan, Dark Blue, or Cinnamon
Willow Green	Grey, Suede Green, Tan, Light Tan, Beige, or Cinnamon

As in the case of the 3.8-liter cars, there were variations to these standards.

Serial-Number Markings

Serial numbers of different sorts are marked on the car in numerous places. The number plate, summarizing chassis, body, engine, and transmission numbers, is located on the horizontal areas in front of the hood latches. On earlier 4.2-liter cars, it was on the right side, and later it was found on the left side. When an auto- matic transmission was fitted, the serial-number plate denoted this fact. Later in production, the plate changed from the traditional Jaguar plate proportions to a more elongated shape, and it was mounted on the left-hand side.

On very late cars, the serial-number plate was changed again, and was moved to the left-hand-side

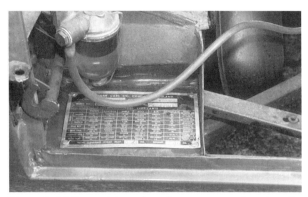

The early 4.2-liter serial-number plates were pop-riveted on the right-hand side of the engine compartment. This is the same position used for all the 3.8-liter cars.

Later on, the serial-number plate was mounted on the left-hand side of the engine compartment.

When an automatic transmission was fitted, a special serial-number plate was used. Note the "AUTOMATIC TRANSMISSION NO." marking in place of the "GEAR BOX NO." marking typically found on these plates. The automatic transmission was available on the 2+2 cars only. This plate should be retained by pop-rivets.

door panel. The date of manufacture was stamped on the plate. The engine, transmission, and body numbers were no longer included.

As in the case of the 3.8-liter cars, cars sold in California received an additional plate, with the letter J and the last two digits of the year of the car. This small aluminum plate was usually mounted near the factory serial-number plate.

The chassis numbers on post-1967 U.S.-specification cars were also displayed on the left side of the windshield on a small aluminum plate that could be seen from outside the car.

An RHD Series I 1/2 car is shown without a driver's side window chassis-number plate in *E-Type: End of an Era*, and an RHD Series II is shown without a window chassis-number plate.

The engine number on early 4.2-liter cars is stamped on the block above the oil filter, on the back of the cam chain area of the head, on the edge of the flywheel, and on the number plate. Later on, the engine numbers stamped on the head and above the oil filter were deleted, but the number was stamped on the block on the left-hand side where the bellhousing butts against it.

The transmission number is stamped only on the iron transmission case and on the number plate. There is no transmission number stamped on the top of the case, as was the case with the 3.8-liter cars.

The body number on early 4.2-liter cars is stamped on a pressed plate affixed to the rear of the body, under where the license plate goes, and on the number plate.

On Series II cars, the body number plate is found in the same region, but mounted off-center to the right.

As in the case of the 3.8-liter cars, the body number was often written in crayon on the body and frame in numerous places.

The differential number is stamped on the bottom of the differential housing case. This may have been omitted on later cars.

During Series II production, an elongated serial-number plate was adopted. It was mounted on the left-hand side of the engine compartment.

The very last Series II cars had this number plate on the left-hand door panel.

A California J66 plate mounted in a different location.

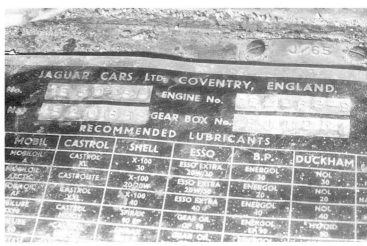

As with the 3.8-liter cars, special plates were added by the state of California. J/65 means 1965 Jaguar.

This windshield-frame-mounted chassis-number plate was required by U.S. regulations.

Later cylinder heads did not have the engine-number stampings that were found on the earlier cars.

On later cars, the engine number was stamped on the rear left-hand side of the block, near the bellhousing.

A serial-number plate is shown on the inner left wheelwell of the hood of an early RHD 4.2-liter car in *The Jaguar E-Type: A Collector's Guide.*

Changes at engine numbers 7R.6305/6 and 7R.38105/6: About August 1969, the engine number stamping was moved from the area above the oil filter to the left-side bellhousing flange, near to the dipstick.

Labels and Decals

Due to U.S. regulations, cars exported to the United States beginning April 1, 1968, had a tire recommendation plate in the inside of the glove compartment lid, telling the capacity weight of the car, seating capacity and distribution, tire pressure, and tire size. In addition, an information panel was molded in the wall of the tires, but some early tires had a label glued to them. This is listed only by Porter.

A negative-earth warning label was affixed to the heater in the Series I 4.2-liter cars. I am not sure if this label was found on any Series II cars; it appears to be absent from a Series II in Skilleter's book.

The run-in sticker was affixed to the inside of the driver's side of the windshield.

On some cars, a seatbelt-anchorage compliance plack was used. This is sometimes mounted in the area above the right-hand-side number plate, both facing to the right on the side of the footwell, and on the firewall above the right-hand-side number plate. It is also found on the firewall above the left-hand-side number plate. There are 1965 and 1968 versions of this plate.

At least three types of tuning-specification labels were applied to the air cleaners of the cars fitted with emission controls. While the early triangular-shaped air-cleaner plenum was still fitted, this label was made of aluminum and was pop-riveted to the top of the air cleaner.

The tuning-specification place is shown on the rear, carburetor side of the air-cleaner triangle plenum on a very early Series I 1/2 car in *Motor*, January 13, 1968, and on a U.S. model Series II air cleaner in Skilleter's book, but is absent from an English-specification car on the same page.

With the introduction of the later-style air cleaner, this label took the form of a sticker. I am aware of two types of these tuning-specification stickers that were fitted to the late-style Series II air cleaner. I have also seen them mounted farther back on the air cleaner.

A transmission number stamped on the transmission case. Unlike the 3.8-liter cars, no transmission number was stamped on the transmission cover.

An early, centrally mounted body-number plate on the rear of a 4.2-liter body.

A body-number plate mounted on the right rear of a Series II car.

This body number is crayoned on top of the front subframe member, just above the rack and pinion.

This body number written in crayon on the firewall of a Series II 2+2 is typical of the body-number markings found in various places on the car.

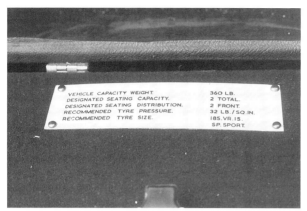

This glovebox-lid specification label is found on later cars.

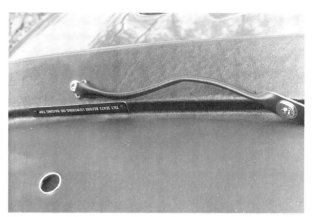

The convertible-top warning label warns to tilt the seat forward before raising or lowering the top.

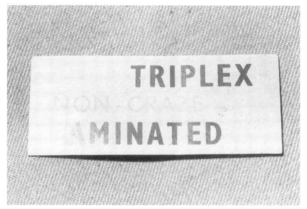

The front view of a Triplex sticker from the bottom center of the windshield of a Series I coupe.

The back view of the Triplex windshield sticker.

These windshield-mounted run-in stickers were mounted on the driver's side of the windshield.

This decal on the bottom center of the rear window of a Series I coupe identifies it as electrically heated.

Small, red plastic stickers were used on at least some of the Stromberg carburetors fitted to the emission-control cars. These say "FOR EMISSION CONTROL SYSTEM, PATENTS APPLIED FOR."

When the serial-number plate was changed to the small, doorjamb-mounted version late in Series II production, the tappet adjustment specification was removed. However, sometime before the number-plate change took place, this tappet information was supplied on a Tappet Clearance sticker affixed to the inner edge of the exhaust camshaft cover.

During Series I 1/2 production, a specification plate with information on the vehicle capacity and tires was added to the inside of the glovebox.

On the convertible top of 4.2-liter cars, there was an aluminum label warning to put the seats forward before lowering or raising the top.

On some Series I cars, a round incuse emission-control certification was on top of the crankcase vent pipe on the front of the cylinder head.

As with the 3.8-liter cars, the early 4.2-liter cars had a Lucas sticker on the coil. This differed from the 3.8-liter coil label in that Negative Earth was printed on it.

A brake-fluid specification sticker is found on some cars. This was sometimes affixed to the back of the heat shield, or on the firewall, just above the heater. On some

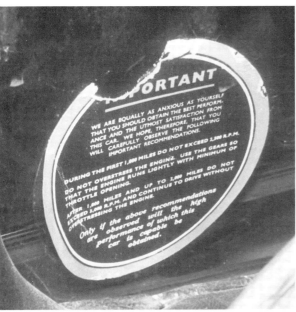

An inside view of a windshield run-in sticker.

This trip-counter-setting sticker is on a Series I car.

The California-approval markings on a Series I crankcase vent pipe.

A Negative Earth coil sticker on a Series I car.

This brake-fluid specification sticker is mounted on the brake and clutch reservoir heat shield of an LHD Series I car.

Brake-fluid specification stickers were mounted on the firewall of some Series II cars, just above the heater.

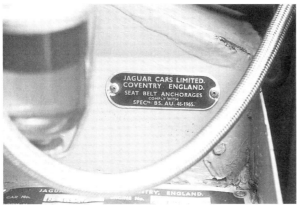

The seatbelt anchorage plates came in at least two types: 1965 and 1968. Here, a 1965-type seatbelt anchorage plate is seen mounted on the side of the footwell, above the right-hand-side number plate.

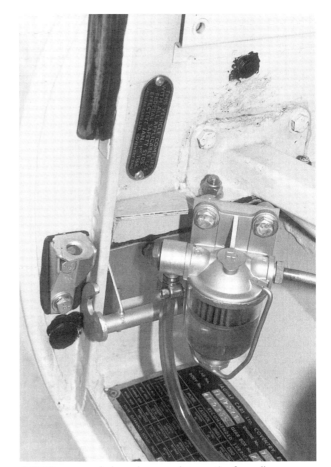

A 1968-type seatbelt anchorage plate on the firewall.

A 1965-type seatbelt anchorage plate on the firewall above the right-hand-side number plate. The undercoating is not original.

A 1968-type seatbelt anchorage plate on the firewall above a left-hand-side mounted number plate.

This tuning plate is pop-riveted on the air cleaner of an early U.S.-specification car.

A tuning specification sticker on the front of a late Series II air cleaner on a U.S.-specification car.

A second type of tuning specification sticker on the front of a late Series II air cleaner on a U.S.-specification car.

A tuning specification sticker mounted toward the rear of the air cleaner on a Series II U.S.-specification car.

When the 4.2-liter cars were introduced, the electrical system was changed from positive to negative ground. This was indicated by a warning label pop-riveted to the top of the heater box.

A tappet-clearance sticker on a late Series II camshaft cover. This information was previously contained on the serial-number plates.

The back of an aluminum marking strap on the master cylinder of a Series II car.

An emissions-control sticker inside the hood, on the back of the right front wheelwell, of a U.S.-specification 1970 Series II car.

A red plastic emission-control sticker on a Stromberg carburetor.

RHD cars, this sticker was fitted on the right-hand side of the firewall, just above the mounting for the brake fluid reservoirs.

Replacement brake-fluid reservoir caps sometimes carried metallic testing labels; see page 88.

On some late U.S.-specification Series II cars, an emission-control sticker was affixed to the inside of the right wheelwell wall, inside the hood.

As in the case of the 3.8-liter cars, the brake master cylinder often carries a strap on it.

Changes at engine numbers 14268/9: About December 1970, the designation of the compression ratio of the engine was changed from a number to a letter, thus H was for high compression, S for standard compression, and L for low compression. This change is listed only in *Jaguar E-Type: The Definitive History*.

The "JAGUAR" nameplate on the camshaft covers of Series I 1/2 and Series II cars came in two types, as discussed previously.

Various other labels appeared on some cars. For example, small rectangular labels were sometimes found on the side of the alternator and on the windshield squirter bottle and motor.

Dated Components

The electrical components and engine block were dated on the 4.2-liter cars in much the same way as on the 3.8-liter cars. Refer to chapter 5 for details.

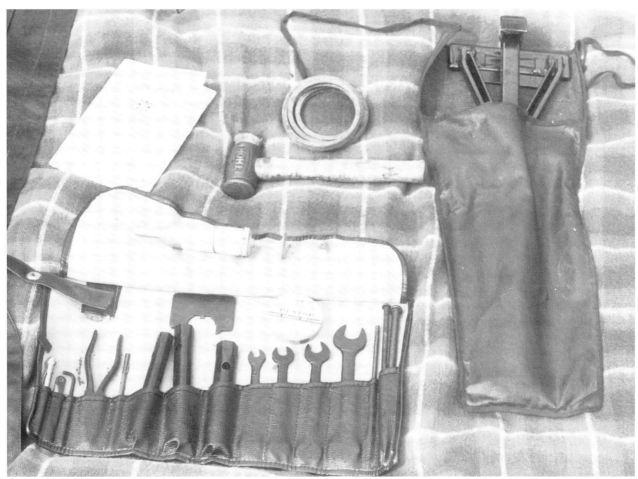

A 4.2-liter Series I tool kit. The adjustable wrench is missing.

Tools

The 4.2-liter cars used a tool roll to contain the tools, similar to most 3.8-liter cars.

A line illustration of the entire tool kit for a Series I 4.2-liter car shown in Jaguar handbook E/131/6. Beneath the illustration is the following inventory of the tools:

Jack
Hammer (copper and rawhide)
Hubcap removal tool
Bleeder tube
Valve timing gauge
Grease gun
Feeler gauge
Screwdriver for contact breaker points
Tire valve extractor
Tire pressure gauge
Adjustable spanner
Pliers
Tommy bar (short)
Box spanner [wrench] (sparking plugs and
    cylinder head nuts)
Box spanner 9/16x5/8 inch SAE)
Box spanner 7/16x 1/2 inch SAE)
Box spanner 3/4x7/8 inch SAE)
Open-ended spanner (11/32x3/8 inch AF)
Open-ended spanner (9/16x5/8 inch AF)
Open-ended spanner (1/2x7/16 inch AF)
Open-ended spanner (3/4x7/8 inch AF)
Tommy bar (long)
Combination screwdriver

While the hubcap removal tool is listed as part of the kit, it was supplied only for cars with earless hubcaps.

For the cars with earless hubcaps, the tool kit included a large brass wrench that fitted around the hubcap and allowed hammer blows to tighten or loosen it. Note that this is a different tool from the one used on the early earless hubcaps, as discussed in chapter 5.

While early cars had the iron, copper, and rawhide hammer of the 3.8-liter cars, the later ones had a single-piece hammer.

When the Series II cars came fitted with the Turbo Disk steel disc wheels, a lug wrench was supplied with the tool kit.

There are variations within the tool kits. For example, there are various makers of the open-end wrenches. Moreover, the small adjustable wrench is unique among

The tool roll and jack, in its bag, were stored inside the spare tire. This view is from a 6,000-mile original Series I 2+2.

Back view of the hubcap wrench.

The early, multipiece knock-off hammer had brass on one side and leather on the other. The main body was iron.

A late, single-piece knock-off hammer.

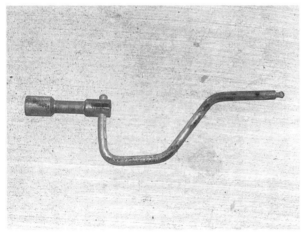

Cars fitted with the Turbo Disk wheels came with a lug wrench.

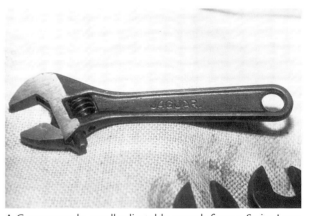

A German-made, small adjustable wrench from a Series I car. These were supplied from other countries as well.

the tools, I believe, in being often supplied by non-British firms. For some 4.2-liter cars, and perhaps for some of the 3.8-liters, this wrench was made in Germany and perhaps other European countries.

Another variation is found in the brake-bleeder hose can, which was supplied by Lockheed or Girling.

In the parts catalog for Series II E-Type open and fixed-head coupes, an air-conditioner dipstick is listed as available for servicing the air conditioning.

Jack

There were at least three styles of jacks. The first type had an attached handle, the second had a detached ratchet handle, and the latest type had a detached handle that was made of a single rod bent into a crank shape. This is the type of jack used with the Series III cars, and it was supplied with the late 1971 cars.

All jacks were supplied with a bag.

A typical painted Dunlop brake-bleeder hose can from a Series I car.

The brake-bleeder hose also came in an embossed Girling can. This one is from a Series I car.

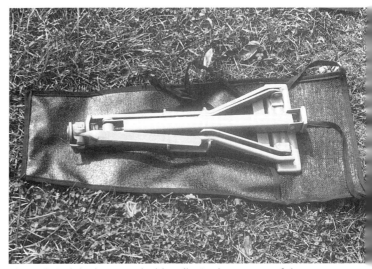

The early jack had an attached handle, in the manner of the late 3.8-liter cars.

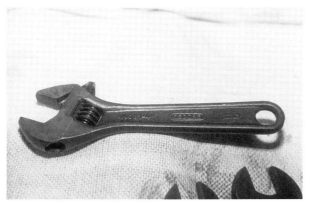

Back view of the German-made wrench. Note the "GEDORE" marking. The small letters to the right read "MADE IN GERMANY."

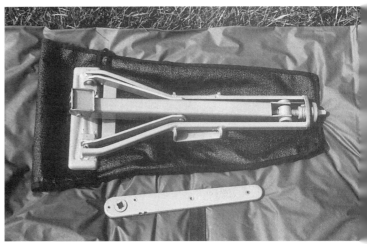

The later jack had a detached ratchet handle.

Literature: Driver's Handbooks

The Series I handbooks came in successive versions, as in the 3.8-liter case. Here the publication numbers are E/131/X, where X ran from 1 up to at least 6.

As in the case of the 3.8-liter cars, a large, foldout lubrication chart was inserted in the back of the handbooks.

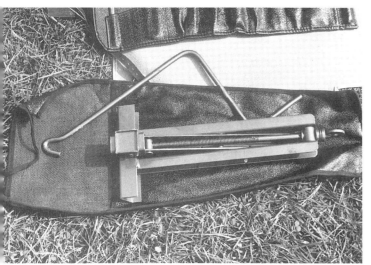

The last style of jack had a detached bent-rod crank handle. This is the same sort used on the early Series III V-12 cars.

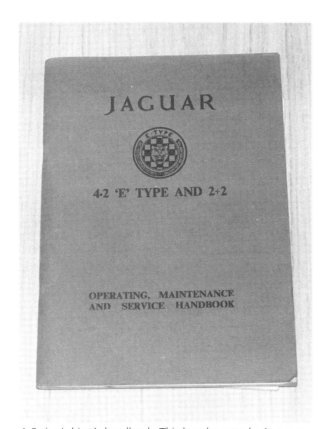

A Series I driver's handbook. This has the same basic proportion and appearance as the 3.8-liter handbooks.

Pouches and Service Vouchers

A typical selection for a Series I car is illustrated here. Even though it is not part of the standard literature package, the U.S.-delivery price sticker is interesting.

Service Manuals

The service manuals for the Series I 4.2-liter cars consisted of a 3.8-liter service manual with a 4.2-liter supplement. The suffixes of the printing numbers of the supplements involved letters as well as numbers.

While the service manual available with most Series I 4.2-liter cars seems to have been the ring-bound type, I know of at least one instance where an early, bolt-bound unnumbered 3.8-liter manual was supplied with a 4.2-liter supplement for a 1967 car. The supplement was much like the usual ones found in the ring-binder type manuals, but it had an introduction section with ghost-views of the entire car. The supplement was publication number E/123A/1.

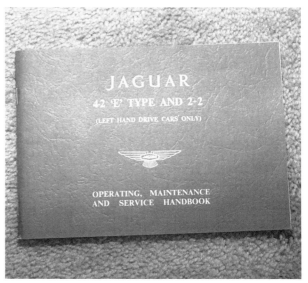

A Series I 1/2 driver's handbook.

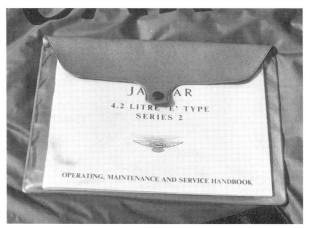

Series II driver's handbook, in its vinyl pouch.

The more common 4.2-liter supplements were the ring-bound type. Their printing numbers went at least as high as E/123B/2.

Spare Parts Catalogs

Unlike the 3.8-liter cars, where there was only one spare parts catalog, J.30, there were at least four types of 4.2-liter spare parts catalogs. J.37 covers the Series I 4.2-liter cars (but does not go quite to the end of the Series I production). It came in its initial version of November 1965, and in a reprint version of November 1969.

J.38 covers the Series I 2+2 cars and, as far as I have been able to determine, came only in the December 1966 version.

I am not aware of any spare parts catalog specifically covering the Series I 1/2 cars.

The Series II cars are covered by at least two catalogs. The first of these is the 1969 Interim Parts Catalog (there is no publication number), which covers the early Series II cars. More complete coverage is given in the microfiche parts listings, a late version of which is labeled Series 2 E-Type Open and Fixed-Head Coupe

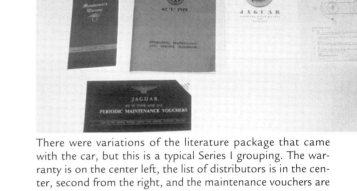

There were variations of the literature package that came with the car, but this is a typical Series I grouping. The warranty is on the center left, the list of distributors is in the center, second from the right, and the maintenance vouchers are on the bottom.

This early bolt-bound manual was supplied with a 1966 Series I 2+2.

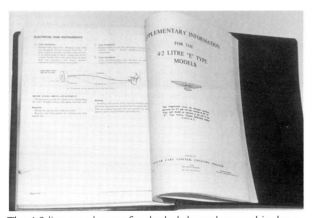

The 4.2-liter supplement for the bolt-bound manual is shown here. This supplement is marked publication number E.123A/1.

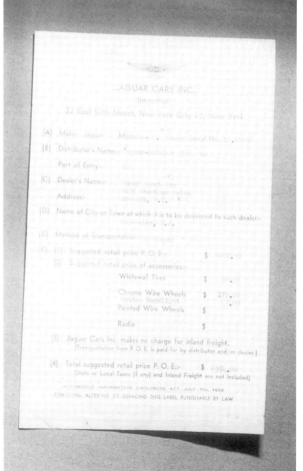

The price sticker from a Series I 2+2 sold new in Amherst, New York.

Parts catalog, part number RTC9873FA, dated January 1979. This is currently available as part number RTC009873FA.

Service Bulletin Books

Jaguar supplied ringed notebooks containing their service bulletins. These were not assigned to a particular model, but covered all Jaguar models over a given period.

Options and Variations: Axle Ratios

A limited-slip differential was standard on early 4.2-liter coupes.

A 3.54:1 differential was used for Series II cars exported to the United States and Canada without limited-slip; a 3.07:1 differential was used for cars exported to these countries with limited-slip; and all other countries had a 3.07:1 differential as standard.

The side-view mirror on a U.S.-specification car.

Top view of a Hickok buckle from a Series I 2+2.

Wheels

The May 1965 issue of *Road Test* stated that chrome wheels are an option, but that 95 percent of the cars sold in the United States have chrome wheels, and painted wheels are available by special order only.

Wire or pressed steel wheels (Turbo Disks) were available for the Series II cars.

Tires and Tubes

As outlined earlier in this chapter, various tires were offered on the 4.2-liter cars over time.

In *Jaguar E-Type: The Definitive History*, Porter stated that the Dunlop SP Sport radials were adopted on the Series I 1/2, but had been an option on the home-market cars since 1965.

Mirrors

With the introduction of the Series I 1/2, the U.S.-specification cars came fitted with a driver's side side-view mirror. This curved-stem exterior mirror, seen mounted on an early Series I 1/2 coupe in *Motor*, January 13, 1968, is stated to be an item specified by the U.S. safety regulations. However, no exterior mirror is shown on an RHD Series II 2+2 in the June 1970 issue of *Car* magazine, so it was not supplied on cars for all markets.

The left-hand sun visor for RHD, FHC cars came with a mirror at special order only.

Seatbelts

Seatbelts are said to be an option on an early LHD coupe pictured in *Road Test* magazine, May 1965.

Changes at chassis numbers 1E.50573/4 and 1E.76888/9 (and certain individual earlier cars): Seatbelts were available for the rear seats.

For the early 2+2 cars, seatbelt anchorages were standard.

In *Motor*, April 30, 1966, in one illustration, seatbelts are mentioned as if standard, but on another page they are cited as optional.

Pictures of 2+2 interiors in the literature show two common seatbelt configurations: seatbelts with shoulder harnesses, and seatbelt mounts with no seatbelts fitted.

Bottom view of a Hickok buckle from a Series I 2+2.

In one case, in *The Jaguar Story*, a 2+2 is shown with front lap belts but no shoulder harnesses.

Autocar magazine, October 12, 1967, in discussing a Series I RHD roadster, stated that seatbelt anchorages were built in, but that seatbelts were an option.

In the parts catalog for open and fixed-head coupes, an escutcheon and screw for the safety harness points of the FHC models are listed as not required when a safety harness is fitted. This indicates that some Series II cars did not come standard with safety harnesses.

There were different sorts of seatbelts fitted to the 4.2-liter cars. Hickok belts with the Jaguar wing stamping were supplied with some early U.S.-specification Series I 4.2-liter cars. Later on, the Kangol magnetically actuated three-point seatbelts were supplied. The upper attachment point on the three-point belts was originally a bolt, but later this was changed to a reel.

Top view of a magnetic Kangol buckle from a late Series II roadster.

Bottom view of a magnetic Kangol buckle from a late Series II roadster.

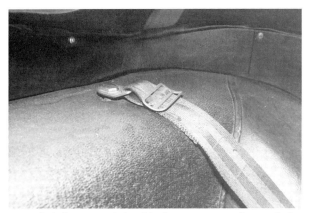

An early bolt-mounted shoulder-harness mount from a Series II car.

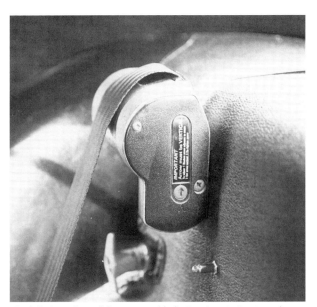

The left view of a reel from Kangol belts in a late Series II roadster.

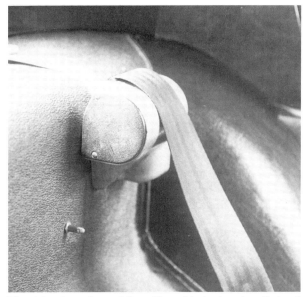

The right view of a reel from Kangol belts in a late Series II roadster.

This unusual nine-band Motorola "RADIOMOBILE" radio is from a 1967 French-specification LHD coupe.

The nine-band radio, with a different band selected to illustrate how it changes bands. Note that the frequency band is different and the right rear knob has been turned.

A typical Blaupunkt radio fitted to a Series I car.

Radio, Suppressor Capacitor, Antenna, and Blanking Plate

Common radios fitted to 4.2-liter Series I cars were the Motorola Radiomobiles and Blaupunkts. A common radio for the Series II cars is the Phillips AM/FM/SW.

An interesting Smith Radiomobile radio was fitted to a French-market 1967 model Series I coupe. It had nine separate bands that were accessed by turning the back knob on the right side. As this knob turned, a cylinder with nine different frequency-label strips on it rotated behind the frequency display window. The frequencies ranged from 600 kHz to 17.9 mHz.

The radio antennas were typically fitted to the cowl, on the same side as the steering wheel.

When no radio was fitted, a blanking plate was fitted by the factory. This plate was apparently the same on all types of 4.2-liter cars; see illustration on page 96.

A suppressor capacitor is shown bolted to the front subframe, next to the alternator, on an early LHD coupe in *Cars Illustrated*, March 1965.

Locking Gas Cap

The locking gas cap (WB.7/8653, Jaguar part number C.12816) is listed as an option in spare parts catalogs November 1969 J.37 and December 1966 J.38. It is listed merely as part number C.12816 in the Interim Parts List and in the open and fixed-head coupe parts catalog. This is the same Jaguar part number as used for the 3.8-liter cap.

174

Another version of a Blaupunkt radio from a Series I car.

A radio marked "JAGUAR" in a Series II 2+2.

A later Blaupunkt radio fitted to a Series I 1/2 car.

Key Fob

The Series I fobs are discussed in parts catalogs November 1969 J.37 and December 1966 J.38, where two key fobs are listed: part number 11/721 with the Jaguar wings, and part number 11/723 with the Jaguar badge.

I think this is the same key fob that was an option on the 3.8-liter cars. A key fob supplied new with a Series I 2+2 is almost identical to the fob that came with an early 3.8-liter roadster, with the only prominent difference being the size of the Made in England lettering on the back of the escutcheon. I know the complete history on the cars these two fobs came from, and in both cases the fobs were supplied by the dealers when the cars were delivered to their first owners.

Hardtop

The removable hardtop was available throughout the production run of 4.2-liter cars. I am not aware of any changes.

Tinted Glass

Tinted glass in the rear coupe window is listed as an option for the Series I cars in catalogs November 1969 J.37 and December 1966 J.38. However, it is not listed in the Series II parts catalogs.

This Phillips AM/FM/SW radio is fitted to a U.S.-specification Series II car. The center button, marked S, is for short-wave operations.

The key fob and keys supplied new with a Series I 2+2. This is basically the same fob seen earlier (although there are minor differences), and is likely the one listed in spare parts catalog J.37.

The back view of the Jaguar medallion on the fob. Contrast the lettering here to the fob shown earlier, supplied new with an early 3.8-liter car.

The early vertical, high-density rear-window defroster wires on a Series I coupe.

A rear-window defroster switch with warning light from a 1967 Series I coupe.

The indicator light for the rear-window defroster on the Series II cars was locate in approximately the same location as the control switch had been on earlier cars.

The late Series II cars all came with a hole in the dash for the rear-window defroster indicator light. When no rear defroster was fitted, the hole was plugged. This plug is on the dash of a 1971 Series II roadster.

The later horizontal, low-density defroster wires on a Series II coupe.

The rear-window defroster switch on the Series II cars was located on the central switch row.

Anti-Mist Element

In *Jaguar E-Type 3.8 & 4.2 6-cylinder; 5.3 V-12*, Jenkinson stated that the coupe rear-window heater element came in with 4.2-liter cars. However, it is discussed as an option for the 3.8-liter cars in chapter 4, so there is some ambiguity here. It is listed as a Series I option in November 1969 J.37 and December 1966 J.38. In both cases there is no mention of starting serial numbers, implying it was available from the beginning of the 4.2-liter production.

A demister switch with integral light is shown on a Series I car in the line drawing in Jaguar handbook E/131/6.

On late Series I 1/2 and Series II cars, the rear-window defroster system was different. The spacing and size of the wires were larger, and the switch was moved to the center switch row. The indicator light remained above the brake warning light.

Later on in Series II production, all cars were produced with a hole for the light. The hole was plugged if there was not a defroster fitted. This applies even to roadsters.

Changes at chassis numbers 1E.21222/3, 1E.32608/9, 1E.50001, and 1E.75001: The rear defroster switch was changed and a warning light was added. The warning lamp dims when the sidelights are on. Dates of April 1966 and July 1967 were given in various sources for this change.

Air Conditioning

Air conditioning became a standard option on the Series I 1/2 cars, but some late Series I cars may have been supplied with it. Mention is made of air conditioning being fitted to an early 4.2-liter coupe in *Autosport* magazine, March 11, 1966, but it is not stated whether or not it was a factory installation.

An air-conditioner dipstick was available for servicing the air conditioning, according to the open and fixed-head coupe parts catalog.

Changes at chassis numbers 1R.1183/4, 1R.9456/7, 1R.20260/1, and 1R.26319/20: The air conditioning was changed from the early type (which did not permit the fitting of power steering) to the later type. As a special note,

the fixed-head coupe catalog states that the late-type installation was also fitted to chassis numbers 1R.1152, 1R.9207, 1R.9451, 1R.9453, 1R.20223, and 1R.20245.

Jaguar E-Type: A Collector's Guide states that Series I cars with air conditioning have an expansion tank mounted on the firewall with a 13-pound cap (in addition to the header tank), as of June 1967.

In the January 1969 issue of *Popular Imported Cars*, a five-bladed fan, with what appear to be aluminum

An air-conditioning receiver mounted on the right-hand side of the engine compartment on a Series II car.

The air-conditioning compressor on a Series II car.

Some air-conditioning receivers were mounted on the left-hand side of the engine compartment.

blades, is shown mounted on the front of the air-conditioner condenser on the front of the radiator of an LHD Series I 1/2 roadster. The associated text says that this fan was fitted on cars with air conditioning. I have seen no other evidence for such a fan.

In a feature on a Series II LHD roadster, *Car and Driver*, May 1969, stated that two cooling fans are operated thermostatically, unless air conditioning is fitted, in which case they are both kept on at all times. No mention of a third fan is made.

Air conditioning is said to be an option (for the Series II), and also last-year Series I 1/2 cars. In *Jaguar E-Type: The Definitive History*, Porter stated that Series II air conditioning was not available on RHD cars.

The air-conditioning receiver had several different mounting positions, as seen in the illustrations.

Transmissions
The Borg-Warner Model B automatic transmission was an option on the 2+2 only.

Flywheel
An optional racing flywheel was available.

Block Heater
A block heater is listed as an option in Jaguar's open and fixed-head coupe Series II parts catalog.

This interior view shows an air-conditioning installation on a Series II car.

An alternate air-conditioning console for a 2+2 car with automatic transmission. Note the absence of a cigarette lighter in the lower right.

A view of the combination alternator and air-conditioning compressor mount. The compressor is removed for a good view of the bracket.

Changes at engine numbers 7E.16335/6 and 7E.54361/2: About July 1968, cylinder block heaters were made standard for Canada. This change is listed only in Porter's *Jaguar E-Type: The Definitive History*.

A 240-volt block heater was available, but not for use in Canada.

Bumper Guards

In *Road Test* magazine, May 1965, the bumper guards are said to be a $60 option, but one that the cars typically come with. The front guards are shown, and it is even suggested that they may be fitted to the cars at the dock. This is in line with Porter's suggestion that the guards on 3.8-liter cars may have sometimes been factory-fitted. The test car shown in *Car and Driver*, February 1965, has a front bumper guard fitted, but none on the rear.

Power Steering

There is some ambiguity in the literature about the fitting of power steering. *Road & Track*, January 1969, stated that power steering was a new option that came in with the 2+2. *Motor* magazine, March 21, 1970, stated that power steering came in as an option after the introduction of the Series II, and therefore wasn't available on very early Series II cars.

Power steering was available on cars with manual transmissions, and one such car, a RHD Series II 2+2, is cited in the November 18, 1970, issue of *Autocar*.

Oil Cooler

Jaguar E-Type: A Collector's Guide states that an oil cooler kit was available as an option for all Series I cars from April 1969.

Top view of the optional power-steering rack and pinion assembly on a Series II.

Bottom view of a power-steering rack and pinion assembly on a Series II.

Front view of a power-steering pump on a Series II.

Rear view of a power-steering pump on a Series II.

A power-steering fluid reservoir on a Series II car.

Chapter 8

4.2-LITER ENGINE, DRIVETRAIN, AND CHASSIS COMPONENT CHANGES

This chapter covers changes made to the 4.2-liter E-Type's engine, drivetrain, chassis, and other mechanical parts.

Engine: Cylinder Block

Changes at engine numbers 7R.1914/5 and 7R.35388/9: The cylinder block assembly was changed (the core plugs and the block heater were changed), and the front timing cover was changed.

Changes at engine numbers 7R.5541/2 and 7R.37654/5: About June 1969, the water drain spigot on the block was changed to a drain plug, and the fiber washer was deleted, but the copper washer was retained.

Early 4.2-liter cars had a block drain spigot, as found on 3.8-liter cars.

Cylinder Head and Camshaft Covers

Changes at engine numbers 7E.2895/6: The exhaust-side camshaft cover was changed, and the fiber washer on the filler cap was changed to an O-ring.

Changes at engine numbers 7E.6332/3: The exhaust manifold studs were changed.

Changes at engine numbers 7E.7449/50 and 7E.50021/2: In late 1966 or early 1967, the valve guides were fitted with circlips to ensure their location in the head.

Changes at engine numbers 7E.9209/10 and 7E.50962/3: About December 1966, the cylinder head gasket was changed. This change is listed only in Porter's *Jaguar E-Type: The Definitive History*.

Changes at engine numbers 7E.11667/8 and 7E.52686/7: About March 1967, oil seals were fitted to the inlet-valve guides. This change is listed only in Skilleter's *The Jaguar E-Type: A Collector's Guide*.

Changes at engine numbers 7E.17864/5 and 7E.52452/3: About December 1968, the valve seats were changed. This change is listed only by Porter.

Changes at engine numbers 7R.1914/5 and 7R.35388/9: The cylinder head studs, the cylinder head assembly, and gasket set were changed.

Autosport magazine, October 29, 1970, stated that the cylinder head studs were recently increased in length. It was stated in the May 1969 issue of *Car and Driver* that the cylinder head studs were increased in length from 4 to 12 inches.

Changes at engine numbers 7R.2082/3 and 7R.35462/3: The camshaft covers and studs at the front of the head for fixing the camshaft covers were changed for U.S. and Canadian cars only.

Changes at engine numbers 7R.4158/9 and 7R.36599/600: About May 1969, the camshaft cover mounts at the front were changed to countersunk screws.

Changes at engine numbers 7R.8687/8: The cylinder head assembly and the camshaft covers were changed.

Changes at engine numbers 7R.8767/8 and 7R.38894/5: About January 1970, the camshaft covers were changed so that all cars had mounting holes for the emission-control warm-air duct, even if the duct was not fitted.

In *Modern Motor* magazine, March 1971, grooved camshaft covers are shown on a late RHD Series II engine (with three HD8 carburetors) with grooves in the center to accommodate the absent center crossover pipe.

At least some of the early grooved camshaft covers had a separate cast-aluminum "JAGUAR" label attached. The later grooved camshaft covers had this label cast into them. This is the common configuration.

Sometime after the camshaft covers were changed from the traditional polished aluminum to the grooved type, the name "JAGUAR" on the oil-filler cap (on the left camshaft) was deleted. From research of surviving cars: Serial number 1E.17271 (engine numbers 7E.16522–9) had the Jaguar oil-filler cap, and 1E.34580 (engine numbers 7E.14113–9) and 1E.35084 (engine numbers 7E.15872–9) had the blank oil-filler cap.

Interestingly, pictured in *Jaguar E-Type: The Definitive History* is a late six-cylinder engine shown in a Series III E-Type with Jaguar on the oil-filler cap. This may imply that some of the late Series II cars had labeled oil-filler caps. However, Skilleter's *The Jaguar E-Type: A Collector's Guide* featured another six-cylinder Series III car shown without Jaguar on the oil-filler cap. Skilleter indicated that about four of these six-cylinder Series III cars were made, so they are likely very nonstandard and little about the production cars can be deduced from them.

Oil Pan and Plug

Changes at engine numbers 7E.2693/6: The oil pan was changed about April 1965.

Changes at engine numbers 7E.10008/9 and 7E.52154/5: About March 1967, the front seal on the oil pan was changed. This change is listed only in Porter's *Jaguar E-Type: The Definitive History*.

Changes at engine numbers 7R.1345/6 and 7R.35088/9: About December 1968, the pointer for the timing marks was moved from the bottom of the engine to the left-hand side. This change is listed only by Porter.

Changes at engine numbers 7R.5338/9 and 7R.37549/50: About May 1969, the pointer for the timing marks on the crankshaft damper was moved from the left-hand side of the engine back to the bottom of the engine (where it had been before), for cars with air conditioning or power steering. This change is listed only by Porter.

Starter Motor

I am not aware of any changes.

Engine Mounts

I am not aware of any changes.

Crankcase Breather

Changes at chassis numbers 1E.1252/3, 1E.11048/9, 1E.20691/2, and 1E.31077/9: About September 1965, the front cylinder-head cover and the crankcase breather arrangement were changed from the non-U.S. type to a standard type for all cars.

Early Series II cars had domed-nut retaining nuts on the front of the cam covers, in the manner of earlier Jaguars.

Late Series II cars had a block drain plug instead of the earlier spigot.

On the later Series II cars, a Phillips screw was used to retain the front of the cam covers.

Changes at chassis numbers 1E.2050/1, 1E.31806/7, and 1E.51212/3: About May 1968, the breather pipe was changed to the type already fitted to LHD cars.

Oil Filter Assembly

Changes at engine numbers 7E.5169/70: About November 1965, the oil filter changed from felt to paper. This change is listed only by Porter.

Changes at engine numbers 7R.2297/8 and 7R.35582/3: The oil filter assembly was changed.

Timing Chain Cover

Changes at engine numbers 7E.6332/3: The bolt holding the timing chain cover to the cylinder block was changed to allow attachment of the alternator shield.

Crankshaft Damper and Pulley

Changes at engine numbers 7E.10956/7 and 7E.52607/8: About July 1967, the crankshaft damper was changed. This change is listed only in *Jaguar E-Type: The Definitive History.*

Changes at engine numbers 7R.13198/9 and 7R.40325/6: About August 1970, the crankshaft distance piece at the front of the shaft was replaced by a distance piece with an O-ring.

Oil Dipstick

The dipstick on the Series I and Series I 1/2 cars was the same as used on the late 3.8-liter cars. With the introduction of the Series II, it was changed to a type with a red plastic disc on the top.

Early oil-filler caps had an incuse "JAGUAR" marking on them. This was discontinued sometime shortly after the introduction of the finned cam covers.

A late oil-filler cap without markings.

The "JAGUAR" label on the grooved camshaft cover of this late Series I 1/2 is a separate casting from the cover.

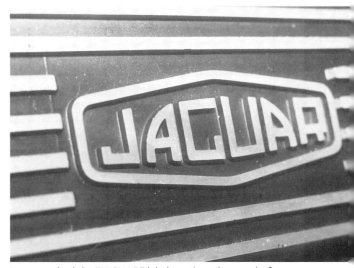

Later cars had the "JAGUAR" label cast into the camshaft cover.

The Jaguar E-Type: A Collector's Guide pictures two early Series II cars. The LHD car has the plastic dipstick, while the U.S.-specification car has the early metal dipstick.

Crankshaft, Connecting Rods, Bearings, Caps, Pistons, and Rings

Changes at engine numbers "7E.1001 to 7E.0000" and then "7E.0000 and subs": The main bearings were changed.

Changes at engine numbers 7E.1336/7: About December 1964, the connecting rods were changed. The new rods have a small hole at the small end to spray oil. This change is listed only by Porter.

Changes at engine numbers 7E.14212/3 and 7E.53742/3: About July 1968, the connecting-rod bearings were changed. This change is listed only by Porter.

In January 1969 the connecting-rod nuts, bolts, and split pins were changed to bolts and plain nuts. The tightening torque was also changed. This change is reported only by Porter.

A bottom-mounted timing mark.

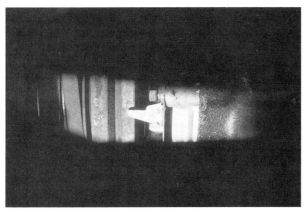

A side-mounted timing mark.

Bottom view of the side-mounted timing mark.

The early Series I 1/2 and Series II oil filter assemblies were similar to those used on the earlier cars.

A late Series II oil filter assembly. Note the large-diameter collar.

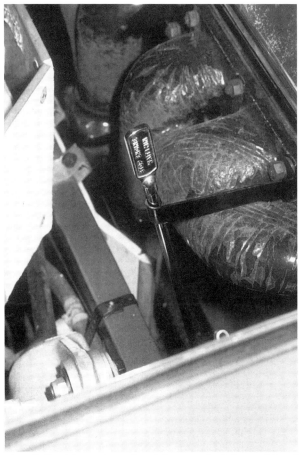

The oil dipstick on the early 4.2-liter cars had the traditional "STOP ENGINE, WAIT 1 MIN" warning cast in the metal.

The later oil dipsticks had the warning on a red plastic insert.

In July 1968 for 9:1 compression engines, the Hepworth-Grandage solid-skirt pistons replaced the Birco split-skirt pistons.

Valves, Valve Gear, Camshafts, Chains, and Sprockets

Changes at engine numbers 7E.50021/2: The shaft assembly for the intermediate timing-chain sprocket was changed.

Changes at engine numbers 7E.50024/5: About September 1966, the intermediate sprocket was changed to cast iron. This change is listed only by Porter.

Changes at engine numbers 7R.8687/8 and 7R.38854/5: About November 1969, the camshafts were changed to give quieter valve operation and longer periods between valve adjustments.

Changes at engine numbers 7R.14074/5: About October 1970, the camshafts were changed so as to have no oil hole in the back. This was to reduce oil consumption.

Oil Pump and Oil Delivery System

Changes at engine numbers 7R.7503/4 and 7R.38501/2: About October 1969, the oil pump shaft was changed from one with a pinned-on inner rotor to one with a pressed-on rotor. This change is listed only in *Jaguar E-Type: The Definitive History*.

Fuel System: Carburetors, Manifolds, and Associated Emission-Control Equipment

Some Series II exhaust manifolds were porcelainized and some were not. On the last U.S.-specification Series II cars, with the central crossover pipe, the exhaust manifolds were not porcelainized, and a shroud was used to direct intake air over the hot exhaust manifolds.

There were three basic styles of crossover pipes used on the emission-control cars. They occurred in the following order: the early rear-mounted crossover pipe, no crossover pipe, and the latest centrally mounted crossover pipe.

Sometimes the plastic damper assembly caps on the tops of the carburetors are found in a light tone instead of the standard black, but I think this is the result of fading with time rather than the existence of a different type of cap. This is illustrated on page 104. Some replacement caps had the "AUC" marking in white letters, as opposed to being cast in as with the caps supplied with the cars (see illustration on page 105).

Changes at chassis numbers 1E.1252/3, 1E.11048/9, 1E.20691/2, and 1E.31077/8: The inlet

The intake-side view of an early air-intake crossover pipe on a U.S.-specification car. These early crossover pipes were polished aluminum.

manifold stud for the water outlet was changed, and a stud and distance piece for the water outlet pipe and breather pipe were added for non-U.S. cars.

Changes at engine numbers 7E.1724/5: About January 1965, the inlet manifold was changed. The pressed-in vacuum fitting was replaced with a screwed-in one. This change is listed only by Porter.

Changes at engine numbers 7E.1881/2: About March 1965, the inlet manifold gasket was changed. This change is listed only by Porter.

Changes at engine numbers 7E.7297/8 and 7E.50021/2: About September 1966, a low-lift carburetor cam was introduced to reduce engine speed when the choke was put on. This included changes in the jet housing of the carburetors.

Changes at engine numbers 7R.1837/8 and 7R.35329/30: The inlet manifold and associated hardware, the carburetors, and accelerator linkage were changed for U.S. and Canadian cars only.

Changed at engine numbers 7R.2082/3 and 7R.35462/3: The rear exhaust manifold, the mixture housing on top of the rear exhaust manifold and its associated hardware, and the clip holding the dipstick were changed for U.S. and Canadian cars only.

On the home-market Series I 1/2 and Series II cars, the carburetors remained three SU HD8s.

The exhaust-side view of an early air-intake crossover pipe on a U.S.-specification car.

The intake-side view of a later engine without an air-intake crossover pipe.

A shrouded exhaust manifold on a later car.

Exhaust-side view of a late air-intake crossover pipe on a U.S.-specification car.

Fuel Filter and Lines

Changes at chassis numbers 1E.1895/6, 1E.16009/10, 1E.21628/9, 1E.34633/4, 1E.51016/7, and 1E.77694/5: About July 1968, the fuel filter was changed to one with more filter area. This change is listed only by Porter.

Changes at chassis numbers 1E.1904/5, 1E.16056/7, 1E.21661/2, 1E.32771/2, 1E.51042/3, and 1E.77700/1: The fuel filter element was changed from gauze to a renewable fiber element. In *Jaguar E-Type: The Definitive History*, Porter cites a date of about July 1968 for this change, while Skilleter, in *The Jaguar E-Type: Collector's Guide*, cites about February 1968. In addition, Skilleter cites chassis numbers 1E.34771/2 instead of 1E.32771/2, and numbers 1E.50142/3 instead of 1E.51042/3.

Changes at engine numbers 7E.9291/2 and 7E.51101/2: About December 1966, the fuel lines from the filter to the carburetors were changed. This change is listed only by Porter.

Air Filter

Changes at chassis numbers 1E.1252/3, 1E.11048/9, 1E.20691/2, and 1E.31077/8: The base assembly for the air intake with three trumpets, and the adapter for the breather pipe were changed to a standard type for all cars (U.S. cars were no different).

Changes at chassis numbers 1E.1464/5, 1E.12521/2, 1E.21214/5, and 1E.32596/7: About September 1966, the air cleaner and its support bracket were changed. This change is listed only by Porter.

Gas Tank

Changes at chassis numbers 1R.1067/8, 1R.7992/3, 1R.20118/9, 1R.25523/4, 1R.35797/8, and 1R.40667/8: About March 1969, the top part of the gas tank was changed.

This charcoal canister on a 1970 Series II roadster was part of the fuel evaporation containment system required by U.S. regulations. It is mounted next to the brake vacuum assist.

The early Series II air cleaners were of the sort used on Series I cars.

The late Series II air cleaners were more compact, and fed into the central crossover pipe.

The early gas tanks had a single vent on the top.

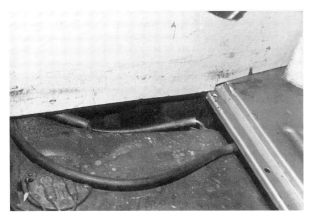
Later gas tanks had multiple vents.

Later 4.2-liter gas tank sumps had a drain bolt on the bottom.

The early 4.2-liter gas tank sumps were similar to the later 3.8-liter sumps; they did not have a drain bolt at the bottom.

Changes at chassis numbers 1R.1392/3, 1R.11051/2, 1R.20485/6, and 1R.27050/1: The gas tank and cap were changed.

The later gas tanks had multiple, small vents on the left-hand side, as opposed to the single vent near the filter aperture.

The drain sump on the later 4.2-liter cars had a drain bolt in the bottom. This change occurred around the time of the Series I 1/2.

Fuel Pump, Mount, and Fuel Lines

The fuel pump was changed from the submerged type to an external type when the 4.2-liter was introduced. However, I am not aware of any design changes.

Fuel-Level Sender Unit

I am not aware of any design changes.

Ignition System: Coil and Bracket

Changes at engine numbers 7E.16754/5 and 7E.54608/9: About July 1968, the coil was changed to one with a push-in high-tension coil wire, and with + and - replacing SW and CB. This change is listed only in *Jaguar E-Type: The Definitive History*.

The coil on Series I 1/2 and early Series II cars was found sometimes mounted on the top of the intake manifold, and sometimes at the front of the cylinder head (the position it was found on in the Series I cars). The later Series II cars had the coil mounted on the right front frame cross-member.

Later replacement Lucas coils can differ markedly from those originally fitted. For example, see the illustrations of the replacement coil with the white plastic insulation cap on page 110.

Distributor

Changes at engine numbers 7R.7973/4 (and 7R.7506): The distributor was changed.

Distributor Rotor, Cap, and Wire Retainers

Changes at engine numbers 7E.2458/9: About April 1965, a waterproof cover was added to the distributor. This change is listed only by Porter.

A suppressor was used on the distributor cap of Series II cars exported to Denmark.

Spark-Plug Wires and Organizers

It appears that all 4.2-liter cars, to the last Series IIs, had the vinyl conduit tube for the spark-plug wires lying in the trough of the cylinder head.

Spark-Plug Caps

The spark-plug caps came in at least two types for the Series I 4.2-liter cars: the oval-top caps and the bow-tie top caps. The bow-tie caps are more typical.

A front-mounted coil on a Series I 1/2 engine.

A coil mounted on the intake manifold of a Series II engine.

The frame-mounted coil on a late Series II.

The SW marking is evident on this early coil.

On later coils, + and - replaced the SW and CB markings on the earlier coils.

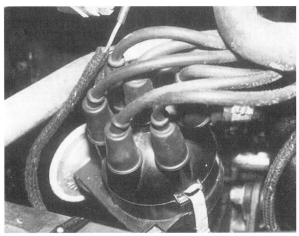

Rubber distributor-cap covers.

Spark Plugs

Champion N.5 spark plugs were used on 4.2-liter Series I cars.

Ballast Resistor

Changes at chassis numbers 1R.1392/3, 1R.11051/2, 1R.20485/6, 1R.27050/1, 1R.35642/3, and 1R.42849/50: About January 1970, a ballast resistor was added to the ignition system.

Cooling System: Radiator and Fan Shroud

Changes at chassis numbers 1E.2050/1, 1E.31806/7, and 1E.51212/3: The radiator was changed to a vertical-flow type, as already fitted to LHD cars. The date for this change is alternately listed as April and July of 1968.

Changes at chassis numbers 1R.1183/4, 1R.9456/7, 1R.20260/1, and 1R.26319/20: The cooling fan cowl was changed.

Changes at chassis numbers 1R.1189/90, 1R.9594/5, 1R.20271/2, and 1R.26401/2: The radiator was changed.

Header Tank

Changes at chassis numbers 1E.2050/1, 1E.31806/7, and 1E.51212/3: About July 1968, the header tank and cap were changed. This change is listed only in *Jaguar E-Type: The Definitive History*.

Water Pump and Pulley

Changes at engine numbers 7E.1404/5: About December 1964, the pulley and water pump were changed to make removal easier. The studs and bolts for the water pump were changed to bolts.

Changes at chassis numbers 1E.2050/1, 1E.31806/7, and 1E.51212/3: About April or July 1968, the water pump assembly was changed to the type already fitted to LHD cars.

Changes at engine numbers 7E.17157/8 and 7E.54836/7: About June 1968, the water pump pulley and

An oval-top spark-plug cap on a Series I 4.2-liter car.

belt were changed to increase pump speed. This change is listed only in *The Jaguar E-Type: A Collector's Guide.*

Changes at engine numbers 7R.1914/5 and 7R.35388/9: The water pump assembly was changed.

Changes at engine numbers 7R.4488/9 and 7R.36957/8: About May 1969, the water pump spindle was changed. This change is listed only in *Jaguar E-Type: The Definitive History.*

Hoses and Clamps

The hose clamps were basically the same as those used in the 3.8-liter cars.

Changes at chassis numbers 1E.1225/6, 1E.10957/8, 1E.20611/2, and 1E.30981/2: About June 1965, the left-hand water-feed pipe to the heater, behind the dash panel, between the water control valve and the heater radiator, was changed.

Changes at engine numbers 7R.1837/8 and 7R.35329/30: The heater-hose return pipe at the right-hand side of the cylinder block was changed.

Changes at chassis numbers 1R.1195/6, 1R.9642/3, 1R.20277/8, and 1R.26428/9: The top water hose from the radiator to the water manifold was changed.

Thermostat

Changes at chassis numbers 1E.2050/1, 1E.31806/7, and 1E.51212/3: The water outlet housing and thermostat

Most 4.2 liter cars had the white-outlined bow-tie spark-plug caps, as found on late 3.8-liter cars.

The spark-plug wire organizing system shown on a Series II car.

A ballast resistor on a late Series II car.

The Series I 4.2-liter header tank and cap were similar to those used on the 3.8-liter cars, but they are not interchangeable. The hose attachment points were different.

Later Series I 1/2 and Series II cars had a header tank mounted on the firewall.

Early cars had no shield around the alternator. This is the early alternator.

housing were changed. The thermostat was changed to the type already fitted to LHD cars. Dates of about April and July of 1968 are cited for this change.

Changes at engine numbers 7R.5263/4 and 7R.37488/9: About May 1969, the thermostat was changed from 74 to 82 degrees Celsius. Some sources cite engine numbers 7R.5262/3 instead of 7R.5263/4, and numbers 7R.37488/9 are not cited.

Changes at engine numbers 7R.14048/9: The thermostat was changed about October 1970.

Charging System: Alternator and Bracket

The alternator heat-shield arrangement went

through at least three configurations during the production run of 4.2-liter cars. The early 4.2-liter Series I cars had no alternator shield, but a metal one was added for the late Series I cars. Early Series II cars had no shield, but one was later adopted.

Changes at engine numbers 7E.6332/3: An alternator shield was added about May 1966. The alternator shield was introduced on all E-Types at the time of introduction of the 2+2.

Changes at engine numbers 7E.6332/3: The bolt holding the timing chain cover to the cylinder block was changed to allow the attachment of the alternator shield.

This shield was added to the alternator about the time of the introduction of the 2+2.

Changes at engine numbers 7E.3422/3: About June 1965, the alternator bracket was changed. This change is listed only by Porter.

Changes at chassis numbers 1R.1012/3, 1R.7442/3, 1R.20006/7, 1R.25283/4, 1R.35010/1, and 1R.40207/8: About January 1969, the alternator was changed to have side-entry cables, for cars not fitted with air conditioning.

When air conditioning was fitted, the alternator was mounted high in front of the engine.

Changes at chassis numbers 1R.9456/7, 1R.26319/20, 1R.35332/3, and 1R.42012/3: About August 1969, a composite bracket was introduced to mount the alternator, air-conditioning compressor, and the power steering pump. This change is listed only by Porter.

Changes at engine numbers 7R.5546/7: The alternator was changed for cars without air conditioning.

Pulleys and Belt

The alternator pulley was different on cars exported to Canada and the United States.

Changes at engine numbers 7E.1404/5: About December 1964, the water pump and pulley were changed to make pump removal easier.

Changes at engine numbers 7E.17157/8 and 7E.54836/7: About June 1968, the water pump pulley and belt were changed to increase pump speed. This change is listed only in *The Jaguar E-Type: A Collector's Guide*.

Changes at engine numbers 7R.5546/7: The alternator belt for cars without air conditioning was changed to a different type for cars exported to the United States and Canada.

Voltage Regulator and Bracket

I am not aware of any changes.

Battery, Cables, Tray, and Mounts

The early batteries were of the tar-topped sort supplied with the 3.8-liter cars.

Later batteries had the long, red plastic single-piece cap. It is reported that this type of battery was supplied originally on 1967 2+2 serial number 1E.75930, a very

At the start of Series II production, there was no shield on the alternator. This is the late alternator.

Later on in Series II production, a second-style heat shield was introduced.

When air conditioning was fitted, the alternator was relocated. Here it is seen mounted in front of the upper camshaft-chain tensioner on a Series II roadster.

The plastic windshield-washer assembly of the late 4.2-liters.

The early 4.2-liter cars used a glass windshield-washer assembly, as seen in this 3.8-liter car.

original car with approximately 6,000 original miles, although this seems in conflict with evidence from the literature that indicates the early cars were supplied with the tar-topped battery.

Electric: Wiring Harness

Changes at chassis numbers 1E.1162/3, 1E.10771/2, 1E.20362/3, and 1E.30856/7 (except 1E.20335): About June 1965, the forward wiring harness and front lamp harness were changed.

Changes at chassis numbers 1E.1164/5 and 1E.20370/1: The forward wiring harness and the instrument panel harness were changed.

Changes at chassis numbers 1E.10753/4 and 1E.30824/5: The instrument-panel wiring harness was changed.

Changes at chassis numbers 1E.1412/3, 1E.11740/1, 1E.20999/1000, and 1E.32009/10: About March 1966, the front wiring harness was changed. This change is listed only by Porter.

Changes at chassis numbers 1E.50165/6 and 1E.75546/7: The forward wiring harness, the instrument panel harness, and the alternator harness were changed.

Changes at chassis numbers 1R.1012/3, 1R.7442/3, 1R.20006/7, 1R.25283/4, 1R.35010/1, and 1R.40207/8: The alternator harness was changed.

Windshield Washer

Changes at chassis numbers 1E.1164/5, 1E.10753/4, 1E.20370/1, and 1E.30824/5: About June 1965, the windshield washer bottle was changed to plastic, and pre-timed operation was deleted.

All Series I 1/2 and Series II cars had the plastic bottle.

On some late 2+2s, the bottle was located farther to the right at the end of the right-hand rocker panel.

Brake-Light Switch

I am not aware of any changes.

Cooling Fan, Relay, and Switch

Changes at chassis numbers 1E.1430/1, 1E.12169/70, 1E.21139/40, 1E.32315/6, 1E.50156/7,

This Lucas battery with one-piece cap was used on late E-Types.

and 1E.76000/1: About September 1966, the cooling fan thermostat was changed. This change is listed only in *Jaguar E-Type: The Definitive History*.

I have seen both screws and studs with nuts used to fasten the thermostats.

Changes at chassis numbers 1E.2050/1, 1E.31806/7, and 1E.51212/3: About April 1968, the single cooling fan was replaced by dual cooling fans, as already fitted to LHD cars. This change is listed only in *The Jaguar E-Type: A Collector's Guide*.

Changes at engine numbers 7R.5263/4: The cooling fan thermostatic switch was changed.

In *Popular Imported Cars* magazine, January 1969, a five-bladed fan, with what appears to be aluminum blades, is shown mounted on the front of the air-conditioner condenser on the front of the radiator of an LHD Series I 1/2 roadster. The associated text says that this fan was fitted on cars with air conditioning. I have seen no other evidence for this, however.

A discussion of a Series II LHD roadster in *Car and Driver*, May 1969, states that two cooling fans operate thermostatically, unless air conditioning is fitted, in which case they both are kept on at all times. No mention of a third fan is made.

Horn and Relay

A horn mute was fitted to Series II cars exported to Holland.

Changes at chassis numbers 1E.1062/3, 1E.10771/2, 1E.20362/3, and 1E.30856/7 (and 1E.20335): The horns were changed about June 1965. In some sources, chassis numbers 1E.1162/3 are cited instead of 1E.1062/3.

Tachometer, Pressure, and Temperature Senders

Changes at chassis numbers 1E.50165/6 and 1E.75546/7: The oil pressure-ignition warning light-switch

The early cooling-fan thermostatic switches were similar to those used on the late 3.8-liter cars. The filler cap here is not original.

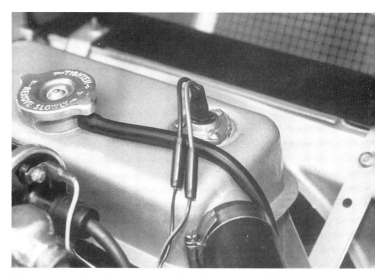

The later cooling-fan thermostatic switches had different mounts for the wires.

A plastic windshield-washer assembly on a Series II 2+2, mounted down and to the right, at the end of the right-hand rocker panel. This car has the steep windscreen and the bonnet-mounted dual-squirter, as opposed to the dual, cowl-mounted squirters of the steep-screen cars. The straps on this bottle are not original; there should be one central rubber strap.

This late cooling-fan thermostatic switch is retained by studs with nuts, instead of the screws found on some cars. The radiator cap and hose clamps seen here are not original.

This metal cap on the clutch reservoir of serial number 1E.16928 may have been original.

adapter at the right-hand side of the cylinder block was replaced by a plug, and a control unit for the ignition warning light was mounted on a frame-fixing bolt.

Changes at chassis numbers 1E.1723/4, 1E.13150/1, 1E.21480/1, and 1E.33090/1: About July 1967, there were numerous changes in the electrical equipment, an ignition warning light replaced the oil pressure switch, and the old oil-pressure switch in the cylinder-block oil gallery was replaced by a plug. This change is listed only by Porter.

Changes at chassis numbers 1R.1586/7, 1R.12955/6, 1R.20722/3, 1R.27869/70, 1R.35787/8, and 1R.43772/3: About April 1970, the fan control thermostat was changed. This change is listed only by Porter.

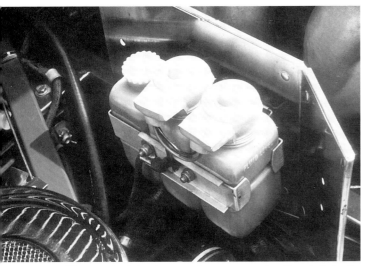

The standard clutch-reservoir cap was made of knurled plastic. The chroming on the heater intake screen retainer is not original. It should be painted black.

Brakes and Hydraulics: Brake and Clutch Fluid Reservoirs and Mounts

Changes at chassis numbers 1E.1483/4, 1E.12637/8, 1E.21234/5, 1E.32666/7, 1E.50007/8, and 1E.75074/5: About September 1966, a rubber cover was added to the tops of the brake-fluid warning terminals. This change is listed only in Porter's *Jaguar E-Type: The Definitive History*.

In spite of this entry about the introduction of rubber caps on the brake fluid reservoirs, I have seen no evidence that any 4.2-liter cars ever came without them.

I am aware of one strange occurrence of a small metal cap being used on the clutch reservoir. This occurred on serial number 1E.16928. The owner said this cap had been on the car when it was new, and that another car next to it in the showroom had the same cap. The normal clutch-reservoir cap is made of a white, knurled plastic. I have not heard nor seen any other evidence of a metal cap being fitted.

Brake and Clutch Reservoir Heat Shield

Changes at chassis numbers 1E.1544/5, 1E.12964/5, 1E.21334/5, and 1E.32887/8: About December 1966, a heat shield was introduced for the headpipes. This change is listed only by Porter.

Hydraulic Lines, Switch, Cylinders, and Activation Mechanism

Changes at chassis numbers 1E.1076/7, 1E.10429/30, 1E.20136/7, 1E.30442/3, 1E.10427, and 1E.20132: The hydraulic pipe from the front flexible hose to the front brake calipers was changed.

Changes at chassis numbers 1E.1412/3, 1E.11740/1, 1E.20999/1000, and 1E.32009/10: About March 1966, new brake and clutch master cylinders and pedal housings were fitted to standardize the two-seater cars with the 2+2 cars, and the brake-light switch was repositioned.

Changes at chassis numbers 1E.1560/1, 1E.13010/1, 1E.21341/2, and 1E.32941/2: About November 1966, the clutch and brake master cylinders were modified to have shorter pushrods to change pedal angles, and to improve the accelerator pedal angle. There was also a change in the accelerator pedal assembly.

Changes at chassis numbers 1R.1060/1, 1R.7829/30, 1R.20101/2, 1R.25438/9, 1R.35098/9, and 1R.40507/8: About March 1969, the master-cylinder spacer (for the clutch?) was changed. This change is listed only by Porter.

Brake Vacuum System

Changes at chassis numbers 1E.1019/20, 1E.10323/4, 1E.20081/2, and 1E.30268/9: The vacuum reservoir was changed.

The 4.2-liter reservoirs may have been supplied new with "TRICO" markings, as illustrated in the 3.8-liter section on page 121.

Miscellaneous: Steering

Changes at chassis numbers 1E.1234/5, 1E.11165/6, 1E.20632/3, and 1E.31243/4: About November 1965, the rack and pinion assembly was changed. This change is listed only by Porter.

Changes at chassis numbers 1E.1412/3, 1E.11534/5, 1E.20992/3, and 1E.31764/5: About March 1966, the steering assembly was changed (a seven-tooth pinion replaced the eight-tooth one) to improve steering when radial-ply tires were fitted.

Heater

Changes at chassis numbers 1E.2038/9 and 1E.21783/4: About April 1968, the dashboard was revised. The heater controls, choke, and switches were changed, and the heater box was changed. I think this is also the introduction of the rocker switches, which I believe was simultaneous with the addition of the glovebox lid (except for the 2+2 cars, which had it earlier). This change is listed only in *The Jaguar E-Type: A Collector's Guide*.

Splash Shields

I am not aware of any changes.

Drivetrain: Bellhousing, Flywheel, Clutch, Slave Cylinder, and Torque Converter

Some early 4.2-liter cars may have had a flywheel

inspection hole in the bellhousing, as on the 3.8-liter cars. Most cars do not have this inspection hole.

Changes at engine numbers 7E.7810/1 and 7E.50046/7: About September 1966, the clutch disc was made a little convex. The new disc is marked with light blue and purple paint near the center. This change is listed only in Porter's *Jaguar E-Type: The Definitive History*.

Changes at engine numbers 7E.13500/1 and 7E.53581/2: About July 1968, the clutch was changed from a Laycock to a Borg and Beck diaphragm type. This change is listed only by Porter.

Changes at engine numbers 7R.2587/8 and 7R.35730/1: About March 1969, the clutch cover assembly was changed to a new one with stronger springs. In some sources, an exception is given for engine numbers 7R.2784 to 7R.2791.

Changes at engine numbers 7E.4606/7: The clutch slave cylinder, return spring, and operating rod were changed.

Changes at engine numbers 7E.12159/60 and 7E.53209/10: About January 1968, the adjustor and pivot pin for the clutch operating rod was changed. This change is listed only by Porter.

The early bellhousings had an inspection hole on the upper left side. A 3.8-liter bellhousing is illustrated here to show an early 4.2-liter feature.

The later bellhousings did not have inspection holes.

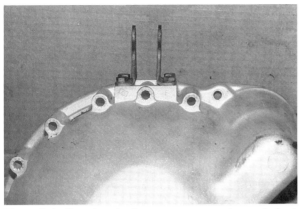

The early bellhousings had a center top attachment bolt. A 3.8-liter bellhousing is illustrated here to show an early 4.2-liter feature.

Later bellhousings did not have the center top attachment bolt. Notice that the raised area in the casting was still supplied for it.

The early rear hub carriers had smooth side walls.

Later rear hub carriers had a dipped-in region on the side.

Changes at engine numbers 7R.9709/10 and 7R.39111/2: About March 1970, the clutch-operating rod was altered to allow greater adjustment tolerances.

Changes at engine numbers 7R.10747/8: The release bearing and cup assembly were changed.

Changes at engine numbers 7E.52275/6: The torque converter housing was changed (for cars fitted with automatic transmission).

Changes at engine numbers 7E.11818/9 and 7E.52716/7: About January 1968, the number of bolts holding the bellhousing to the cylinder block was reduced from nine to eight, with the top one being omitted. This change is listed only by Porter.

Transmission and Mounts

In November 1964, a chamfered idler gear was introduced to reduce gearbox noise.

Changes at chassis numbers 1R.35656/7 and 1R.43164/5: About January 1970, the automatic-transmission selector lever was changed. This change is listed only by Porter.

Changes at engine numbers 7E.51451/2: About September 1966, the automatic-transmission kickdown control rod and cable, and the automatic transmission itself, were changed.

Changes at engine numbers 7R.6572/3 and 7R.38135/6: About August 1969, the oil seal in the speedometer drive gear was changed. This change is listed only by Porter.

Changes at transmission number EJ.245/6: About January 1965, the housing for the rear oil seal, and its gasket, were changed.

Changes at transmission numbers EJ.944/5: About March 1965, the roller bearing on the gearbox constant-pinion shaft was changed.

Changes at transmission numbers EJ.3169/70: The constant pinion shaft was changed to include an oil thrower, and the spacer under the roller bearing was no longer required. This change is listed as occurring both about September 1965 and February 1966.

Changes at transmission numbers EJ.7919/20 and EJS.7919/20: About November 1966, a retaining washer was added to the shift lever.

Changes at transmission numbers EJ.11776/7 and EJS.11776/7: About July 1967, the spring for the synchromesh trust members was changed. This change is listed only in Porter's *Jaguar E-Type: The Definitive History.*

Changes at transmission numbers KE.11768/9 and KJS.2858/9: About March 1970, the clutch release bearing was changed. The new one can be identified by a ridge in the bore of the thrust pad. This change is listed only by Porter.

In *Motor Sport* magazine, April 1966, the transmission is said to be a ZF unit, but I have seen no other evidence for this. In fact, in the May 1969 issue of *Car and Driver,* while discussing an LHD Series II roadster, it is stated that the box is not a ZF. In *Car* magazine, June 1970, the gearbox is referred to as a Jaguar unit, and no mention is made of ZF.

Driveshaft

I am not aware of any changes.

Differential

Changes at chassis numbers 1E.1151/2, 1E.10702/3, 1E.20328/9, and 1E.30771/2: About May 1965, the axle ratio was changed from 3.31:1 to 3.07:1 for all cars except those exported to the United States, Canada, and Newfoundland, which were 3.54:1. Some sources cite chassis numbers 1E.1072/3 instead of 1E.10702/3.

Changes at chassis numbers 1E.10739/40 and 1E.30806/7: The 3.54 rear-end assembly was changed for cars exported to the United States, Canada, and Newfoundland.

Changes at chassis numbers 1E.1177/8, 1E.10783/4, 1E.20396/7, 1E.30861/2 (for 3.07:1 rear ends), 1E.10739/40, and 1E.30806/7 (for 3.54:1 rear ends): About June 1965, the rear end changed to a type with driveshaft flanges as part of the driveshafts.

Changes at chassis numbers 1E.1886/7, 1E.15981/2, 1E.21619/20, and 1E.34602/3: About September 1967, the Powr-Lok differential was discontinued as standard, except for the U.S. 3.54:1 ratio axle. This change is listed only in *The Jaguar E-Type: A Collector's Guide.*

Changes at chassis numbers 1R.1243/4, 1R.9939/40, 1R.20334/5, and 1R.26575/6 (except numbers 1R.9929/30 were cited instead of 1R.9939/40, I believe in error): The final drive unit was changed.

Chassis: Front Wheel Hubs

I am not aware of any design changes.

A-Arms and Pivots

As with the 3.8-liter car, the A-arms of the 4.2-liter cars came in both dark and light finishes. I believe the dark finishes were black paint, while the light-finished ones were plated. From the evidence I have found, it appears the dark A-arms were found only on some early 4.2-liter Series I cars, and subsequently all A-arms were bright.

Changes at chassis numbers 1E.1038/9, 1E.10337/8, 1E.20097/8, and 1E.30291/2: About March 1965, the sealing at the front ball joints was improved.

The early 4.2-liter cars had eared hubcaps and forged center hubs on the wire wheels, as used on the 3.8-liters.

Turbo Disk wheels were available as an extra-cost option on the Series II cars.

Changes at chassis numbers 1E.1046/7, 1E.10337/8, 1E.20099/100, and 1E.30301/2 (and 1E.1021, 1E.20083, and 1E.30271): The left-hand tie-rod lever was changed.

Changes at chassis numbers 1E.1076/7, 1E.10429/30, 1E.20136/7, and 1E.30442/3 (and 1E.10427 and 1E.20132): The front suspension was changed.

Front Torsion Bars

Changes at chassis numbers 1E.50874/5 and 1E.77406/7: About July 1968, the diameter of the torsion bars was increased. This change is listed only in *Jaguar E-Type: The Definitive History.*

Changes at chassis numbers 1R.1775/6 and 1R.20954/5: About August 1970, larger diameter torsion bars were fitted to RHD cars.

Front Shock Absorbers

I am not aware of any design changes.

Front Antiroll Bar

I am not aware of any design changes.

An original one-ounce wheel weight.

Rear Wheel Hubs and Carriers

Changes at chassis numbers 1E.1236/7, 1E.10978/9, 1E.20638/9, and 1E.31002/3: The rear hub carrier and its oil seal were changed.

Changes at chassis numbers 1E.1762/3, 1E.15109/10, 1E.21488/9, and 1E.34302/3: About July 1967, the rear hub carriers were changed. This change is /listed only by Porter.

While the early 4.2-liter rear hub carriers have the same appearance as the 3.8-liter ones, later on in 4.2-liter production the shape of the casting was changed. The early-type casting has smooth side walls, while the later type has the side walls dipped in near the lower pivot mounting points.

Radius Arms, Trailing Arms, and Halfshafts

Changes at chassis numbers 1E.1925/6, 1E.16720/1, 1E.21668/9, 1E.34850/1, 1E.51066/7, and 1E.77704/5: In the first part of 1968, grease nipples were reintroduced on the halfshaft universal joints. In some references, chassis numbers 1E.16126/7 are cited instead of 1E.16720/1, and numbers 1E.50166/7 are cited instead of 1E.51066/7.

Rear Springs, Seats, and Spacers

Changes at chassis numbers 1E.1376/7, 1E.11363/4, 1E.20899/900, and 1E.31526/7: About November 1965, the rear coil springs were changed. This change is listed only by Porter.

Changes at chassis numbers 1E.1489/90, 1E.12692/3, 1E.21253/4, and 1E.32684/5: About September 1966, a rubber seat was added to the top of the spring in the rear transmission mount, and the spring retainer was changed. This change is listed only by Porter.

As in the 3.8-liter cars, I am not aware of any deviations from a black-painted finish on the rear springs.

Rear Shock Absorbers

Changes at chassis numbers 1E.1292/3, 1E.11120/1, 1E.20762/3, and 1E.31176/7: About November 1965, the rear shock absorbers were changed. This change is listed only by Porter.

Rear Antiroll Bar

I am not aware of any design changes.

Brakes

Changes at chassis numbers 1E.1046/7, 1E.10337/8, 1E.20099/100, and 1E.30301/2 (and 1E.1021, 1E.20083, and 1E.30271): Shields were added to the front brake discs about February 1965.

Changes at chassis numbers 1E.1046/7, 1E.10337/8, 1E.20099/100, and 1E.30301/2 (and 1E.1021, 1E.20083, and 1E.30271): The bolt and washer mounting for the front caliper to the stub axle carriers was changed.

Changes at chassis numbers 1E.1076/7, 1E.10429/30, 1E.20136/7, and 1E.30442/3 (and 1E.10427 and 1E.20132): About March 1965, the front calipers were altered to move the bleed screw to the inner side of the assembly.

With the introduction of the Series II, the brakes were changed to Girling.

Changes at chassis numbers 1R.1243/4, 1R.9939/40, 1R.20334/5, and 1R.26575/6: The mounting of the rear brake calipers to the final drive unit changed, and the adapter plate was discontinued.

Changes at chassis numbers 1R.1410/1, 1R.11302/3, 1R.20509/10, 1R.27173/4, 1R.35647/8, and 1R.42993/4: About November 1969, the front flexible brake hose was changed.

Parking Brake

Changes at chassis numbers 1R.35421/2 and 1R.42400/1: About March 1970, the handbrake lever was changed to one with a different material in the pivot pin and lever. This change is listed only in Porter's *Jaguar E-Type: The Definitive History*.

Front Wheelwells and Engine Compartment Undershields

Changes at chassis numbers 1E.1386/7, 1E.11546/7, 1E.20936/7, and 1E.31778/9: About March 1966, more mud shield was fitted to the front frame. This change is listed only by Porter.

Wheels, Weights, and Hubcaps

With the onset of the U.S. regulations came the change from the eared to the earless hubcaps. As in the case of the 3.8-liter cars, earlier Series I 4.2-liter cars shipped to Germany had the early version of the earless hubcaps (as mentioned in chapter 6). The U.S.-regulation earless hubcaps had three rounded lobes instead of the two square lobes of the early earless variety.

The newer three-lobed version was introduced for the U.S. market on the Series I 1/2 cars. Standardization of earless hubcaps for all cars came in after the introduction of the Series II. Therefore, some non-U.S. Series II cars have eared hubcaps.

An original narrow-whitewall Dunlop RS.5 tire on a Series I car.

An original Dunlop SP Sport on a Series I 1/2 car. Note the earless hubcap and cast center hub typical of these later cars.

Another change that occurred around the same time was the introduction of the cast center hubs.

Changes at chassis numbers 1E.1813/4, 1E.11534/5, 1E.21517/8, 1E.34338/9, 1E.50911/2, and 1E.77474/5: New wheels with the forged center hub and straight spokes were introduced for the chrome wire wheels only. Some sources cite chassis numbers 1E.15486/7 instead of 1E.11534/5. Dates of May 1967 and July 1968 are cited for this change.

Changes at chassis numbers 1E.1852/3, 1E.15752/3, 1E.21578/9, 1E.34457/8, 1E.50971/2, and 1E.77601/2: About July 1968, a forged hub was introduced for the painted wire wheels. This change is listed only by Porter.

Changes at chassis numbers 1R.1053/4, 1R.20072/3, and 1R.35098/9: Earless hubcaps were introduced on RHD cars (as on the LDH cars) about February 1969.

RHD Series II cars are shown with and without eared hubcaps.

While most 4.2-liter cars seem to have had chrome wheels, painted wheels were also available.

The more expensive disc wheel option came in after the introduction of the Series II, and therefore was not available on early Series II cars. The disc wheel option cost more than the standard wire wheels.

The original wheel weights found on the Series I 4.2-liter cars were marked with the weight, and clipped to the rim of the wheel in the usual way.

Tires and Tubes

The early 4.2-liter cars had the Dunlop RS.5s, but Dunlop radials were used later. The first radials were SP.41s, and they were first fitted as standard in England in October 1965. As with the later 3.8-liter cars, when whitewalls were fitted, they were the narrow type.

Changes at chassis numbers 1E.1408/9, 1E.11714/5, 1E.20977/8, and 1E.32008/9: About March 1966, the standard tires were changed to Dunlop SP.41 HR tires, except for cars exported to Australia, Canada, Newfoundland, New Zealand, or the United States. This change is listed only in Porter's *Jaguar E-Type: The Definitive History*.

In *Motor* magazine, January 13, 1968, it is stated that radial tires came in with the Series I 1/2 cars, but I believe that they were standard earlier.

Changes at chassis numbers 1E.1919/20, 1E.16098/9, 1E.21668/9, 1E.34846/7, 1E.51058/9, and 1E.77704/5: About July 1968, the tires were changed to Dunlop SP Sport, and whitewalls were used for cars exported to the United States. This change is listed only by Porter.

Motor magazine, September 7, 1968, pictures a Series I 1/2 roadster with tires that are stated to be Dunlop SP Sport VR. *Jaguar E-Type: The Definitive History* stated that the Dunlop SP Sport radials were adopted on the Series I 1/2, but had been an option on the home-market cars since 1965. *Car and Driver*, May 1969, in discussing an LHD Series II roadster, stated that the tires are 185VR15 Dunlop SPs. And a RHD Series II 2+2 came with Dunlop SP Sport tires in *Car* magazine, June 1970.

At least some loading and tire specification plates from late Series II cars indicates "185.VR.15, SP.SPORT" tires.

According to *Modern Motor*, March 1971, Dunlop Aquajet tires were standard on a late RHD Series II coupe (an Australian car).

The tires on the 4.2-liter cars were either blackwalls or narrow whitewalls. In *Jaguar E-Type: The Definitive History*, Porter stated that for the Series II, the U.S.-delivery cars were fitted with whitewalls, and that for other markets a different whitewall was available as an option.

Typical unpainted subframe bolts on a Series I car.

mount and the firewall. I have seen this strip affixed both with a bottom mounting and with a top mounting.

Rear Subframe, Mounts, and Stops

Changes at chassis numbers 1E.1408/9, 1E.11714/5, 1E.20977/8, and 1E.32008/9: About March 1966, special rear suspension bump-stops were used to avoid fowling the new Dunlop tires. This change is listed only by Porter.

Tubing and Cables

I am not aware of any changes.

Exhaust System

The exhaust manifold changed in the U.S.-specification cars as the crossover-pipe arrangements changed. This is discussed earlier in this chapter.

Rear Pipes and Resonators

The Series I 4.2-liter cars had the usual short large-diameter section and long small-diameter section resonators.

Resonators with slightly turned-down tips are shown on a coupe in the July 1966 issue of *Road & Track*. These may be aftermarket units, but the car in question appears from the text to be new.

Changes at chassis numbers 1E.1598/9, 1E.13181/2, 1E.21379/80, 1E.33119/20, 1E.50155/6, and 1E.75991/2: About December 1966, the mufflers changed from being welded to the tailpipes to being clipped to them. This change is listed only by Porter. A similar change occurred earlier during 3.8-liter production at chassis numbers 850178/9, 860011/2, 875607/8, and 885058/9.

Changes at chassis numbers 1E.1689/90, 1E.13846/7, 1E.21450/1, 1E.33708/9, 1E.50640/1, and

Front Subframe

Changes at chassis numbers 1R.1187/8, 1R.9569/70, 1R.20269/70, 1R.26386/7, 1R.35352/3, and 1R.42117/8 (but 1R.3532/3 and 1R.42117/8 were not included): The front subframe assembly changed.

As discussed in chapter 6, there seems to be a question about the painting of the subframe bolts, at least on the 3.8-liter cars. All the information I have been able to gather on the 4.2-liter cars indicates that the bolts were unpainted.

On some late Series II cars, the frame grounding strip is fitted between the upper-right front subframe

The grounding strips on the late Series II cars were also mounted on the top of the subframe bolt.

A bottom-mounted grounding strip from the front subframe to the firewall on a late Series II roadster.

The splayed-out resonators of the Series II cars.

1E.76933/4: About July 1967, the linkage between the tailpipes was changed from bolted to welded. This change is listed only in *Jaguar E-Type: The Definitive History*. This change would bring the inter-tailpipe mounting configuration back to the welded type of the 3.8-liter cars of 1961.

With the restyling of the Series II rear end, the resonators had to splay around the license plate.

The circular-type muffler clamps, as used on the 3.8-liter cars, were used on the 4.2-liter cars, at least into Series I 1/2 production.

Exhaust Heat Shields

I am not aware of any changes.

Chapter 9

5.3-LITER BODYWORK AND INTERIOR COMPONENT CHANGES

Exterior: Headlights and Trim

As with earlier models, Lucas headlights were used in the Series III cars. Series III lighting systems came in a wide variety of configurations. The lighting configuration for RHD cars changed at chassis numbers 1S.1211/2 and 1S.50972/3 and again at 1S.1775/6 and 1S.51705/6. Different lighting systems were used for cars exported to the United States and Canada, those exported to Italy, and those exported to France. There was a change in the lighting system for cars shipped to other countries than those named here at 1S.25467/8. The lighting configuration changed again at chassis numbers 1S.22333/4, for cars shipped to the United States and Canada.

Quartz-halogen headlights were available as an option.

Parking and Brake Lights and Trim

The sidelights were of one type for RHD cars, while two types were used on LHD cars. Different front ancillary

The removable connector in the windshield-washer line can be seen just to the right of the shock absorber and above the inner part of the upper front left-side A-arm.

lighting systems were used on cars shipped to the United States and Canada. The lights used on cars shipped to Italy were changed at chassis numbers 1S.72624/5.

The rear lights for cars shipped to the United States, Canada, Mozambique, Portugal, Angola, and Greece were changed at chassis numbers 1S.50144/5 and 1S.71035/6 and again at 1S.51761/2 and 1S.74822/3. The rear lights on cars shipped to countries not listed here were different and were changed at chassis numbers 1S.51761/2 and 1S.74822/3.

License-Plate Lights and Trim

I am not aware of any changes.

Back-up Light and Trim

Changes at chassis numbers 1S.1004/5, 1S.20024/5, 1S.50227/8, and 1S.71836/7: The reverse light was changed for cars going to all countries except Algeria, Ivory Coast, Morocco, New Caledonia, Senegal, and South Vietnam.

Changes at chassis numbers 1S.20711/2 and 1S.73523/4: The reverse light was changed for cars going to Algeria, Ivory Coast, Morocco, New Caledonia, Senegal, and South Vietnam.

Changes at chassis numbers 1S.1296/7 and 1S.20409/10, for cars not shipped to the United States and Canada, 1S.20168/9, for cars shipped to the United States and Canada, 1S.51225/6, 1S.73210/1, for cars not shipped to the United States and Canada, and 1S.75266/7, for cars shipped to the United States and Canada: The back-up light was changed. This change did not apply for cars destined for Algeria, Ivory Coast, Morocco, New Caledonia, Senegal, and South Vietnam.

Wiper Arms, Blades, and Windshield Squirter Nozzles

Changes at chassis numbers 1S.1004/5, 1S.20024/5, 1S.50202/3, and 1S.71475/6: About November 1971, a removable connector (part number C.33835) was added to the line from the pump to the hood-mounted windshield squirters to make hood removal easier.

Series III cars used these wire-frame wiper blades.

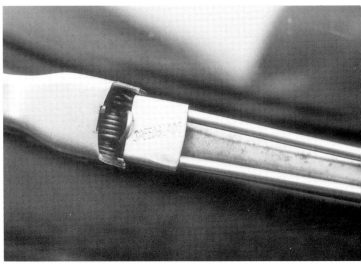

The wire-frame wiper blades were marked "SPEEDBLADE" in slanted letters. They were also marked "MADE IN ENGLAND" on the end of the main body, but this marking is not showing in the picture.

Changes at chassis numbers 1S.1700/1, 1S.21850/1, 1S.51618/9, and 1S.74515/6: The windshield squirter nozzles were changed.

The original wiper blades were the "wire frame" type, and were marked "SPEEDBLADE" near their mounting point to the arm.

Bumpers

In response to continuously tightening U.S. federal safety regulations, the bumper overriders were changed. The first style was chrome with a rubber pad on the front. Later, elastomeric overriders were used front and rear for U.S.-market cars. The change to the fully elastomeric bumpers came first at the front of the car and later at the rear.

The rear elastomeric "Nordel" bumpers were fitted to a steel reenforcing box that was itself attached to the rear sheet metal. I have been told by a DuPont employee that the name for the "Nordel" elastomer was derived from the words "NORthern DELaware," the original location of the DuPont company.

Changes at chassis numbers 1S.21028/9 and 1S.73855/6, for cars shipped to the United States and Canada: About January 1974, the rubber bumper overriders were added as a result of the U.S. federal 5 mph impact requirements. While most sources cite 1S.23239/40 and 1S.74585/6 as the introduction of these bumper overriders, the factory parts books seem to cite only chassis numbers 1S.21028/9 (only for cars shipped to the United States and Canada) for the introduction of the rear overriders, and 1S.21028/9 and 1S.73855/6 (only for cars shipped to the United States and Canada) for the introduction of the front overriders. No change in the rear-end sheet metal is cited for coupes. Roadster UD1S.21221, a very original

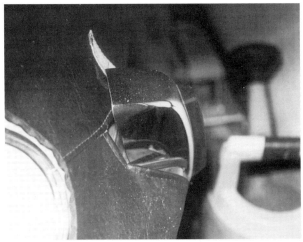

The original bumper overriders of the Series III cars had small rubber bumpers on their front surfaces, but were otherwise very close to earlier designs.

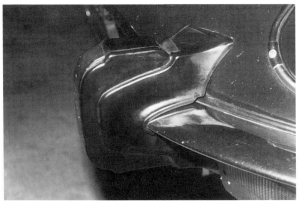

The "Nordel" elastomer bumper overriders. While generally considered to be unattractive, they did meet the ever-tightening U.S. regulations. These are the first of two types of elastomeric overriders. The later type was similar to the rear elastomeric bumper overriders of Figure 5-128, in that they were more squared-off and did not have the metal strip along the leading edge.

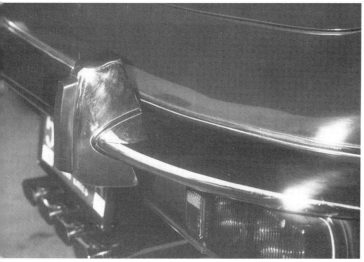

This early-style overrider is steel, with a small rubber pad. This rear overrider is fitted to a transition car carrying the long "Nordel" overriders on the front.

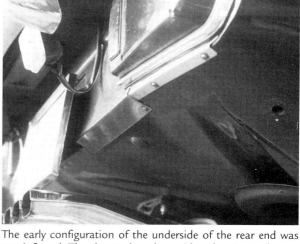

The early configuration of the underside of the rear end was unreinforced. The chromed steel overrider, showing in the upper left-hand corner, was attached to the bumper and not itself directly fastened to the bodyshell. This was as E-Types had been since their introduction in 1961.

In the final configuration, the long elastomeric overriders were fitted to both the front and rear.

This reenforcing section was added when the Nordel elastomer overriders were introduced to meet rear impact requirements. The elastomeric overrider, showing along the upper left side of the picture, is directly mounted to the fabricated steel frame fixed to the rear of the bodyshell to the left of and below the taillight lens in the picture.

car still in the hands of the first owner, is fitted with rubber overriders and impact tubes on the front, but steel overriders with small rubber pads (and no reenforcing box on the body) on the rear-end. Perhaps the rubber overriders came in on the front at 1S.21028/9 and 1S.73855/6 and at the rear at 1S.23239/40 and 1S.74585/6.

These overriders were not available on home-market cars.

Grille Trim

Changes at chassis numbers 1S.1006/7, 1S.20075/6, 1S.50264/5, and 1S.72256/7: The clips for the top trim piece of the main air intake were changed.

Vent Trim

I am not aware of any changes.

Door Handles

I am not aware of any changes.

Top Door Trim

I am not aware of any changes.

Convertible-Top Trim

Russ observes that convertible-top snaps were not installed prior to early 1972, but were present on 1973 and 1974 model year roadsters.

External Markings and Decorative Trim

I am not aware of any changes.

Windshield and Pillars

I am not aware of any changes.

Side Windows, Trim, Frames, Winding Mechanisms, and Sealing Rubber

I am not aware of any changes.

Wing Vents

Changes at chassis numbers 1S.51012/3 and 1S.72660/1: The leading section of the rear quarter windows was changed.

Rear Window

A heated rear window was available as an option, and at chassis numbers 1S.50590/1 and 1S.72332/3, the optional electrically heated rear window was changed.

Front License-Plate Mount

A black-painted, steel number plate mount was mounted to the lower right front of the hood, just under and to the right of the air-intake, for cars shipped to the United States, Canada, and Germany.

Changes at chassis numbers 1S.21028/9, for cars shipped to the United States and Canada, 1S.21727/8, for cars shipped to Germany, 1S.73855/6, for cars shipped to the United States and Canada, and 1S.74400/1, for cars shipped to Germany: The front license-plate mount was changed.

License-Plate Holder

I am not aware of any changes.

Interior: Instruments and Controls

Changes at chassis numbers 1S.1112/3 and 1S.20102/3, for cars not shipped to the United States and Canada, 1S.20024/5, for cars shipped to the United States and Canada, 1S.50685/6 and 1S.72333/4, for cars not shipped to the United States and Canada, and 1S.71369/70, for cars shipped to the United States and Canada: About July 1971, the water temperature gauge was changed. Numerous unofficial sources cite only chassis numbers

This is the front license-plate mount in-situ on the lower right side of the air intake on a U.S.-market 1974 roadster. Its elevated position on the side of the aperture avoided the problem of the license plate scraping on the ground when the hood was raised. On the six-cylinder cars, this had been a problem that required an elaborate cam and connecting rod mechanism to tilt the plate up.

1S.20024/5 and 1S.71369/70 and state that the change was the removal of the red warning marking on the gauge and that this applied only for cars shipped to the United States. The factory parts books cite the full set of six transition numbers, with U.S. and Canada distinctions, as listed above, but do not describe the change. Possibly there are other changes besides the removal of the red marking.

Changes at chassis numbers 1S.23239/40: Changes were made to the dashboard switchgear.

Changes at chassis numbers 1S.1004/5, 1S.20024/5, 1S.50166/7, and 1S.71247/8: The instrument panel electronics were changed.

Changes at chassis numbers 1S.1004/5, 1S.20024/5, 1S.50204/5, and 1S.71493/4: The center dash clock was changed from a Smiths type to a Kienzle type.

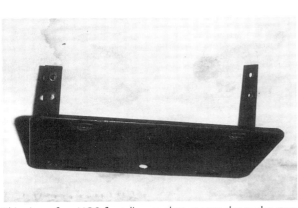

This view of an NOS front license-plate mount shows the staggered dual-hole tangs that were used to affix it to the sheet metal.

The early water temperature gauges had a red section on the far right of their scale.

Later U.S.-export cars had a water gauge without a red warning section at the right of the scale.

The Smiths clock was replaced with this Kienzle unit with radially oriented numerals and a central set-knob. It was mounted in the same center dash position as the earlier clock.

Changes at chassis numbers 1S.1039/40, 1S.20090/1, 1S.50378/9, and 1S.72318/9: About March 1972, the choke and heater controls were reconfigured into a symmetrical arrangement.

Changes at chassis numbers 1S.1162/3, 1S.20134/5, 1S.50874/5, and 1S.72449/50: About March 1972, the cable and pinion gear control of the defroster control flap was changed to a cable and connecting rod.

The early-style Smiths clock had the setting knob in the upper left, and the rate-adjusting screw on the upper right.

Cold-air footwell vents were introduced about March 1972. These were controlled by knobs mounted on the outside walls of the footwells, toward the door apertures.

A seatbelt warning light was mounted between the tachometer and speedometer on later U.S. market cars, but was reportedly omitted on all RHD cars.

Switches and Controls

Changes at chassis numbers 1S.1697/8 and 1S.21790/1: The choke control was changed.

Changes at chassis numbers 1S.1740/1, 1S.21984/5, 1S.51654/5, and 1S.74626/7: The air-distribution knobs were changed from the old serrated types (as used on Series II E-Types and S-Type sedans) to a type with raised knurling, and the vertical anodized metal labels were riveted next to the choke and heater controls. There is uncertainty about the 1S.51654/5 and 1S.74626/7 numbers, with some sources citing 1S.51655/6 and 1S.74627/8.

A special version of the switch indicator strip was used when the heated rear window option was fitted.

Indicator Lights

I am not aware of any changes.

Cigar Lighter

Like the Series II cars, the cigar lighter was mounted on the console, above the radio. When air conditioning was fitted, it was relocated to the front of the armrest-storage area.

Changes at chassis numbers 1S.1004/5, 1S.20024/5, 1S.50192/3, and 1S.71448/9: The cigar lighter was changed.

Ignition Switch and Key

Changes at chassis numbers 1S.1231/2, 1S.20174/5, 1S.51048/9, and 1S.72686/7: About April 1972, the lock on the steering column was changed from a Britax unit to a Waso unit. The earlier Britax unit had a single-piece metal key (Jaguar blank number RTC 0817B) while the later Waso key (Jaguar blank number RTC 0816B) had a black rubber handle molded on it.

Grab Handle

I am not aware of any changes.

Steering Wheel and Column

About December 1971, the location of the mounting bolts for the steering column lock was changed.

Changes at chassis numbers 1S.1004/5, 1S.20024/5, 1S.50166/7, and 1S.71233/4: About December 1971, the retaining bolts for both steering-column universal joints were changed to bolts with longer shanks.

On later cars, the heater control under the choke had an indicator label mounted beneath it. Note also here that the heater-control knob is still of the early type with incus serrations.

This view of the choke and vent-control area of an early car shows an unlabeled heater-control knob.

The heater-control knob label on this late car has the label riveted to its right, and now has two arrows, one still "DE-FROST," but now an "INTERIOR" arrow has been added. The same progression of labels occurred simultaneously on the vent controls on both sides of the dash, i.e., both next to the heater controls on the left side and the choke on the right side.

This early U.S.-market car was not fitted with the seatbelt warning light. Home-market cars also were supplied without this warning light.

On this later U.S.-market car, the seatbelt warning light was installed between the two main instruments.

Changes at chassis numbers 1S.1442/3, 1S.20920/1, 1S.51317/8, and 1S.73371/2, or 1S.73720/1: About December 1972, the pinion valve in the rack and pinion was changed. There is disagreement about the changeover numbers for the coupe, so I have listed the two sets of cited changeover numbers here.

About January 1973, the power-assisted rack and pinion assembly was changed. The new version was designated by a "W" prefix.

Pedals

Changes at chassis numbers 1S.1004/5 and 1S.50175/6: About July 1971, the brake pedal was changed on cars fitted with automatic transmissions.

Changes at chassis numbers 1S.20024/5 and 1S.71485/6: The stop on the accelerator pedal mechanism was changed.

Mirror and Mounts

Changes at chassis numbers 1S.20115/6 and

View from below of the early Britax ignition switch.

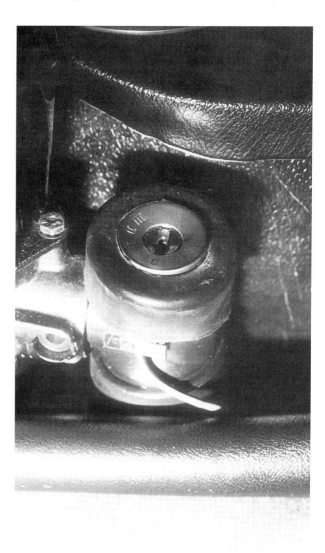

The later Waso ignition switch was bulkier than its predecessor.

1S.72489/90: The interior mirror for cars exported to France was changed.

Changes at chassis numbers 1S.20168/9 and 1S.72660/1: About April 1972, a remote control was added to the external mirror for cars shipped to the United States and Canada.

Interior Lights

I am not aware of any changes.

Handbrake Lever

Changes at chassis numbers 1S.1151/2, 1S.20121/2, 1S.50871/2, and 1S.72356/7: About December 1971, the handbrake was changed.

Dash Top

I am not aware of any changes.

A spare ignition key was screwed to the firewall. This is the later rubber-handled key that was used with the Waso steering-column/ignition lock.

The early handbrake was shorter than its successor.

The early cars did not have a fresh-air vent control. The speaker mounted on the footwell wall is an aftermarket unit.

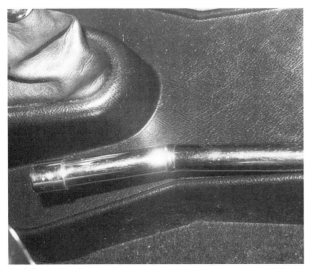

Besides being longer (note how far it overlaps the shift-lever rise in the console), the later handbrake lever was bent up and to the left at the end.

On later cars, a separate fresh-air vent control was added on the upper outer wall of the footwells.

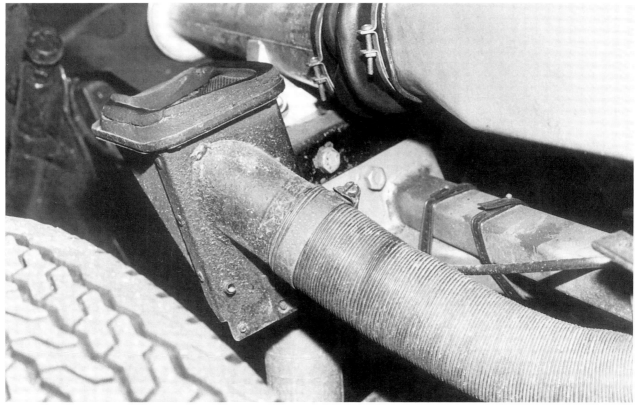

The new fresh-air vents in the footwells supplied air from two of these feeds, each consisting of a box with a screen filter at its inlet connected to a corrugated tube. The filter boxes were mounted on either side above the tops of the front shock absorbers.

Defroster Ducts and Vents

Changes at chassis numbers 1S.1235/6, 1S.20172/3, 1S.51015/6, and 1S.72681/2: About April 1972, the fresh-air vents with control levers were introduced.

Dash Materials and Trim

I am not aware of any changes.

Glovebox

I am not aware of any changes.

Sun Visors

I am not aware of any changes.

Under-dash Trays

When a tape player was specified as an optional extra, the passenger's side portion of the under-dash tray was not supplied.

Console Frame, Trim, and Components

In the Series III cars, the center console was a vacuum-formed assembly trimmed in simulated leather. Different console units were used for cars fitted with air conditioning.

Under-console Area

I am not aware of any changes.

Carpets and Interior Trim

Changes at chassis numbers 1S.1235/6, 1S.20180/1, 1S.51073/4, and 1S.72690/1: The carpets were changed.

Changes at chassis numbers 1S.72661/2: The headliner used was changed in color from beige to grey.

The trim on the rear-wheel arches of the coupes was changed twice. On very early cars, Ambla with piping was used. Later the piping was discontinued. Lastly, the trim was changed to "foam slabs." This change is cited only in Porter's *Original Jaguar E-Type*.

Seats and Mounts

Headrests were an option on cars shipped to the home market, and were either compulsory or optional in other markets.

Changes at chassis numbers 1S.72660/1: The upper squab of the rear seat was changed for cars shipped to Australia, the United States, and Canada. Cars shipped to these markets were fitted with a different upper squab than for other markets throughout production.

Convertible-Top Frame and Hardware

I am not aware of any changes.

Convertible-Top Cloth and Window

I am not aware of any changes.

Convertible-Top Cover

I am not aware of any changes.

Hardtop Mounting Equipment

I am not aware of any changes.

Hood Release

I am not aware of any changes.

Trunk Release

I am not aware of any changes.

Bodywork: Front Fenders

I am not aware of any changes.

Hood Center Section

I am not aware of any changes.

Hood Hinges and Lifts

Hood-lifting struts for cars shipped to the United States and Canada were different from those used for cars shipped to other markets.

Hood Latches

I am not aware of any changes.

Rubber Stops

I am not aware of any changes.

Rear Tub Sheet Metal, Firewall, and Underside

The bodyshell underwent changes during the production run of the Series III at these chassis numbers:

1S.21028/9, for cars shipped to the United States and Canada, 1S.23239/40, for cars shipped to the United States and Canada, 1S.2484/5 and 1S.23758/9, for cars not shipped to the United States and Canada, 1S.51012/3 and 1S.72660/1, 1S.51015/6 (including 1S.51013, 1S.51014), 1S.72681/2 (including 1S.72676 and 1S.72677 for cars not shipped to the United States or Canada), 1S.72660/1 (including 1S.72567 and 1S.72579, for cars not shipped to the United States or Canada), 1S.51415/6 (including 1S.51392) and 1S.73950/1, and 1S.73855/6.

Cockpit Sheet Metal

I am not aware of any changes.

Doors

Changes at chassis numbers 1S.1579/80 (including 1S.1550, 1S.1553, and 1S.1555) and 1S.21169/70: Changes were made to the door sheet metal, for cars not shipped to the United States and Canada.

Door Hinges and Supports

I am not aware of any changes.

Door Latches

Changes at chassis numbers 1S.1579/80 (including 1S.1550, 1S.1553, and 1S.1555), 1S.21169/70, 1S.51415/6 (including 1S.51392), 1S.73950/1, for cars not shipped to the United States and Canada, and 1S.73855/6, for cars shipped to the United States and Canada: The door latch mechanism was changed.

Trunk Sheet Metal

In conjunction with the introduction of the Nordel bumper overriders, the rear of the bodyshell was reenforced.

Trunk Lid

I am not aware of any changes.

Trunk Hinges and Supports

I am not aware of any changes.

Fuel Filler Recess, Lid, and Hinge

I am not aware of any changes.

Trunk Panels, Mat, and Flooring

I am not aware of any changes.

Trunk-Lid Sealing Rubber

I am not aware of any changes.

Exterior and Interior Colors

From March 1971 to October 1972, the following colors were offered:

Exterior	Interior
Ascot Fawn	Red, Beige, Cinnamon
Black	Red, Cinnamon, Grey
British Racing Green	Suede Green, Beige, Cinnamon
Dark Blue	Red, Light Blue, Grey
Light Blue	Dark Blue, Grey, Light Blue
Old English White	Black, Red, Dark Blue, Light Blue
Pale Primrose	Black, Beige
Regency Red	Beige, Grey
Sable	Beige, Grey, Cinnamon
Signal Red	Black, Red, Beige
Silver Grey (Silver Grey available by special order)	Black, Red
Warwick Grey	Red, Dark Blue, Cinnamon
Willow Green	Grey, Suede Green, Beige, Cinnamon

From October 1972 to the end of production, these colors were offered:

Exterior	Interior
Azure Blue	Dark Blue, Biscuit, Cinnamon
British Racing Green	Biscuit, Moss Green, Cinnamon
Dark Blue	Red, French Blue, Russet Red
Fern Grey	Moss Green, Olive, Tan

The main serial-number plate for the Series III cars was pop-riveted in the engine compartment on the top center of the firewall. This was in contrast to the six-cylinder cars that had these plates mounted on the right- or left-hand sides of the engine compartment, above the front ends of the rocker panels.

Serial-Number Markings

The main serial-number plate was attached to the upper part of the center of the firewall on 1971 to 1973

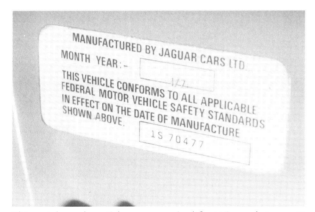

This serial-number sticker was required for U.S.-market cars. It is similar to the late Series II cars, except it is a sticker instead of a plate, and is light instead of dark. This is the early version.

On later cars, the serial-number sticker was still located in the same location, but contained more information. Other variants of these stickers were used, with format changes and different weights.

The windshield-frame-mounted chassis-number plate continued to be required by U.S. regulations and was almost identical to those used on the late Series II cars. The latter I have typically seen with the serial-number prefix, "1R," anodized on the plate with the rest of the number stamped in, while the early Series III plates have the "1S" prefix anodized on them. Also note the "Triplex" windshield glass marking indicating that this windshield is the optional "Sundym" type.

Later on the windshield-frame-mounted chassis-number plate was supplied with no part of the chassis number anodized in, so the entire number was stamped in. Also note the "MADE IN ENGLAND" marking reverse anodized in this later plate. Some later plates continued the "MADE IN ENGLAND" marking, but had a "U" anodized in as the first letter of the serial number. Note the Jaguar head run-in sticker on the lower left.

This view of the top rear of the engine block shows the engine serial-number stamping. The "FED" stamping indicates the engine meets the U.S. federal emission specifications.

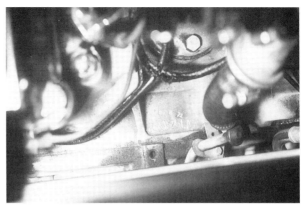

This later engine block has the serial number stamped farther back and the "FED" marking omitted.

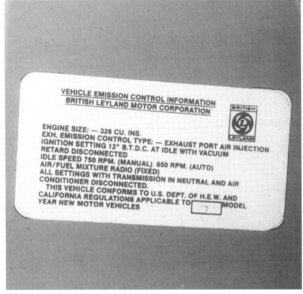

Located on the inside of the hood, on the back of the right front wheelwell, the emissions-control sticker of the early Series III cars was only slightly different from those of the Series II cars. Compare with Series II illustration.

On later Series III cars, this much more extensive emissions label was affixed to the back of the right-front wheelwell, in the same location as the earlier sticker.

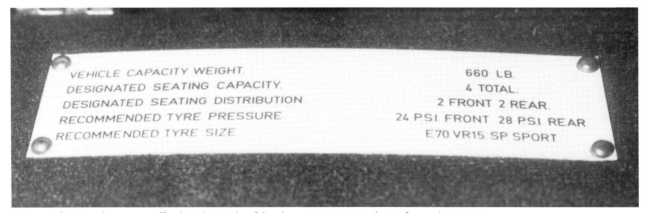

This specification plaque was affixed to the inside of the glove-compartment door of an early Series III car.

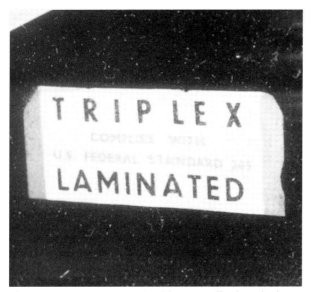

This "TRIPLEX LAMINATED" sticker was affixed to the lower center of the windshield.

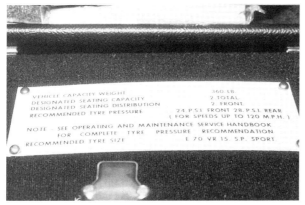

Later in production, additional information was added to the glove-compartment specification plaque.

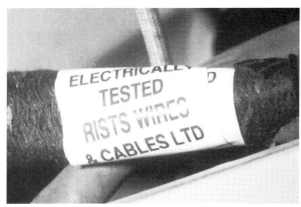

The wiring harness was wrapped with this "ELECTRICALLY TESTED RISTS WIRES & CABLES LTD" sticker.

model year cars. Russ states that the small brass "MADE IN ENGLAND" plaque normally pop-riveted on the firewall beneath the main number plate was not used on cars shipped to the home market.

The chassis number, as well as the date of manufacture, was imprinted on a label that was affixed to the rear face of the door aperture. This label changed several times throughout the Series III production run. The chassis number was also stamped in the engine compartment, under the heater.

As with the late Series II cars, the body number plate was mounted in the rear license-plate recess.

The engine serial numbers were stamped on the top of the engine block, at the rear.

Labels and Decals

The emission sticker on the inside wall of the right front wheel well was used only on cars exported to the United States. This sticker comes in at least two types. On the early cars, it was a small, rectangular sticker, very similar to those used on late Series II cars. Later it was

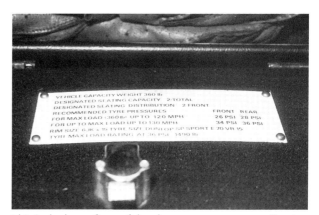

This is the latest form of the glove-compartment specification plaque.

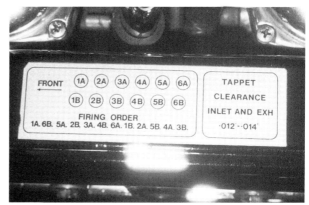

Initially, separate firing-order stickers were used for cars shipped to the United States and Canada versus those shipped to other markets, but after engine number 7S.14000 only one type of sticker was used. It was applied to the top of the left air filter.

changed to a larger, nearly rectangular sticker with additional tuning information imprinted on it.

The wiring harness had a label stating "ELECTRICALLY TESTED RISTS WIRES & CABLES LTD" on it. Tags were attached to the wire to the brake reservoir and the wire to the differential pressure sensor.

When the optional heated rear window was fitted, it carried a "TRIPLEX ELECTRICALLY HEATED" decal on it, as illustrated on page 162.

The heater blower motor carried a black sticker with white lettering giving the "SMITHS" name and with arrows indicating the rotation direction for both positive and negative ground configurations. All 4.2-liter and 5.3-liter cars were negative ground. A similar sticker was applied on the underside of the heater, next to the fan motor housing.

A round sticker stating, "ENGINE INITIALLY FILLED WITH PREMIUM OIL 20W/40" was applied

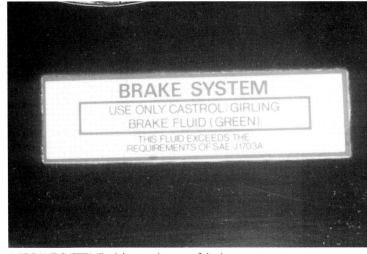

A "BRAKE SYSTEM" sticker on the top of the heater.

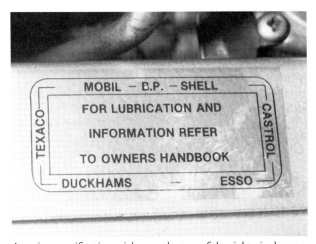

A tuning specification sticker on the top of the right air cleaner.

This "BLUECOL" sticker, in blue and white, was affixed to the top of the surge tank.

This red warning sticker was affixed to the starter relay, which was mounted to the center of the firewall.

A "TRICO" sticker on the side of the windshield washer fluid bottle.

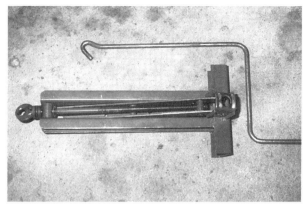

The jack used with the Series III cars came in grey on the early cars but was later painted blue.

This hubcap wrench was supplied when wire wheels were fitted.

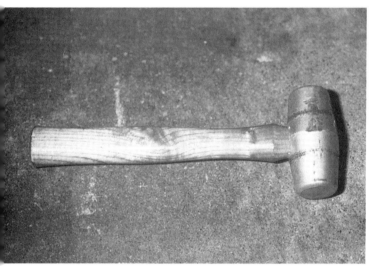

As with the late six-cylinder cars, this single-piece head hammer was supplied to turn the hubcap wrench.

on the left air-cleaner, next to the firing order and tappet clearance sticker.

A "BLUECOL" antifreeze sticker was affixed to the top right-side of the header tank. The red emission stickers on the front of the carburetors were applied only on 1971 model year cars. The air-conditioning compressor had a "Frigidaire" sticker on it.

Tools

The hubcap wrench and solid hammer were supplied with cars equipped with wire wheels. According to Russ, cars shipped to North America had no other tools, although the factory parts book shows a full toolkit.

Jack

On very early cars, the jack and its handle were painted grey. Subsequently, they were painted medium blue. This type of jack was also used on the late Series II cars.

Literature

The standard Series III literature packet included a driver's handbook, lubrication and maintenance chart, service handbook, U.S. safety instructions (where applicable), radio and automatic transmission pamphlets (if fitted with these options), and a plastic pouch to hold them all. The driver's handbook had publication numbers A.181/X, where X was the revision number.

Options and Variations: Axle Ratios

Changes at chassis numbers 1S.21575/6 and 1S.74260/1: About March 1973, the 3.31:1 rear end was introduced for cars sent to the United States and Canada, and the 3.07:1 was fitted to cars sold in other countries. The 3.54:1 rear end was no longer available on manual transmission cars.

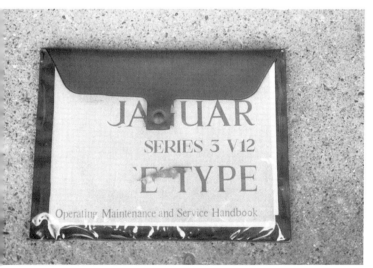

The Series III driver's handbook in its pouch

View of the inside of the Series III driver's handbook. Note that the car is denoted here as "Series 3," instead of the more common "Series III." The header strip to the Jaguar parts book refers to the car as "SERIES THREE," in one case and "Series 3" in another.

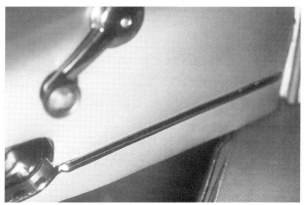

This view of the interior of a left-side door of an early Series III U.S.-market car shows the original configuration with the full trim strip and no remote-adjust for the mirror.

Wheels

Initially the Series III cars were fitted with steel disc wheels painted silver-grey and fitted with chrome trim rings. Chrome-plated steel disc wheels or chrome-plated wire wheels were available as options. Chrome-plated steel disc wheels became standard for the 1973 model year.

Tires and Tubes

Whitewall tires were available as an option.

Headlights

Quartz-halogen headlights were available as an option.

Mirrors

Door and fender mirrors were optional in some countries and were required in others. One interior mirror configuration was required for exports to France. Door-mounted mirrors were required for exports to the Netherlands, Austria, Belgium, Denmark, Holland, Switzerland, the United States, and Canada.

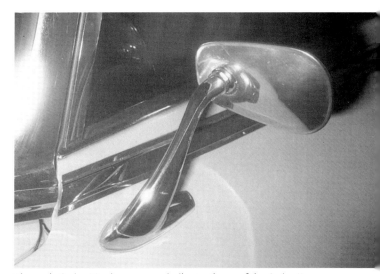

The early Series III mirrors were similar to those of the Series II, and they could only be adjusted from outside the car. Compare with Series II mirror.

The remote-control mirrors on the later Series III cars were larger to accommodate the control mechanism. This is the inside view of the later U.S.-market Series III mirror.

This lever was mounted on the inside of the driver's door of the late U.S.-market Series III cars for remote control of the mirror.

Changes at chassis numbers 1S.20168/9 and 1S.72660/1: About April 1972, a remote control was added to the external mirror for cars shipped to United States and Canada.

Seatbelts and Seatbelt Warning System

Inertia-reel seatbelts were supplied in both Kangol and Britax types. For a few countries, a bent wire guide was used on the upper outer corners of the seats to guide the seatbelts. While the factory parts books show these as fitted throughout production, Russ states that this bracket was introduced for 1973 model year cars.

Changes at chassis numbers 1S.20168/9, for cars shipped to the United States and Canada, and

1S.72660/1, for cars shipped to the United States and Canada: About May of 1972 seatbelt alarms were added.

Changes at chassis numbers 1S.23239/40: Changes were made to the seatbelt warning system.

Radio, Suppresser Capacitor, Blanking Plate, and Antenna

A tape-player-equipped radio was offered as an option, as was a power antenna. Later British-Leyland radios had the British-Leyland symbol on their tuning plates, while early ones did not.

Russ states that the early 1971 model year cars did not have British-Leyland radios, as the radios at that time were dealer-installed options, but that subsequently British-Leyland radios were the only ones available.

The early Series III cars had Kangol seatbelt latches similar to the late Series II cars.

A Kangol inertia-reel mechanism on an early Series III coupe.

Seatbelt alarms were added to later U.S.-market cars, and the latch design was changed. The alarm-actuation wires can be seen on this late-style latch.

An inspector's sticker can be seen on this Kangol inertia-reel mechanism.

Locking Gas Cap

A locking gas cap was an option in the United Kingdom only. I believe this unit is identical to the one available on Series I cars and illustrated on page 97.

Key Fob

As with earlier cars, a key fob was available as an option. It was teardrop-shaped, with a round escutcheon bearing a front-on view of a Jaguar cat.

Anti-Mist Element: Coupe

A heated rear window was available as an option, and at chassis numbers 1S.50590/1 and 1S.72332/3, the optional electrically heated rear window was changed. These windows employed the vertical, high-density wires, as used on Series I coupes. I am not sure if Series III cars were also fitted with the horizontal, low-density wire windows as used on the Series II coupes.

Air Conditioning

Air conditioning was available as an option, at least on LHD cars. Skilleter has stated that due to location of the blower motor in the footwell interfering with the steering column, no RHD cars could be fitted with air conditioning.

Hardtop

A removable hardtop was available as an option on all roadsters. Russ states that his sources indicate the hardtop was available in black or white. I have never seen a factory-painted white removable hardtop, and Russ makes this same statement. Porter states that the hardtop was available only in black, as does the factory parts book, and I believe this to be the case.

Tinted Glass

"Sundym" tinted glass was available as an option in both the coupe and roadster.

Side Lights

The side lights could be ordered as an option in the home market.

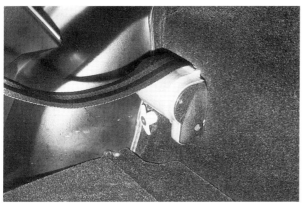

The mounting arrangement for a Kangol Reflex inertia-reel mechanism on a later Series III roadster.

The British-Leyland radio, as fitted by the factory to an early Series III car. Note that this car is fitted with air conditioning, and the cigar lighter has been relocated away from its standard position above the radio to the front of the armrest-storage area.

The base of the optional antenna had a teardrop shape, with the point facing downward.

Transmissions

Due to the increased wheelbase of the Series III, the automatic transmission option was available in both the coupe and roadster. Previously, it had been available only on the 2+2, which for the six-cylinder cars was the only long-wheelbase variant.

The automatic transmission changed at engine numbers 7S.4336/7, and again at engine numbers 7S.8929/30.

This later British-Leyland radio differs from earlier models in that the British-Leyland symbol is imprinted on the left of the dial. Note the cigar lighter mounted in its standard position above the radio.

The four-speed manual transmission was standard on Series III cars.

Changes at chassis numbers 1S.2449/50, for cars not shipped to the United States and Canada, 1S.23418/9, for cars not shipped to the United States and Canada, and 1S.23239/40, for cars shipped to the United States and Canada: The manual and automatic transmission housings changed.

Flywheel

I am not aware of any changes.

Block Heater

A Bray block heater was offered as an optional extra.

Bumper Guards

I am not aware of any changes.

Paint

In 1972 a special silver-grey metallic paint was offered as an optional extra.

Power Steering

For the first time, power steering was standard and not an option.

Changes at engine numbers 7S.7784/5: The mount for the power-steering pump was changed.

Oil Cooler

I am not aware of any changes.

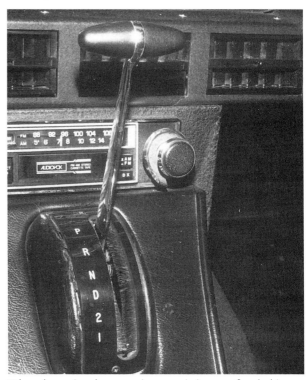

When the optional automatic transmission was fitted, this was its control lever. This picture is from a Series III roadster, which was now on the long wheelbase of the 2 + 2 and could, for the first time, be fitted with the automatic transmission option.

Chapter 10

5.3-LITER ENGINE, DRIVETRAIN, AND CHASSIS COMPONENT CHANGES

Engine: Cylinder Block

Changes at engine numbers 7S.4020/1: The thrust bearings were changed.

Changes at engine numbers 7S.4064/5: The bolts for the crankshaft pulley were changed.

Changes at engine numbers 7S.4509/10: About December 1971, the thrust bearings on the crankshaft were altered to have beveled corners on their inner side. The new bearings were gold colored.

Cylinder Head, Camshaft Covers, and Associated Fittings

Changes at chassis numbers 1S.1303/4, 1S.20557/8, 1S.51246/7, and 1S.73336/7: About June 1972, a support bracket was added between the intake manifold and the front part of the rain shield.

The vacuum tubing was changed at engine numbers 7S.7685/6, and again at engine numbers 7S.8929/30.

The early rain shields had only two mounts.

Underview of a late rain shield showing the fastening bracket between the new front mount and the top of the intake manifold.

Later rain shields had three mounts. The new one was located farthest toward the front of the shield, and inward, toward the center of the engine.

The early cam covers had the "JAGUAR" label cast into them in the same manner used for the late Series II six-cylinder cars. To the left of the "JAGUAR" label is the early-type oil-filler cap, without handle and with fluted edges, much in the style of the caps used on the six-cylinder XK engine that preceded the V-12. The early-style cast engine-lifting ring can be seen along the lower edge of the picture, just right of center. These were continued far through the production run, at least into the 1974 model year.

Underview of an early rain shield showing the absence of the front mount.

Changes at chassis numbers 1S.22271/2 and 1S.74768/9: From about March 1973, cars sold in West Germany had engines meeting the ECE 15 European emission specification.

Changes at chassis numbers 1S.2449/50 and 1S.23418/9: From about October 1974, cars sold in all countries except the United States, Canada, and Japan had engines meeting the ECE 15 European emission specification.

Later cars were fitted with emission controls regardless of their destination. These included an air pump that forced air into the exhaust ports of the heads.

At one point, the cast "JAGUAR" name in the front of the cam covers was discontinued. In its place was a flat region in the casting and a gold-and-black sticker

with the name "JAGUAR" printed on it. Russ states that this change took place at engine numbers 7S.3904/5 at about the transition from 1973 to 1974 model years.

Changes at engine numbers 7S.4663/4: The lifting rings attached to the engine were changed. The early rings were cast and the later rings were fabricated from sheet steel.

Oil Pan and Plug

I am not aware of any changes.

Starter Motor

The starter motor was changed at engine numbers 7S.3708/9, and again at engine numbers 7S.4097/8.

Changes at engine numbers 7S.7000/1: About May 1972, the starter motor and flywheel (for manual transmission cars) or driven plate (for automatic transmission cars) were changed.

Engine Mounts

Changes at engine numbers 7S.8833/4: The engine mounts were changed.

Crankcase Breather

Changes at engine number 7S.8178/9: The engine breather configuration was changed.

Oil Filter Assembly

I am not aware of any changes.

Oil Cooler Assembly

The bolts retaining the oil cooler assembly were changed early in production.

Timing Chain Cover

I am not aware of any changes.

Crankshaft Damper and Pulley

I am not aware of any changes.

Oil Dipstick

Changes at engine numbers 7S.4663/4 (including 7S.4560 and 7S.4621, excluding 7S.4879): Changes were made to the dipstick and its mounting hardware.

On this early car, there are no clamps on the rubber connector between the intake horn and the plenum.

The later Series III cars had a flat region cast onto the front of the cam covers where a "JAGUAR" sticker was placed. Note the later-style oil-filler cap, now without flutes but with a handle cast in. Unlike the earlier caps, which were bare aluminum, these later caps were finished in black. The late-style engine-lifting ring, fabricated from sheet steel, can be seen in the lower right quarter of the picture.

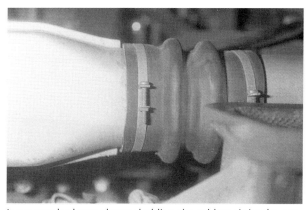

Later cars had two clamps holding the rubber air-intake connector.

This red emission decal was used on early carburetors only. It is similar but not the same as those used on Series II cars.

In the emission-control plumbing configuration on the early U.S.-market cars, the gulp valve was mounted below and to the rear of the throttle linkage. It is seen below the throttle mast in the lower right quadrant of the picture. Also clearly evident here are the early-type spherical throttle control-rod ends. Note also the alphanumeric string cast into the throttle disc, which is absent from the later disc.

On this later car, the gulp valve is located to the front of the throttle linkage and at the same height above the engine. Note on this late car the late-type cylindrical throttle control-rod ends.

Crankshaft, Connecting Rods, Bearings, Caps, Pistons, and Rings

Changes at engine numbers 7S.5501/2: The pistons were changed.

Changes at engine numbers 7S.6309/10: About May 1972, the pistons were changed to a lighter version.

Changes at engine numbers 7S.7154/5: About June 1972, the oil-feed holes were deleted from the con-rod big-end bearings.

Changes at engine numbers 7S.7855/6: About October 1972, the oil-feed holes in the small ends of the con rods were discontinued.

Changes at engine numbers 7S.8188/9: About December 1972, the main bearings were changed to a new version with better lining material.

Changes at engine numbers 7S.10798/9: About May 1973, the crankshaft was changed to the one used on the XJ12.

Valves, Valve Gear, Camshafts, Chains, and Sprockets

About October 1973, cams with new profiles were fitted to cars sold in the United States and Canada.

Changes at engine numbers 7S.17073/4: About November 1974, the tappets were changed.

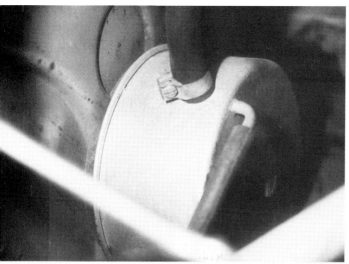

The early cars had metal carbon canisters. They were mounted in the engine compartment, in front of the right-side footwell.

Carbon canisters with a black plastic housing were used on the later cars. Note the corrugated air-intake pipe running into the footwell just above the canister. These ducts were used only on later cars.

Oil Pump and Oil Delivery System

Changes at engine numbers 7S.12064/5: About July 1973, the oil pump was changed to one with a different housing.

Changes at engine numbers 7S.7377/8: The oil-line plumbing to the heads was changed, and the oil pressure sender unit mounting was changed.

Fuel System: Carburetors and Manifolds

Changes at engine numbers 7S.2823/4: About December 1971, the carburetor gaskets were changed to a new style having insulating properties. The new gaskets were pink, and after they were fitted, the separate insulators were no longer required.

The rubber connectors between the air-intake horns and the carburetor input plenum were held in place with clamps only after the 1971 model year.

The carburetors on the emission-controlled engines were marked to show that they met the emission standards. Russ states that on 1971 model year cars this was a red dot, and on later cars it was blue.

Changes at engine numbers 1S.4663/4, for cars shipped to the United States, Canada, and Japan, automatic-transmission cars, and 1S.4560 to 1S.4621, for the United States, Canada, and Japan, automatic-transmission cars: The balance-pipe and gulp valve plumbing between the left and right intake manifolds was changed.

Changes at engine numbers 7S.4879/80, non-emission-control engines: The air balance pipes were changed.

Changes at engine numbers 7S.4663/4, for cars shipped to the United States and Canada, and 7S.4879/80, for cars not shipped to the United States and Canada: The carburetors were changed.

Changes at engine numbers 7S.8178/9: Exhaust gas carburetor preheat was added and the carburetor

The original location of the coil and ballast resistor was at the right front of the engine, just in front of the right-side cam cover.

float-chamber vents were changed for U.S. market cars.

Changes at engine numbers 7S.8178/9, for cars shipped to the United States and Canada, and 7S.8670/1, for cars not shipped to the United States and Canada: Changes were made to the fuel-delivery system and carburetors.

Changes at engine numbers 7S.9733/4: The exhaust gas carburetor preheat was changed.

Changes at engine numbers 7S.8670/1, for emission-control engine cars shipped to Sweden, Japan, and EEC countries: The balance-pipe and gulp valve plumbing between the left and right intake manifolds was changed, as well as the thermostatic vacuum system.

On later cars, the coil and ballast resistor were located at the right-rear of the engine.

Changes at engine numbers 7S.14000/1, for emission-control cars shipped to the United States, Canada, and Japan: The thermostatic vacuum system was changed.

Throttle Linkage

Changes were made to the throttle linkage at engine numbers 7S.13501/2, and again at engine numbers 7S.14662/3.

Fuel Filter and Lines

Changes at chassis numbers 1S.21028/9 and 1S.73855/6 for cars shipped to the United States and Canada: About December 1972, a sealed fuel system was introduced. The new system used a carbon canister.

Changes at chassis numbers 1S.1664/5, 1S.21661/2, 1S.51616/7, and 1S.74311/2: About March 1973, the fuel filter was changed to one with a metal bowl, and it was located on the right side of the trunk bulkhead.

The OPUS transistor ignition was located on top of the engine, next to the distributor.

Air Filter

The air filter retaining bolts were changed at engine numbers 7S.4663/4, for cars shipped to the United States and Canada, and 7S.4879/80, for cars not shipped to the United States and Canada, and again at engine numbers 7S.8178/9, for cars shipped to the United States and Canada, and 7S.8670/1, for cars not shipped to the United States and Canada.

Changes at engine numbers 7S.8670/1: The air-cleaner adapters were changed for cars other than those going to the United States and Canada.

Changes at engine numbers 7S.8178/9, for cars shipped to the United States and Canada: The air-cleaner adapters were changed.

Air-Injection Pump

Changes at engine numbers 7S.9033/4, for emission cars: About February 1973, the air-injection pump was altered on emission-controlled engines. The new pump incorporated an air filter.

Changes were also made to the air-distribution pipes at this point.

Gas Tank

I am not aware of any changes.

Fuel Pump, Mount, and Lines

I am not aware of any changes.

Fuel-Level Sender Unit

I am not aware of any changes.

Ignition System: Coil and Bracket

Changes at chassis numbers 1S.1021/2, 1S.20090/1, 1S.50317/8, and 1S.72317/8: Changes were made to the ignition system.

Changes at engine numbers 7S.9678/9: About February 1973, the ballast resistor and coil were moved to the right rear of the engine. This made the drive belts easier to get at.

The early radiator cowling was made of fiberglass, similar to that used in the early six-cylinder E-Types. The thick cross section of the fiberglass cowling is evident here where the air-intake horn passes through it.

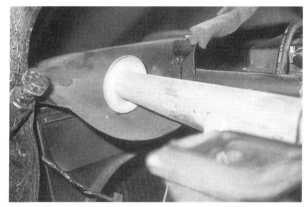

The radiator shroud of later cars was made of sheet metal, and the air-intake horns did not pass through it.

This is the B.U.T.E.C. voltage regulator as originally fitted to the Series III cars.

This Prestolite voltage regulator is a replacement unit.

The light-colored braided wire cover on the positive battery cable.

Changes at engine numbers 7S.16209/10: About February 1974, a high-load coil and an amplifier were specified.

Early coils, up to 1974, have an oval Lucas sticker, while coils for 1974 have a label with a rectangular section with the words "BALLASTED COIL" on it.

Transistor Ignition

The transistor ignition unit was mounted on top of the engine. About 1980, a kit was offered by the factory to relocate the unit in front of the engine where it would be cooler.

Distributor

The distributor was changed at engine numbers 7S.4663/4 (emission-control engines, including 7S.4560 to 7S.4621), and again at engine numbers 7S.4879/80 (non-emission-control engines).

Distributor Rotor, Cap, and Wire Retainers

Problems with the resistivity of the rotor caused it to be changed early in production.

Spark-Plug Wires and Organizers

The spark-plug wires were changed early in production.

Spark-Plug Caps

I am not aware of any changes.

Spark Plugs

About October 1972, the N9Y spark plugs were changed to N10Y.

Ballast Resistor

Changes at engine numbers S.7559/60: About August 1972, a printed-circuit ballast resistor was introduced, Lucas number 47229.

Cooling System: Radiator and Fan Shroud

Changes at engine numbers 7S.4879/80, non-emission-control engines: The thermostatic vacuum system was changed.

Changes at engine numbers 7S.8443/4: About February 1973, the thermostatic vacuum switch (and related plumbing) on the right rear coolant pipe was discontinued on non-emission-control engines.

In early 1972, the radiator cowling was changed.

Header Tank

I am not aware of any changes.

Water Pump and Pulley

Changes at engine numbers 7S.7784/5: About October 1972, the water pump and its hoses were changed.

Hoses and Clamps

Changes at chassis numbers 1S.1004/5, 1S.20024/5, 1S.50226/7, and 1S.71729/30: The cooling system plumbing was changed.

Thermostat

The thermostat housing underwent frequent changes during production, at least including changes at these engine numbers: 7S.4663/4 (including 7S.4560 to 7S.4621, emission-control engines), 7S.4879/80, non-emission-control engines, 7S.9336/7, 7S.12546/7, 7S.14000/1.

Charging System: Alternator and Bracket

I am not aware of any changes.

Pulleys and Belt

I am not aware of any changes.

Voltage Regulator and Bracket

The B.U.T.E.C. voltage regulators were apparently fitted throughout production, but "Prestolite" replacements are often seen.

Battery, Cables, Tray, and Mounts

Early cars were fitted with a Lucas Pacemaker P/N CP 13/11-8 battery, while later cars had a Lucas P/N XC55/8.

Changes at chassis numbers 1S.1004/5, 1S.20024/5, 1S.50226/7, and 1S.71684/5: About December 1971, the battery and its tray and hold-down were all changed, and the colors of the battery cables were changed: positive from red to blue and negative from black to brown. Russ states, however, that his research does not support the battery-cable-color change, and he has observed on Series III cars only the positive cable covered by a white cloth braid and bare braided wire on the negative.

Electric: Wiring Harness

The parts book lists numerous changes to the wiring harness throughout production. Changes are listed for chassis numbers: 1S.1004/5 and 1S.20024/5, 1S.50204/5 and 1S.71493/4, 1S.50263/4 and 1S.72169/70, 1S.1178/9 and 1S.20152/3, 1S.50885/6 and 1S.72567/8, 1S.1264/5 and 1S.20248/9, 1S.51164/5 and 1S.72952/3, 1S.23239/40, and for engine numbers: 7S.2251/2, 7S.7377/8, 7S.9696/7, and 7S.14000/1.

Russ reports that the wiring harness on early cars had a green tracer thread in the black cloth covering that was lacking on later cars, and that late in production, the ties used to retain the harness were changed to translucent or clear plastic.

Windshield Washer
I am not aware of any changes.

Brake-Light Switch
I am not aware of any changes.

Cooling Fan, Relay, and Switch
I am not aware of any changes.

Horn and Relay
Changes at chassis numbers 1S.2125/6, 1S.23237/8, 1S.52008/9, and 1S.75183/4: The horns were changed.

Tachometer, Pressure, and Temperature Senders
Changes at chassis numbers 1S.1004/5, 1S.20063/4, 1S.50263/4, and 1S.72204/5: The coolant temperature sensor was changed.

Brakes and Hydraulics: Brake and Clutch Fluid Reservoirs and Mounts
I am not aware of any changes.

Brake and Clutch Fluid Reservoir Heat Shield
I am not aware of any changes.

Hydraulic Lines, Switch, Cylinders, and Activation Mechanism
Changes at chassis numbers 1S.1178/9, 1S.20152/3, 1S.50885/6 (including 1S.50826), and 1S.72567/8: The hydraulic brake pipes near the master cylinder changed.

Brake Vacuum System
I am not aware of any changes.

Miscellaneous: Steering
I am not aware of any changes.

Heater
I am not aware of any changes.

Splash Shields
I am not aware of any changes.

Drivetrain: Bellhousing, Flywheel, Clutch, and Slave Cylinder
Changes at engine numbers 7S.7000/1: About May 1972, the starter motor and flywheel (for manual transmission cars) or driven plate (for automatic transmission cars) were changed.

Transmission and Mounts
Changes at chassis numbers 1S.2449/50, for cars not shipped to the United States and Canada, 1S.23418/9, for cars not shipped to the United States and Canada, 1S.23239/40, for cars shipped to the United States and

The impact tube ran from behind the front bumper overrider and terminated inside the hood. The inside end was adjustable in length to allow proper contact with the mating pad on the front of the subframe.

This locating pad was fitted to the front of the front tubular space frame to serve as a butting-point for the rear of the impact tube. It was mounted just in front of and above the top shock-absorber mount.

Canada: The manual and automatic transmission housings changed.

Changes at engine numbers 7S.9714/5: About February 1973, the modified Model 12 Borg Warner automatic transmission was introduced. This was the same transmission used on the XJ12.

Changes at engine numbers 7S.13999/14000 (associated with gearbox number KL.6771/2): About October 1973, synchromesh sleeves were changed.

Changes at engine numbers 7S.14340/1 (associated with gearbox number KL.7097/8): About October 1973, the gearbox countershaft was changed. The new one was made of a different material.

Changes at transmission numbers KL.4240/1: About January 1973, there was a change in the needle bearings.

Changes at engine numbers 7S.8981/2: Changes were made to the gearbox.

The automatic transmission changed at engine numbers 7S.4336/7 and 7S.8929/30.

Changes at engine numbers 7S.14000/1: The rear transmission mount was changed.

Driveshaft

I am not aware of any changes.

Differential

Changes at chassis numbers 1S.1092/3, 1S.20098/9, 1S.50591/2, and 1S.72331/2: About November 1971, the teeth on the ring and pinion gears were modified (new parts marked 4HA-016-54 and 4HA-017-54 respectively). At this same point, a tag labeled "7.5" was attached to the case.

Changes at chassis numbers 1S.21575/6 and 1S.74260/1: About March 1973, the 3.31:1 rear end was introduced for cars sent to the United States and Canada, and the 3.07:1 was fitted to cars sold in other countries. The 3.54:1 rear end was no longer available on manual transmission cars.

Chassis: Front Wheel Hubs

I am not aware of any changes.

A-Arms and Pivots

I am not aware of any changes.

Front Torsion Bars

Changes at chassis numbers 1S.50064/5 and 1S.70412/3: The torsion bars and front shock absorbers were changed.

Changes at chassis numbers 1S.1347/8, 1S.20568/9, 1S.51262/3, and 1S.73371/2: About June 1972, the torsion-bar adjuster cam profile was raised.

Front Shock Absorbers

I am not aware of any changes.

Front Antiroll Bar

Changes at chassis numbers 1S.2125/6, 1S.23237/8, 1S.52008/9, and 1S.75183/4: The front roll-bar mounts were changed.

Changes at chassis numbers 1S.2808/9 and 1S.25320/1: The antiroll bar couplings were changed.

Rear Wheel Hubs and Carriers

About June 1973, the steel rear-hub spacer was replaced by a phosphor bronze spacer.

Radius Arms, Trailing Arms, and Halfshafts

Changes at chassis numbers 1S.50166/7 and 1S.71177/8: The lower wishbone in the rear suspension was changed.

Rear Springs, Seats, and Spacers

I am not aware of any changes.

Rear Shock Absorbers

I am not aware of any changes.

Rear Antiroll Bar

I am not aware of any changes.

Brakes

Changes at chassis numbers 1S.1662/3, 1S.21605/6, 1S.51609/10, and 1S.74265/6: About April 1973, the cooling ducts to the rear brakes were changed to increase ground clearance.

Parking Brake

I am not aware of any changes.

Front Wheelwells and Engine Compartment Undershields

I am not aware of any changes.

Wheels, Weights, and Hubcaps

Initially the Series III cars were fitted with steel disc wheels painted silver-grey and fitted with chrome trim rings. Chrome-plated steel disc wheels or chrome-plated wire wheels were available as options. Chrome-plated steel disc wheels became standard for the 1973 model year.

Tires and Tubes

I am not aware of any changes.

Front Subframe

The front subframe was changed at chassis numbers 1S.1021/2, 1S.20090/1, 1S.50184/5, and 1S.71310/1, and again at chassis numbers 1S.50313/4 and 1S.72317/8.

Changes at chassis numbers 1S.1659/60, 1S.21169/70, for cars not shipped to the United States and Canada, 1S.21028/9, for cars shipped to the United States and Canada, 1S.51582/3 and 1S.73966/7, for cars not shipped to the United States and Canada, 1S.73855/6, for cars shipped to the United States and Canada: The hood-support subframe (between the hood and the main front subframe) was changed.

The V-12 cars initially came standard with four-outlet tailpipes.

This view of the rear of a later car shows the dual-outlet tailpipe.

Changes at chassis numbers 1S.21028/9, for cars shipped to the United States and Canada, 1S.73966/7, for cars not shipped to the United States and Canada, and 1S.73855/6, for cars shipped to the United States and Canada: The front subframe was changed. It was at this point the front bumper impact tubes were added.

Rear Subframe, Mounts, and Stops

Changes at chassis numbers 1S.1209/10, 1S.20168/9, 1S.50967/8, and 1S.72661/2: About April 1972, the factory began supplying brackets on the center cross beam and the lower mounts of the rear shock absorbers for use during shipping of the car, but not for towing purposes.

Tubing and Cables

I am not aware of any changes.

Exhaust System

I am not aware of any changes.

Rear Pipes and Resonators

Changes at chassis numbers 1S.1740/1, 1S.22045/6, 1S.51317/8 or 1S.51616/7, and 1S.74311/2 or 1S.74661/2: About March 1973, the four-outlet tailpipes were replaced by tailpipes with two outlets. There is disagreement about the changeover numbers for the coupe, so I have listed the two sets of cited changeover numbers here.

Exhaust Heat Shield

I am not aware of any changes.

Chapter 11

FASTENERS

The subject of fastening devices used in the Jaguar E-Type is broad, including nuts, bolts, screws, straps, and retainers. While this chapter is not meant to be a final or definitive treatment of the subject, at least a brief treatment seems appropriate for a book such as this. The illustrations of the bolt-head markings are representative of those to be found originally on the cars, but many variants exist with slightly different lettering and marking, and quality of markings. Bolts changed throughout production of the E-Type, and they are illustrated here roughly in chronological order, with early bolts first.

BEES 45R55 bolt with wide-spaced lettering, as typically used on earlier cars.

BEES 45R55 bolt with narrow-spaced lettering, as typically used on earlier cars.

GKN R-UNF bolt without dividing lines and with narrow spacing, as typically used on earlier cars.

GKN R-UNF bolt without dividing lines and with wide spacing, as typically used on earlier cars.

GKN S bolt with dividing lines, as typically used on later cars.

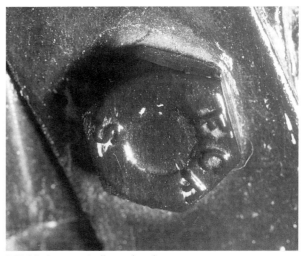

FCF S bolt, as typically used on later cars.

CRANES S bolt, as typically used on later cars.

R O S bolt without dividing lines on a V-12 rain shield.

R O S bolt with dividing lines, as typically used on later cars.

R O T bolt with full dividing lines, as typically used on later cars.

The heads of the sheet-metal screws used to hold the heater box together had rounded shoulders and flat tops. This same type of head was used on machine screws used in various places, for example, retaining the chrome trim over the outlet at the rear of the hood bulge.

Beveled chromed nut on a Series I 3.8-liter carburetor. I believe the bevels on these bolts faced out during original assembly.

Locknut on the front frame of an early car.

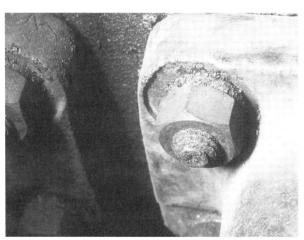

Brass nuts on steel bolts with steel spring lock washers were used to retain the exhaust manifolds to the head.

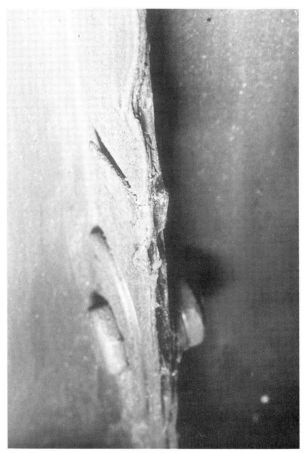

This is a view of the inner-side of the joining region between the outer front fender and the center section of the hood. It shows the bent-back arms of the brass retaining clip that holds the chrome beading on the top of the fender, and a hex-headed bolt with elongated washer holding the fender to the hood center section.

These large Phillips-headed bolts with elongated washers were used to assemble the hood. Hex-headed bolts were also used.

Castellated locknut with cotter on the top mount of a front shock of a 3.8-liter car.

This BEES bolt holding a heater mount to the firewall is used in conjunction with a spring lock washer followed by a flat washer.

Flat brass washers were used under the small domed chrome nuts used to hold the cam covers down, and in other places around the cylinder head.

In other places, for example the retaining bolts for the air-cleaner canister, serrated locknuts were used instead of spring lock washers.

The triangular air-cleaner plenums were held to the three-trumpet base assembly on the carburetors with two sets of these wing nuts. They were used with spring lock washers and large-diameter flat washers.

In some locations, the serrated locknuts were used alone. This is one of three LINREAD R bolts retaining the thermostatic switch blanking plate on the intake manifold assembly.

Specialty bolts, such as this hollow brass bolt retaining the banjo connector to the fuel-filter assembly, were typically not marked. Fiber sealing washers were used here, while similar hollow steel bolts used on cylinder-head oil lines used copper sealing washers.

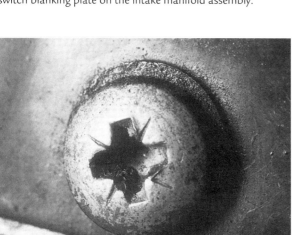

Most of the Phillips screws had these slash marks stamped into them 45 degrees off from the main pattern. One exception was the headlight glass-cover retaining ring screws.

The pop-rivets used on some of the early cars had a flattened region on their tops, near the center.

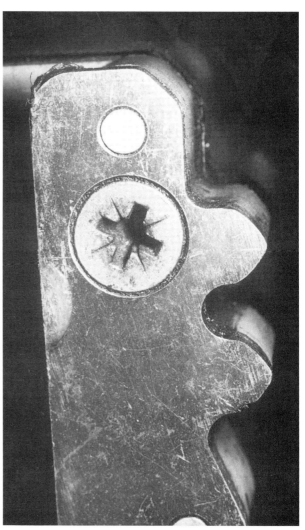

This flat-head door latch Phillips screw also shows the slash marks.

These sheet metal nuts were used with special coarse-thread screws to retain the lower engine-compartment shields to the inner ends of the rocker panels.

These clamps were used on the vacuum-assist lines for the power brakes.

These plastic retaining strips were used throughout E-Type production to hold various wires, lines, and hoses in place.

Chapter 12

PRODUCTION RATES AND SURVIVAL

Relationships Between Serial Numbers

A question often asked about the early cars is: what is the order of a particular car within overall E-Type production, not just within its number series? For example, chassis number 875026 has body number R.1044, engine number R.1037-9, and transmission number EB.137 JS. Clearly this is the twenty-sixth of all LHD roadsters made, but where does it stand in the overall E-Type production? Is it the thirty-seventh, since it has engine and transmission number 37? Are engine and transmission numbers always related? Is it the forty-fourth of all roadsters produced (since the roadster and coupe bodies were numbered in two separate series)?

These questions are hard to answer. As will be seen, these are probably good guesses, but there are enough exceptions to this logical order to make them only guesses.

As an attempt to help with questions of production order, I have plotted some of the data from my register for E-Types. The following plots relate the various chassis, body, and engine numbers in various ways in an attempt to show how they relate.

As illustrated, the engine and transmission numbers were, for the most part, directly related to one another.

Also illustrated is the relationship of the four chassis number series to the engine numbers. In order to conveniently plot them all in one figure, I first subtracted the numerical prefixes from the chassis numbers by subtracting 850000, 860000, 875000, and 885000 from the RHD roadsters and coupes and the LHD roadsters and coupes, respectively. It is immediately apparent that the production rates for the four series were very different, with the highest production rate for the LHD roadsters and lowest for the RHD coupes. For example, chassis number 875336 (engine R.1484-9), the 336th LHD roadster made, was likely produced earlier than chassis number 860005 (engine R.1522-9), the fifth RHD coupe made.

It is also evident that there were some glitches in the production. Not all engine and chassis numbers in a given series were sequentially related. On the whole, however, there is a reasonably rational relationship between engine numbers and the chassis numbers in a given series.

It is also interesting to note that at about engine number R.2400 there was a decrease in the LHD roadster production rate, and at about engine number R.3300 there was an increase in LHD coupe rate. The two rates remained about the same for some time thereafter.

Another illustration relates the four chassis number series to body number. Recall that there are two body number series here, the R for roadsters, and the V for the coupes. There are fewer glitches here, and the production rates remain about the same in each series.

Register of E-Types

Since 1975 I have kept a register of surviving E-Types. It began as a register for aluminum-bodied XK-120s and 1961 E-Types, but grew over time to encompass later six-cylinder E-Types as well. However, the majority of the registered numbers are still early E-Types. Each entry typically consists of at least the chassis number, the owner's name, and address or telephone number at the time of its entry into the register. Often other information is included, such as history on the car and its owners, the condition of car, a listing of some of the details, its sales history, and its body, engine, transmission, rear-end, and radiator serial numbers. In some cases, information has been gathered exclusively from articles, and no contact was made. This is indicated in the registration form later in this chapter.

A list of the registered cars as of this printing follows. The most recent contact date is contained in parentheses. I have obtain some of this information through letters, phone calls, and second hand through nonowners. In these cases I have not seen the cars. In addition, some of the information is quite old and will be outdated. In other cases, however, I have extensive information.

Below I have listed only the chassis and other serial numbers. While typically the dates given here indicate that the particular car was in existence at that time, in some instances they specify only the date at which the most recent information on the car was received. In these cases, the car's whereabouts may not be known, or the car may not even still be in existence.

Additional information is contained in my *Early E-Type Production and Registration Handbook*.

RHD E-Type Roadsters
850001 (prototype number 4), R.1001, R.1099-9
850002 (prototype number 5), R.1002
850003, R.1004
850004, R.1011
850005, R.1013
850006 (lightweight number 1), R.1015
850007, R.1017, R.1026-9, EB.129CR
850008
850009
850010
850011 (April 1991)
850012, R.1025
850013, R.1031
850014
850015
850016
850017 (June 18, 1993)
850018, R.1029

850019 (April 1991)
850020 (April 1991)
850021 (April 1991)
850022 (April 1991)
850023 (April 1991)
850024 (April 1991)
850025
850026 (April 1991)
850027
850028 (April 1991)
850029 (April 1991)
850030, R.1165 (October 7, 1991)
850031
850033 (April 1991)
850034, R.1157-9
850041
850045 (November 24, 1993)
850055 (January 23, 1979)
850057 (January 23, 1979)
850064 (September 1988)
850075 (January 23, 1979)
850082 (April 1991)
850084 (April 1991)
850085, R.1351-9 (September 1988)

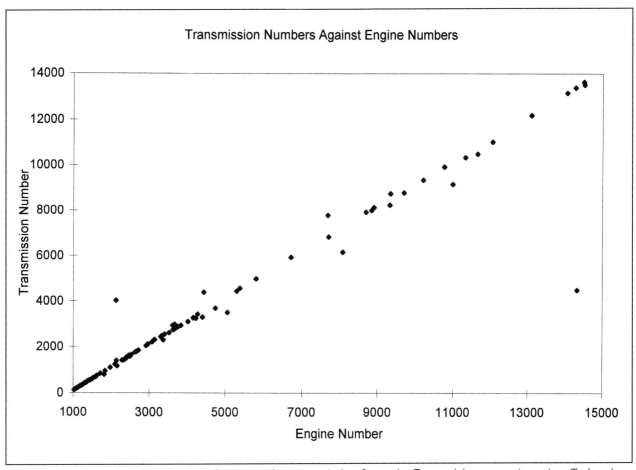

Transmission numbers plotted as a function of engine numbers. Numerical prefixes and suffixes, and the compression-ratio suffix, have been removed. The almost linear relationship indicates the engines and transmissions were kept in reasonably good order during production.

850086, R.1342-9 (September 1988)
850087 (May 1986)
850095, R.1491-9 (September 1988)
850096 (April 1991)
850099 (April 1991)
850108 (April 1991)
850118, R.1682, R.1693-9, DA20594/C20019 (August 12, 1993)
850122, R.1680, R.1622-9, EB.732JS (June 18, 1993)
850152, R.1738, EB.925JS (July 10, 1991)
850155 (April 1991)
850157 (April 1991)
850158 (January 23, 1979)
850161 (April 1991)
850179 (April 1991)
850186 (January 23, 1979)
850210, R.1789, R.2137-8, EB.4022JS (June 18, 1993)
850238, R.2102, R.2152-9, EB.1391JS (August 28, 1976)
850259, R.2378, R.2542-9, EB.1664JS

850274 (September 11, 1976)
850293, R.2431, R.2677-9, EB.1782JS, radiator: P2091 over 9828 (August 24, 1993)
850322, R.2949-9 (June 18, 1993)
850354, R.2935, R.3632-9, EB.2751JS (June 18, 1993)
850357, R.2938, R.3619-8, R.2938 (January 5, 1994)
850414
850533, R.5700-9 (June 18, 1993)
850562, R.4199 (April 1991)
K850817 (April 1986)
1E.1934, 7E.14765-9 (June 18, 1993)
1R.1255 (June 18, 1993)

RHD E-Type Coupes
860001, V.1008
860002
860003, V.1014, R.1424-8, EB.538JS (April 1991)
860004
860005, V.1026, R.1522-9, EB.632JS (April 1994)

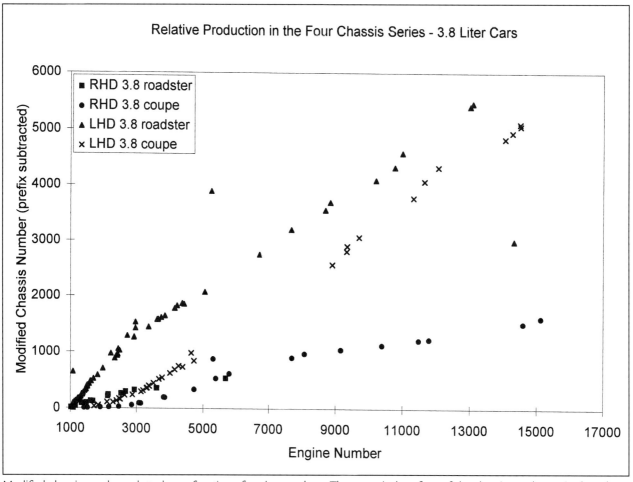

Modified chassis numbers plotted as a function of engine numbers. The numerical prefixes of the chassis-number series have been subtracted off. For the engine numbers, numerical prefixes and suffixes, and the compression-ratio suffix, have been removed. This illustrates the changing relative production rates in the four chassis-number series. At first LHD roadsters had the highest production rate, and RHD coupes had the lowest. Note that after a while, however, the LHD coupe production rate approximated that of the LHD roadsters. The occasional glitches indicate parts getting out of numerical sequence during production.

860006 (April 1991)
860007
860008 (April 1991)
860009
860010
860011
860012, R.1910-8 (June 18, 1993)
860013
860014
860015
860016
860017, V.1245, R.2170-9, EB.1170JS
860018 (April 1991)
860019 (April 1991)
860020 (April 1991)
860021
860022 (April 1991)
860023 (April 1991)
860024 (April 1991)
860025, V.1166, R.2468-9, EB.1595JS (April 1991)
860026 (April 1991)
860027 (April 1991)
860031 (April 1991)
860037
860050 (November 1976)
860053, V.1308, R.2864-9 (April 13, 1994)
860078 (January 23, 1979)
860084, V.1380 or V.1386, R.3137-9, EB.2308JS (June 18, 1993)
860088, V.1359, R.3083-9, EB.2219JS (June 18, 1993)
860116 (December 8, 1982)
860191, V.1819, R.3869-9 (January 5, 1994)
860194, V.1795, R.3838-8, EB.2939JS (June 18, 1993)
860334, R.4743-9, EB.3695JS (June 18, 1993)
860530, V.2527, R.5397-9, EB.4567JS (November 13, 1992)
860574 (January 23, 1979)
860613, R.5814-9, EB.4986JS (June 18, 1993)
860876, V.3758, R.5312-8, EB.4437JS (November 20, 1991)
860900, V.3828, R.7718-8, EB.6834JS (July 1, 1991)
860973, V.4331, R.8087-9, EB.6169CR (June 18, 1993)
861044 (June 17, 1993)
861045, R.9166-9 (June 18, 1993)
861126, V.5503, RA.1394-9 (June 18, 1993)
861213, V.6006, RA.2491-9, EB.10089 or EB.10689JS (June 18, 1993)
861229, RA.2811-9 (June 18, 1993)
861512, RA.5598-9 (~1993)
861616, RA.6132-9 (April 1991)
1E.20368 (June 18, 1993)
1E.20497, 4E.21332, 7E.3407-9, EJ.2484 (June 18, 1993)
1E.20705, 4E.21842, 7E.4155-9, EJ.3206 (June 18, 1993)
1E.20900, 4E.22459, 7E.5303-9, EJ.4289 (June 17, 1993)
1E.21136, 4E.23448, 7E.7071-9, EJ.6186 (~1993)
1E.21528, 4E.25916, 7E.13312-9, EJ.14548 (June 18, 1993)
1E.21914, 4E.27726, 7E.8270-9, KE.2209 (June 18, 1993)
1R.20290 (January 5, 1994)

LHD E-Type Roadsters

875001, R.1003 (June 5, 1989)
875002, R.1005
875003, R.1006
875004
875005 (April 1991)
875006 (April 1991)
875007 (April 1991)
875008 (April 1991)
875009 (April 1991)
875010 (February 11, 1990)
875012
875013 (March 1993)
875015
875022, R.1046, R.1049-9, EB.157JS (June 18, 1993)
875023, R.1042, R.1057-9, EB.160JS (May 13, 1990)
875024 (June 22, 1994)
875025 (April 1991)
875026, R.1044, R.1037-9, EB.137JS, radiator: 217 (January 1992)
875027 (January 21, 1987)
875038 (April 1991)
875045, R.1068, R.1071-9, EB.179JS (July 19, 1989)
875047 (January 21, 1987)
875048 (April 1991)
875049 (April 1991)
875050 (April 1991)
875051, R.1077, R.1054-9, EB.159JS (September 1988)
875053, R.1081, R.1101-9, EB.204JS (March 3, 1987)
875054 (April 1991)
875066, R.1094, R.1107-9, EB.209JS (April 1, 1991)
875071, R.1120-9 (June 7, 1979)
875077 (October 1984)
875078 (November 24, 1993)
875090, R.1138, R.1086-9, EB.188JS (April 13, 1994)
875091 (July 1994)
875095 (March 17, 1982)
875096, R.1099, R.1123-9
875105 (June 1984)
875109, R.1129, R.1138-9, EB.239JS (September 1993)
875115, R.1182, R.1125-9, EB.227JS (September 11, 1977)
875123 (November 24, 1987)
875124, R.1123, R.1172-9, EB.271JS (July 1980)
875125 (August 11, 1978)
875127 (June 1990)
875130, R.1189, R.1169-9, EB.278JS (April 18, 1994)
875131 (January 15, 1987)
875137 (June 1990)
875138, R.1224, R.1200-9, EB.310JS, radiator: 400 (May 28, 1994)
875139 (June 1994)
875140, R.1211, R.1202-9, EB.308JS, radiator: 5545 (September 1988)
875143, R.1167, R.1222-9 (November 1982)
875145 (June 1986)
875147, R.1228-9 (April 22, 1977)
875151 (June 1979)
875159 (June 1994)

875165, R.1270, R.1276-9, EB.374JS (November 18, 1980)
875166, R.1281, R.1277-9, EB.380JS, radiator: 303 (March 6, 1987)
875167, R.1273, R.1269-9 (March 1993)
875168, R.1274, R.1231-9, EB.328JS, radiator: 358 (September 14, 1976)
875179, R.1285, R.1263-9, EB.368JS (June 8, 1980)
875184, R.1291, R.1282-9, EB.383JS (September 13, 1991)
875186, R.1263, R.1289-9, EB.402JS (January 12, 1987)
875190, R.1300-9 (October 1987 I think)
875206, R.1295, R.1326-9, EB.431JS (July 25, 1980)
875214, R.1275-?
875222 (August 11, 1978)
875223 (February, 1989)
875227 (February 4, 1993)
875235, R.1360, R.1361-9, EB.460JS (December 1978)
875236, R.1366 (November 11, 1976)
875241 (February 4, 1993)
875250, R.1361, R.1347-9, EB.451JS (November 1982)
875251, R.1362, R.1375-9, EB.486JS (December 1975)
875254, R.1376 (January 1992)

875274, R.1373, R.1395-9, EB.508JS (July 20, 1980)
875276 (January 1988)
875282 (August 1975)
875283? (October 1987)
875294 (December 4, 1993)
875300 (May 9, 1994)
875304, R.1433, R.1435-9, EB.547JS (January 6, 1987)
875305 (November 24, 1993)
875314 (May 3, 1991)
875317 (September 1988)
875320, R.1449, R.1452-9, EB.550JS (August 21, 1977)
875324 (August 7, 1981)
875325, R.1460-9 (October 15, 1980)
875333, R.1460 (December 4, 1993)
875336, R.1479, R.1484-9 (July 1980)
875340, R.1460 on the body number plate, R.1455 on the main ID plate (December 4, 1993)
875366? (February 23, 1984)
875368 (October 31, 1976)
875378, V.1437, R.1492-9, EB.601JS (September 13, 1987)
875382, R.1465, R.1528-9, EB.637JS (November 8, 1989)
875391, R.1549, R.1500-9, EB.597JS (February 5, 1993)

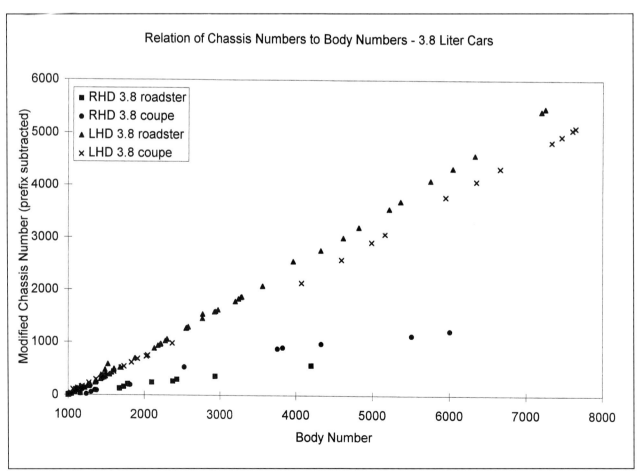

Modified chassis numbers plotted as a function of body numbers. The numerical prefixes of the chassis-number series have been subtracted off. For the body numbers, numerical prefixes have been removed, and the two body-number series use the same horizontal axis scale. As with the transmission/engine plot, the relationship is quite linear.

875399 (November 11, 1979)

875407, R.1501, R.1518-9, EB.617JS (April 20, 1994)

875427, R.1576, R.1573-9, EB.676JS (February 23, 1975)

875437 (September 1988)

875474, R.1606, R.1633-9, EB.746JS (April 14, 1984)

875476, R.1492 on the body number plate, R.1489 on the main ID plate, R.1610-9, EB.711JS (April 13, 1994)

875494, R.1609, EB.755JS (September 17, 1994)

875522, R.1688, R.1705-9 (April 1991)

875584, R.1530, R.1831-9, EB.799JS (March 1984)

875614 (April 7, 1978)

875642, R.1085-9 (December 27, 1975)

875647 (May 1990)

875648 or 468 (July 1991)

875673 (June 1986)

875692 (March 12, 1976)

875700, R.1881, R.1988-9, EB.1100JS (˜ 1991)

875729 (September 1989)

875834 (July 29, 1980)

875868 (March 1990)

875883, R.2132, R.2347-9, EB.1426JS (October 15, 1981)

875921 (January 1987)

875932, R.2180, R.2423-9, EB.1548JS (April 13, 1994)

875935 (July 1990)

875946 (March 1, 1992)

875947 (July 1994)

875949 (˜ 1982)

875953 (July 1990)

875954, R.2210 on the body number plate, R.2202 on the main ID plate, R.2436-9, EB.1553JS (March 3, 1976)

875958, R.2212, R.2418-9, EB.1538JS, radiator: 1777 (January 1975)

875967, R.2218, R.2228-9 (July 13, 1980)

875971 (September 1988)

876024, R.2276, R.2490-9, EB.1601JS (April 25, 1994)

876052, R.2301, R.2447-9, EB.1564JS, radiator: 1876 (October 26, 1987)

876208 (July 19, 1986)

876260, R.2550, R.2927-9, EB.2055JS

876270, R.2558, R.2931-9, EB.2061JS, radiator: 1437 (March 6, 1987)

876289, R.2578, R.2729-9, EB.1847JS (June 11, 1990)

876340 (March 1993)

876397

876423, R.2971-9? (˜ 1991)

876430 (October 1975)

876447, R.2784 on the body number plate, R.2763 on the main ID plate, R.3373-9, EB.2305JS (February 10, 1993)

876474 (January 27, 1989)

876486 (August 1975)

876495 (before June 1993)

876531, R.2877 on the body number plate, R.2867 on the main ID plate and written on dash panels, R.2973-9, EB.2122JS (May 31, 1994)

876577, R.2925, R.3653-9, EB.2760JS, radiator: 3017 (March 3, 1976)

876581, R.3639-9 (September 20, 1975)

876585, R.2943, R.3674-9, EB.2988JS (November 1975)

876613 (March 1976)

876615, R.2973, R.3764-9, EB.2873JS (January 20, 1977)

876643, R.3871-9 (July 24, 1980)

876779, R.3209, R.4163-9, EB.278JS (September 18, 1993)

876826, R.3252, R.4229-9, EB.3247JS (August 22, 1991)

876857, R.3285, R.4437-9, EB.4387JS (February 10, 1992)

876867, R.3295, R.4382-9 (April 26, 1977)

876905 (January 2, 1989)

876916 (October 5, 1992)

877071, R.3563, R.5062-9, EB.3507JS (August 11, 1992)

877268 (July 1990)

877311 (April 3, 1979)

877371 (June 17, 1993)

877545 (˜ 1977)

877546, R.3963, EB.4338JS (June 7, 1994)

877615? (May 1990)

877656 (September 7, 1975)

877752, R.4326, R.6725-9, EB.5944JS (April 21, 1977)

877831 (˜ 1989)

877996, R.4617, RA.5326-9, EB.4500JS (January 28, 1992)

878183 (before June 1993)

878201, R.4819, R.7692-9, EB.7799JS (July 9, 1993)

878263 (May 31, 1994)

878551, R.5216, R.8700-9, EB.7934JS (November 14, 1991)

878693, R.5359, R.8849-9, EB.8007JS (May 1990)

878830 (October 15, 1975)

878888, R.5261-8 (July 1989)

879093, R.5751, RA.1208-9?, EB.9342JS (September 7, 1991)

879325, R.6039, RA.1769-9, EB.9925JS (October 1987)

879336 (July 24, 1992)

879578, R.6330, RA.1997-9, EB.9156JS (September 17, 1994)

879855 (July 1989)

879876 (March 1993)

1E.10128, 7E.1275-8, EJ.322 (October 21, 1991)

1E.10512, 4E.1591, 7E.2323-9, EJ.1382 (September 7, 1991)

1E.10548, 7E.2534-8 (February 26, 1992)

1E.11387 (May 1990)

1E.11849 (March 1993)

1E.11976, 4E.3410, 7E.6723-9, EJ.5851 (June 10, 1990)

1E.12070, 4E.3505, 7E.6757-9, EJ.5376 (January 8, 1992)

1E.12615, 4E.4146, 7E.8179-9, EJ.7350 (July 13, 1992)

1E.12763, 4E.4229, 7E.8416-9, EJ.7474 (September 9, 1989)

1E.12871 (September 1991)

1E.13003, 4E.4547, 7E.8993-9, EJ.8452 (September 9, 1989)

1E.13057, 4E.4680, 7E.9114-9, EJ.8572 (November 29, 1992)

1E.13321, 4E.5002, 7E.9791-9 (August 11, 1992)

1E.13466, 4E.5154, 7E.10101-9, FJ.10617 (August 20, 1992)

1E.13538, 4E.5240, 7E.10329-9, EJ.11019 (June 18, 1993)
1E.13584, 4E.5293, 7E.10299-9, EJ.10952 (September 7, 1991)
1E.14223 (March 1990)
1E.14349 (April 1990)
1E.15161 (July 1991)
1E.15267, 4E.7082, 7E.12937-9, EJ.14038 (September 9, 1989)
1E.15673, 4E.7533, 7E.13580-9 (February 1993)
1E.15705, 4E.7583, 7E.13656-9, EJ.14846 (November 10, 1991)
1E.16928, 4E.8981, 7E.159619, FE.2357 (September 17, 1994)
1E.17212, 4E.9294, 7E.16445-9, KE.134 (September 20, 1991)
1E.17271, 4E.9336, 7E.16522-9, KE.323 (September 17, 1994)
1E.17665, 4E.9756, 7E.17141-9, KE.1028 (September 28, 1993)
1E.1776, 4E.7060, 7E.12933-9, EJ.13786 (June 18, 1993)
1E.17808, 4E.9928, 7E.17289-9, KE.1226 (January 8, 1992)
1E.17973 (July 1989)
1E.18224, 4E.10399, 7E.18133-9, KE.1863 (December 1, 1991)
1E.18282, 4E.10454, KE.1560 (September 7, 1991)
1R.7944, 4R.2019, 7R.2785-9, KE.2997 (September 9, 1989)
1R.7972 (September 1989)
1R.8276, 4R.2377, 7R.3663-9, KE.5049 (July 27, 1992)
1R.8569, 4R.2694, 7R.42509, KE.5508 (September 18, 1993)
1R.8701, 4R.2842, 7R.4435-9, KE.6030 (September 18, 1993)
1R.8848, 4R.3010, 7R.4544-9, KE.5917 (April 6, 1990)
1R.10015, 4R.4296, 7R.6340-9, KE.7742 (November 18, 1992)
1R.10852 (October 1982)
1R.11074, 4R.6501, 7R.8164-9, KE.94601 (January 21, 1992)
1R.11169, 4R.5599, 7R.8311-9, KE.9580 (September 9, 1989)
1R.11824, 4R.6366, 7R.9496-9, KE.10730 (December 3, 1992)
1R.11998, 4R.6575, 7R.9723-9, KE.10259 (September 11, 1991)
1R.12526, 4R.7064, 7R.10535-9, KE.11786 (September 9, 1989)
1R.13090, 4R.7705, 7R.11887-9, KE.13301 (August 19, 1991)
P1R.13288, 4R.7960, 7R.12121-9, KE.13483 (October 15, 1989)
1R.13431 (May 1990)
1R.13587 (September 1989)
1R.13661, 4R.7807, 7R.12672-9, KE.13989 (August 12, 1992)
P2R.14101, 4R.8889, 7R.13269-9, KE.14669 (December 26, 1991)

2R.14326, 4R.9093, 7R.13917-9, KE.14312 (November 1, 1992)
2R.14615 (September 9, 1989)
2R.14816 (June 1990)
2R.14828 (April 1990)

LHD E-Type Coupes
880411?, R.7195, RA.4025-9, EB.1244JS (September 9, 1989)
880462, R.7243, RA.4102-9, EB.12182JS (May 19, 1990)
885001 (prototype number 6), V.1001
885002 (prototype number 7), V.1002
885003 (prototype number 8), V.1003
885004, V.1004
885005, V.1005
885006
885007, V.1007
885008 (April 1991)
885009 (April 1991)
885010 (June 22, 1994)
885013 (April 1991)
885018 (February 4, 1993)
885034, V.1037 on the body number plate, V.1154 on the main ID plate, R.1725-9, EB.840JS (April 27, 1994)
885047 (January 3, 1993)
885051, V.1093, R.1849-9, EB.951JS (January 17, 1979)
885053 (October 1985)
885066 (January 1992)
885082 (December 1981)
885099 (May 1986)
885104, V.1099, R.2300-9, EB.1413JS, radiator: 596 (April 30, 1994)
885107, V.1064, R.2117-9, EB.1233JS (May 10, 1992)
885117 (February 15, 1990)
885130, V.1128, R.2400-9, EB.1481JS, radiator: 1678 (September 9, 1989)
885145 (May 1990)
885153 (November 9, 1987)
885156, V.1177, R.2509-9, EB.1579JS, radiator: 5155 (October 5, 1991)
885161? (July 1990)
885168, V.1191, R.2478-9, EB.1623JS (March 1993)
885227 (March 1993)
885230, V.1278, R.2647-9, EB.1763JS (April 13, 1994)
885236, R.2883-9 (March 31, 1982)
885241 (January 1989)
885261 (January 1979)
885293, V.1374 on the body number plate, V.1362 written on back of dash, and the number Jaguar assigned to the car, R.3148-9, EB.2317JS (June 7, 1994)
885312, V.1435, R.3206-9 (February 20, 1981)
885354, V.1493, R.3309-9, EB.2443JS (February 18, 1994)
885358, V.1526 on the body number plate, V.1497 on the main ID plate, R.3331-9, EB.2486JS (April 12, 1994)
885376 (May 1981)

885387 (May 5, 1989)

885390, V.1526, R.3403-9, EB.2550JS, radiator: 2664 (December 29, 1992)

885397, R.3384-9 (October 19, 1978)

885442, V.1607, R.3527-9, EB.2619JS (September 11, 1977)

885465 (January 3, 1993)

885477 (January 1992)

885501 (December 30, 1992)

885517, V.1703, R.3693-9, EB.2810JS (April 13, 1994)

885541, V.1740, R.3786-9 (August 11, 1992)

885620, V.1839 on the body number plate, V.1837 on the main ID plate, R.4020-9, EB.3107JS (July 18, 1993)

885685, V.1917, R.4158-9, EB.3262JS (July 16, 1991)

885733, V.2029, R.4399-9, EB.3300JS, radiator: 2353 (January 1975 ?)

885748, V.2048, R.4276-9, EB.3425JS (February 1, 1988)

885842, R.4731-9 (May 1975)

885980, V.2368, R.4653-9, EB.3584 JSO on plate, EB.8694JS on transmission (˜ 1975)

886038 (April 12, 1977)

886182 (October 1985)

886184 (March 1993)

887129, V.4071 (September 9, 1989)

887576, V.4595, R.8910-9, EB.8143JS (˜ 1975)

887816, R.9329-9, EB.8250JS (March 3, 1992)

887911, V.4988, R.9343-9, EB.8750JS (May 7, 1992)

888069, V.5160, R.9696-9, EB.8791JS (February 9, 1994)

888778, V.5950, RA.2331-9, EB.10339JS (June 18, 1993)

889076, V.6351, RA.2662-8, EB.10498JS (September 9, 1989)

889325, V.6662, RA.3079-9, EB.11030JS (September 7, 1991)

889640 (May 1990)

889703 (January 5, 1994)

889796 (January 5, 1994)

889834, V.7328, RA.5057-9, EB.13157JS (February 19, 1993)

889941, V.7459, RA.5276, EB.13394JS (October 3, 1992)

890061, V.7599, RA.5516-9, EB.13518JS (August 4, 1989)

890099, V.7639, RA.5500-?, EB.13632JS (September 16, 1993)

890872 (March 1993)

890909 (no date)

K898183 (April 1986)

1E.30284, 4E.20393, 7E.1703-9, EJ.706 (November 16, 1993)

1E.30488, 4E.20658, 7E.2262-9, EJ.1254 (August 27, 1989)

1E.30687, 4E.20976, 7E.2783-9, EJ.1826 (August 19, 1991)

1E.30779, 7E.3014-9 (˜1989)

1E.31148, 4E.25658, 7E.11968-9, EJ.12726 (July 23, 1991)

1E.31823, 7E.5767-9, EJ.4833 (May 1990)

1E.32160, 7E.6696-9 (May 7, 1992)

1E.32528, 4E.23720, 7E.7551-9, KE.2585 (September 18, 1993)

1E.32999 (March 1993)

1E.33077 (March 1990)

1E.33095, 4E.24504, 7E.8065-9, EJ.7009 (September 17, 1994)

1E.33458, 4E.24924, 7E.10208-9, EJ.10726 (October 25, 1993)

1E.33544, 4E.25018, 7E.10300-9, EJ.10947 (April 30, 1993)

1E.33576 (August 12, 1981)

1E.34148 (or 1E.31148), 4E.25658, 7E.11968-9, EJ.12726 (August 19, 1991)

1E.34580, 4E.26272, 7E.14113-9, EJ.15548 (May 1990)

1E.34774, 4E.26502, 7E.14443-9, EJ.15764 (˜ 1991 or 2)

1E.34831, 4E.26565, 7E.14592-9, EE.1206 (November 13, 1991)

1E.35084, 4E.26896, 7E.15872-9 (June 10, 1990)

1R.25001 (May 1990)

1R.26776, 4R.22194, 7R.6917-9, KE.7075 (January 21, 1994)

1R.27691 (June 1990)

P2R.28287, 4R.24140, 7R.12975-9, KE.14330 (September 1989)

P2R.28613, 4R.24616, 7R.14493-H, KE.16762 (July 24, 1990)

LHD E-Type 2+2s

1E.75930, 4E.51106, 7E.50983-9, EJ.8842 (˜ 1990)

1E.76635, 4E.52035, 7E.52036-9, EJ.S10183 (December 10, 1991)

1E.76942, 4E.52599, 7E.52610-9, EJ.10238 (January 10, 1992)

1E.77577, 4E.53502, 7E.53507-9, EJ.S14481 (September 18, 1993)

1E.77645 (˜1990)

1E.77675 (September 1989)

1R.40269, 4R.35303, 7R.35479-9, KJS942 (December 26, 1991)

1R.41173BW, 4R.36366, 7R.32650-9?, 33958 (September 18, 1993)

1R.42449 (August 12, 1981)

P1R.42612BW, 4R.38166, 7R.38271-9, 37485 (September 9, 1989)

P1R.43288BW, 4R.38979, 7R.87583-9 (January 19, 1993)

P1R.43577BW, 4R.3933, 7R.39424-9, 41431 (December 5, 1991)

P1R.43622BW, 4R.39013, 7R.39095-9, 41319 (September 9, 1989)

Early E-Type Registration Form

To register your car, please fill in all the boldface lines. If possible, any other information would be appreciated.
Send to: REGISTER · Box 2626 · Ann Arbor, MI 48106

I. Serial Numbers and Specifications

Chassis number _____

Body number _____

Engine number _____

Transmission number _____

Radiator number _____

Differential number _____

Axle ratio _____

Block date (near dipstick) _____

Original exterior color _____

Original interior color _____

II. Ownership

Current owner _____

Today's date _____

Address _____

City _____

State and Zip Code _____

Telephone number _____

Previous owners to first owner (use back of form if needed)

1. _____

2. _____

3. _____

III. History

Please give any interesting facts on the history of your car: _____

_____

_____

_____

(Please attach copies of historic documents such as delivery papers, bills of sale, and so on, if possible.)

IV. Condition

Please give a description of the condition of your car. _____

_____

_____

(Please attach photographs if possible.)

V. Market Information

Most recent sale price of the car $ _____   Date _____

Recent offers on the car _____   Date _____

_____   Date _____

Appendices

REFERENCE CARS

The following is a partial listing of the chassis numbers of cars used in the researching of this work. Many more cars were examined than are listed here, but their chassis numbers were either not available or were not recorded. The contributions of these cars vary from serving as extensive photography and research subjects to merely contributing a piece of information.

RHD E-Type Roadsters
850007, 850034, 850086, 850087, 850259, 850274

RHD E-Type Coupes
860005, 860025, 860084

LHD E-Type Roadsters
875023, 875026, 875045, 875051, 875053, 875066, 875071, 875096, 875105, 875109, 875115, 875124, 875140, 875143, 875147, 875165, 875166, 875168, 875179, 875186, 875190, 875206, 875214, 875222, 875223, 875235, 875236, 875250, 875251, 875254, 875274, 875282, 875283, 875304, 875320, 875325, 875336, 875340, 875378, 875382, 875407, 875427, 875474, 875522, 875584, 875648, 875883, 875954, 875958, 875967, 876052, 876260, 876270, 876289, 876577, 876581, 876585, 876615, 876643, 876867, 877752, 878693, 879093, 879325, 880462, 1E.11976, 1E.12763, 1E.13003, 1E.15267, 1E.16928, 1E.17271, 1R.7944, 1R.8848, 1R.11169, 1R.12526, P1R.13288, 2R.14615, UD1S.21221, UE1S.24721BW

LHD E-Type Coupes
885002, 885034, 885051, 885130, 885168, 885312, 885358, 885397, 885442, 885733, 885748, 885842, 885980, 887129, 887576, 889076, 890061, 1E.30488, 1E.31823, 1E.34580, 1E.35084, P2R.28287, P2R.28613

LHD 2+2 E-Type Coupes
1E.75930, 1E.77577, P1R.42612BW, P1R.43622BW, 1S.70477

REFERENCE LITERATURE

Official Jaguar Undated Publications

J.30, Spare Parts Catalog for Jaguar 'E' Type Grand Touring Models, Aug. 1961

J.30, Spare Parts Catalog for Jaguar 'E' Type Grand Touring Models, June 1963 Reprint (AL1)

J.38, Jaguar 4.2 'E' Type '2+2' Spare Parts Catalog, Dec. 1965

Jaguar/Daimler Interim Parts List, 1969 Jaguar 'E' Type, open, fixed head coupe, 2+2 models

J.37, Spare Parts Catalog for Jaguar 4.2 'E' Type Grand Touring Models, Nov. 1965, Nov. 1969 Reprint

Series 2 E-Type Open & Fixed Head Coupe Parts Catalog, Jan. 1979, microfiche

RTC9875FA, Jaguar Parts Catalogue, Series 3 'E' Type Open 2-Seater, 1986

RTC9876FA, Jaguar Series 3 E-Type 2+2 Fixed Head Coupe Parts Catalogue, January 1979

Official Jaguar Undated Publications

Jaguar 'E' Type Operating Maintenance and Service Handbook, Jaguar Cars Ltd., Coventry, England, Publications No. E/122/1

Amendments and Additions to the Jaguar 'E' Type Operating, Maintenance and Service Handbook. A small pamphlet included with some E/122/1 books

Jaguar 'E' Type Operating, Maintenance and Service Handbook, Jaguar Cars Ltd., Coventry, England, Publication No. E/122/6

Jaguar 'E' Type Grand Touring Models Service Manual, Issued by Jaguar Cars Ltd., Coventry, England. This early version has no listed publication number

Jaguar 3.8 'E' Type Grand Touring Models Service Manual, Issued by Jaguar Cars Ltd., Coventry, England, Publication No. E/123/5

Supplementary Information for 4.2 Liter 'E' Type and 2+2 Cars, Issued by Jaguar Cars Ltd., Coventry, England, Publication No. E.123/2

Jaguar 4.2 'E' Type & 2+2 Operating, Maintenance and Service Handbook, Jaguar Cars Ltd., Coventry, England, Publication No. E/131/6

Magazines

The Autocar, March 17, 1961; April 26, 1963; May 14, 1965; Feb. 18, 1966; June 10, 1966; Oct. 12, 1967; April 25, 1968; April 25, 1968; Nov. 18, 1970

Autosport, Dec. 14, 1962; Aug. 21, 1964; Oct. 23, 1964; March 11, 1966; Aug. 5, 1966; Oct. 29, 1970

Canada Track and Traffic, May 1961

Car, Nov. 1965; June 1970

Car and Car Conversions, Oct. 1966

Car and Driver, May 1961; Dec. 1961; July 1963; Feb. 1965; April 1966; May 1969; April 1982

The Car Collector, Dec. 1978

Cars Illustrated, Nov. 1963; March 1965

Classic and Sportscar, April 1986

The E-Jag News Magazine, August 1976, March 1982

Jaguar International Magazine, March 1986

Jaguar Quarterly, April 1991

The Milestone Car, Winter 1974

Modern Motor, Nov. 1961; March 1971

The Motor, March 22, 1961; May 22, 1961; Feb. 21, 1962; Oct. 31, 1964; March 12, 1966; April 30, 1966; Jan. 13, 1968; Sept. 7, 1968, Sept. 14, 1968; Dec. 20, 1969; March 21, 1970

Motor Magazine, March 15, 1961

Motor Racing, April 1961; May 1961; April 1966

Motor Sport, April 1961; July 1962; Jan. 1965; April 1966; April 1967

Motor Trend, July 1961

Motoring Life, 1961; 1963

Newsletter of the Jaguar Club of Northwest Ohio, July 1984

Popular Imported Cars, Jan. 1969

Road & Track, May 1961; April 1964; April 1966; July 1966; Oct. 1966; June 1969; Aug. 1969; Jan. 1969; Sept. 1974

Road Test, May 1965

Science & Mechanics, Dec. 1968

Special Interest Autos, Dec. 1979

Sports Car World, Oct. 1963

Sporting Motorist, 1966

Worlds Fastest Sports Cars, 1966

Books

E Type: End of an Era. Harvey, C., St. Martin's Press, New York, 1977.

European Automobiles of the 50's and 60's. Martinez, A., and Nory, J-L. Vilo, Inc., New York, 1982.

Jaguar. Lord Montagu of Beaulieu. A. S. Barnes & Co., Inc., Cranbury, New Jersey, 1967.

Jaguar: Britain's Fastest Export. Lord Montagu of Beaulieu. Ballantine Books Inc., New York, 1971.

Jaguar E-Type: The Definitive History. Porter, P. Foulis, Haynes, Yeovil, Somerset, England, 1989.

Jaguar E-Type 3.8 & 4.2 6-cylinder; 5.3 V-12. Jenkinson, D. Osprey Publishing Limited, London, 1982.

The Jaguar E-Type: A Collector's Guide. Skilleter, P. Motor Racing Publications, London, 1979.

Jaguar Sports Cars. Skilleter, P. Haynes, GT Foulis & Co. Ltd, Sparkford, Yeovil, Somerset, 1975.

Jaguar V-12 E-Type, A Guide to Authenticity. Russ, R. T. Spirit Press, Del City, Oklahoma, 1991.

Original Jaguar E-Type. Porter, P. Bay View Books, Ltd., Bideford, Devon, England, 1990.

The Jaguar Story. Wherry, J.H. Chilton Book Co., Philadelphia, 1967.

The New Jaguar Guide. Williamson, H.W. Sports Car Press, New York, 1964.

INDEX